Debate on Europe

1815-1850

Debate on Europe

1815-1850

GEORGE RUDÉ

Harper & Row, Publishers
New York, Evanston, San Francisco, London

LIBRARY OF CONGRESS CATALOG NUMBER: 79–165157

STANDARD BOOK NUMBER: 06–136070-8

CONTENTS

Introduction

This book is not the usual historian's history, but a history of the histories written by others. Its theme is the different views and interpretations of historians of the half-century of European history between Waterloo and the termination of the revolutions of 1848. It is (and I think this would be a generally acceptable view) a most significant period, covering such important developments as the settlement of Europe after the Napoleonic Wars, the attempt to achieve a "Concert of Europe" based on the diplomacy of the Great Powers, the challenge to that settlement and "Concert" by the rising forces of liberalism and nationalism, the revolutions of 1830 and 1848, and (in Britain and France, in particular) the rise of working-class movements and a new industrial society. By and large, therefore, whether we consider 1848 to have been a "turning point," a "beginning" or an "end," the face of Europe had, by the middle of the century, changed impressively from what it had been at its inception. So much, then, would perhaps be generally agreed on by historians of today. Yet no two historians would agree, in writing a book of this kind, on the themes to select or the order of priorities to give them. The selection of themes naturally poses problems of its own. In making my selection, I have attempted to strike a balance between such "material" factors as industrial revolution and the growth of cities and those more ideological or political factors such as the conflict of ideas, political movements and revolutions. In so doing, I make no more claim to strict objectivity or "value-freedom" on my part than I do for any of the historians whose work I am discussing. It will be evident, for instance, that, in a volume supposedly concerned with Europe as a whole, I have paid far more attention to England and France than I have to Italy or Germany, that Spain has received scant treatment, and that Russia, Poland and Scandinavia have been virtually neglected altogether. It will also not escape the reader that, after my first chapter, I have devoted little space to diplomacy and the relations between the Powers. (That I have almost completely neglected wars is reasonable enough, as the period was remarkably free of them. There were, in fact, only two wars in Europe during these years, both of them in 1848.) Such a selection is obviously not unrelated to what historians have written about the period; but, even more, it reflects the author's own interests and preoccupations, his prejudices and order of priorities, and, of course, his competence to handle some themes better than he can handle others.

So the book is a study of historical controversy over a limited period and embracing a limited number of themes. But if the period and the issues are limited, the divergences in historians' views about them are remarkably wide. Yet why, the reader may ask, do historians, holding broadly similar ideas of what history is all about, often differ so widely in its interpretation? Briefly—though this is by no means the whole answer—it is because they belong to different countries, classes and generations; they have access to different types of evidence; and they hold differing social, political and religious views. In short, their interpretations of the past are colored, to a greater or a lesser degree, by nationality, class, generation, political affiliation and religion, and by the availability of records and their particular research techniques; and some of these variables react in turn on one another. This is, as I say, not the whole story (a historian's purely private choices naturally play a part); but if Mr. Carr is right in calling history "a dialogue between the present and the past," then it follows that there can be no single received or universal truth in its writing and that the "varieties of history" (to use Fritz Stern's expression) must be largely attributed to factors such as these.

Now let us look at some of these variables a little more closely, starting with the writer's country of origin. After all, it is not surprising that historians should be as responsive to the call of their own national past as anybody else. Every nation tends to see its past in its own way, and every teen-age schoolboy knows that an Englishman's view of the Boer War is not likely to be identical with that of a Dutchman or a German, any more than Englishmen and Americans have agreed with Russians, Frenchmen and Germans over the origins of the two world wars. For our period, partly because it is a little more remote, historians tend not to divide so sharply or dramatically along purely national lines, yet such divisions certainly play a part. A French historian, for example, looking back on the Peace Settlement of 1815, may find it hard to view it in the same detached spirit as an American or an Englishman. To him it must, almost inevitably, be a symbol of defeat and, therefore, something more or less deplorable; and, in our first chapter, we quote Mr. E. H. Dance's view that whereas to an Englishman the Peace of Vienna tends to appear as a landmark on the road to peace, to a Frenchman it appears rather as a source of conflict and disorder. Or take the example of the revolutions of 1848, which affected Frenchmen, Italians and Germans, but not Englishmen or Americans. Not surprisingly, we find a far more *personal* and *committed* attitude adopted by the former than by the latter, and this is even more true of Germans than of Italians or Frenchmen. For to Germans 1848 has stood (rather as 1815 to Frenchmen) as a symbol of defeat, which has been re-lived again and again as a kind of traumatic experience, and one that has, even more sharply than in other countries, divided nationalists from liberals and Prussians from other national groups. Again, a historian, looking at another country's history, may bring to its study experiences that are more particularly related to his own country's past. Mr. Hugh Stretton, in his book *The Political Sciences,* cites the example of Elie Halévy, the French historian of England in the nineteenth century, who picked out from England's history those qualities making for stability and integration. "From all the conditions necessary for them [writes Stretton], he chose those which warded off particular alternatives—alternatives chosen as likely—and dangerous—for the English system. But sometimes he took these alternatives from recent French history, choosing what he valued most as the most dangerous causes of its most destructive conflicts."[1]

More obtrusive perhaps than this "nation-gap" is the "generation-gap" that divides one group of historians from another. Returning to

1. Hugh Stretton, *The Political Sciences* (New York, 1969), p. 275.

Mr. Carr's dictum about history being a dialogue between the present and the past, we should hardly expect that past—in this instance the years 1815 to 1850—to have looked the same in the 1850s as it has looked in 1900 or in the 1960s. To illustrate the point, I have tried in the last chapter to contrast the "immediate" views of some of the survivors of 1848 with the longer-term views of historians of later generations. But this is an extreme case and perhaps so obvious as to be hardly worth the mention. More subtle variations in perspective may be noted between one generation and the next, though even these may become sharply distinctive if some new experience, such as a war or a revolution, intervenes. In our first chapter, for example, we shall see how British and American historians (though not noticeably the French) revised their attitudes to the Peace Settlement of 1815 in the light of their experience of the First World War and the problems it brought in its train. It was at this time that Sir Charles Webster, Harold Temperley and others began to give a new and more friendly "look" to the Congress System and the policies of Metternich and Castlereagh, whose problems now appeared to be not dissimilar to those facing the statesmen assembled, a century later, at Versailles. To others, the Concert of Europe, and even the notorious "Holy Alliance," began to assume a new respectability as the forerunners of the League of Nations; and we shall find that similar considerations underlay the work of a number of American historians (Henry Kissinger among them) after World War II. Similarly, we shall see that the experience of Nazism and the Second World War brought about a dramatic reassessment of Germany's past in the work of certain British and French historians. In our last chapter, we cite the example of A. J. P. Taylor and Sir Lewis Namier, who saw the weakness of liberalism in the German revolution of 1848 not only as being deeply rooted in the German national character, but as the sure guarantee of the militarism and despotism of the future. Others, once the Nazi menace had receded, have been more inclined to reinterpret the events of 1848 in the light of the new alignments and antagonisms of the Cold War; while others again, during this postwar period, have reacted, less dramatically, to the rapid social and industrial changes taking place

around them and have given a new social and economic dimension to
their interpretation of the past.

The "generation-gap," however, operates on another level as well.
It is not simply a matter of the later generations of historians holding
different opinions from their predecessors; there is also a difference in
their style of work and presentation. In this sense, a great deal of the
history written in the nineteenth and early twentieth century appears
to us to be old-fashioned and archaic, and may justly be said to have
become superseded by the more competent, more complete and more
significant work of their successors. In this volume, I have devoted a
certain amount of space to work of this kind, not so much for any
particular merit that it might seem to possess as for its reflection of
the ideas and values of the generation in which it was conceived.
Apart form this consideration, there is, for example, nothing in particular to recommend to the present-day reader in the work of Debidour
or Hearnshaw on the diplomatic and political history of Europe, of
York on the Holy Alliance, Cecil on Metternich, Dareste and Hall on
the Restoration, Muir on nationalism, E. R. Taylor on Methodism,
Poplimont on Belgium, Lucas-Dubreton on the July Monarchy, Orsi
or the Berkeleys on Italy, Walton, Hume and Butler Clark on Spain,
or Cayley, Saint-Amand and Léger on the revolutions of 1848. All
these works may be said, without much exaggeration, to bear too
heavily the imprint of the generation in which they were written and
to be by now outmoded and outdated. There are other historians as
well whose work in our eyes appears a little antiquated, yet who, for
their pioneering efforts, are perhaps more worthy of respect: Alison
Phillips, with his study of the organization of European peace, and
possibly Sir John Marriott and Von Sybel; and dare I add Veit Valentin, the liberal historian of the German revolution of 1848? To a
somewhat different category belong three great pioneers of the history
of Germany, Italy and England in the nineteenth century, men who
have had a remarkable influence on the historians of their countries,
yet whose work, apart from its literary and historiographical importance, has now been largely superseded. I refer to the Prussian-nationalist historian Treitschke and to two great early twentieth-century

liberals, Croce and Trevelyan. In addition, there are others, whose work, although it appeared forty—or even a hundred—years ago, has survived remarkably the test of time and still continues to exert an active influence on historians today. Among the more recent of those mentioned in this book are Elie Halévy and Dorothy George, the latter with her pioneering study of London in the eighteenth century. Among those writing a century ago, who can certainly not be said to have become superseded, are Tocqueville, Marx and Engels; and I make no apology for citing them so frequently in some of the chapters that follow.

But even more important as a cause of the controversies that divide historians have been their social and political "values" or affiliations. Man is a political animal and, once more, the historian is no exception. As he responds to the call of nationality or generation or religion, so he responds equally or with even greater vigor to the promptings of his political assumptions. The response may be a muted or a subtle one, or it may be crude and blatant, and even grotesque; but, in one guise or another, his work cannot escape it altogether. In this volume, there are examples given of a wide variety of political response. A few of these are of the crude or grotesque type, such as the Vicomte de Poncins's book on the "secret powers behind revolutions" and some of the neurotic fantasies of German-nationalist historians (accorded a certain degree of respectability in their day) regarding the sinister machinations of liberals, freemasons and Jews. More often, however, the works cited are those of respectable scholars, whose sociopolitical assumptions, though often subtly disguised, are nevertheless unmistakable. To distinguish them I have freely used such labels as "nationalist," "Tory" or "conservative"; "Whig" or "liberal" (with a small "l" unless a specific party affiliation is intended); and "socialist" or "Marxist." The labels are supposed to be reasonably objective definitions and not to separate goats from sheep or to be either approbatory or condemnatory, though I realize that my own particular aversions and affinities are occasionally brought into play. In this context, I have generally affixed the label Tory or conservative to historians who (before 1918 at least) approved of the Vienna Settlement, who have disapproved of the revolutions of 1830 or 1848, have applauded the social effects of industrialization, have preferred Cavour to Mazzini or Tories to Whigs, have praised Guizot, Metternich and Bismarck, have frowned on trade unions and the Anti-Corn Law League, have defended Church and aristocracy and have, in general, been somewhat contemptuous of "patterns" and "progress" in history. I have termed Whig or liberal, on the other hand, those who have been critical of Vienna, Bismarck and Metternich (though not necessarily of Guizot or Cavour), have applauded liberalism and liberal-national (though not often social) revolutions, praised the Reform Bill and the Anti-Corn Law League, been partial to religious dissenters, played down working-class movements, and placed a high premium on constitutional development, parliamentary debate, orderly progress and the "forward march" of ideas. Again, a Marxist has been one who (following Marx and Engels) has seen history in terms of class struggle, has put "matter" before ideas (though often giving weight to both) and "people" before Parliament, has praised all revolutions and expressed as strong a commitment to trade unions, the *menu peuple* and the working classes as liberals have to Parliament and radical *bourgeoisie,* and as conservatives have to Metternich, the monarchy or the Church of England. But these are, of course, generalizations, which never exactly fit and are certainly not intended to apply to every author mentioned in this book. Some historians are inevitably more Tory or more liberal than others, and there are (as Mr. Stretton reminds us) different shades of Whig, conservative and Marxist; and a man who may reasonably be classified as a conservative in one context may not appear to be so in another. (Nationalism may play tricks in this respect; we shall later note the case of Treitschke's "non-conservative" view of Metternich.) Stretton rightly distinguishes the "romantic" conservative from the conservative of the "stockbroking" type, and points to the streak of radicalism that lurks in the former while being singularly lacking in the latter.[2] In a later chapter, we shall observe something of this quality in the work of Dr. Kitson Clark. Again, we shall distinguish between the old-style "Whiggishness" of Croce and Trevelyan and the later, more socially

2. Stretton, *Political Sciences,* pp. 38–9.

oriented, liberalism of certain of their followers. Mr. Stretton believes that, in this respect, Marxists are more consistent—certainly more so than conservatives. "To be conservative about the present," he writes, "is often to be radical about some at least of the past"; whereas "to be Marxist about the present is usually to be Marxist about the past." This is true enough as far as it goes. But it must be added that some Marxists are more subtle and perceptive and less given to dogmatic pronouncements than others; and this often makes them better historians and, no doubt, better Marxists, too. In this respect, we may perhaps contrast the work of E. J. Hobsbawm with that of some of the earlier Marxist, or near-Marxist, historians whose names appear in this book.

The question of "values," therefore, whether inspired by country, political association or contemporary experience, is an all-important one in assessing and explaining the varying interpretations of historians. This is all the more so, as "values" affect not only the sort of books they write and the judgments they make, but also the records they consult, the questions they ask and the methods they use to prepare and to present their answers. Of course, in some cases the element of choice is less elastic than in others. Some records, in fact, are more or less imposed on historians by the field they choose to work in. Several of the works considered in our opening chapter, for example, being conventional exercises in diplomatic history, are based on records as appropriate to the needs of any one historian as the next, thus significantly reducing the variety of questions asked. The same cannot be said, however, of the works of social history, the history of population and of industrial and political revolution, the "new" economic history, or the socio-economic interpretations of political history that are discussed in the following chapters. Here the element of choice, both in regard to the records themselves and the questions that may be asked of them, becomes considerably extended. This is not to say that the "newer" history is more divisively polemical than the history that came before (it is, in fact, rather the reverse); but, being concerned with "new ways" and new methods of enquiry, the sting of controversy over principles and personalities is often replaced by that over method and the problems which should most properly command the historian's attention. A comparatively small proportion of this "newer" history has been contributed to the study of Europe in the early nineteenth century; but some, as we shall see, has found a place in this volume. Thus we shall note the debate over the industrial revolution and the British standard-of-living, Chevalier's and Pouthas's work on cities and population, Tilly's and Gossez's studies on French popular movements, the work of the *Annales* school (Morazé and Jean Lhomme, for example) on nineteenth-century France, the "new look" given by Thompson and Hobsbawm to the study of the British working class, Demarco's social interpretation of the *Risorgimento,* and the kind of questions asked by Hamerow about the nineteenth-century history of Germany.

But, if a large part of the political polemic has gone out of the newer history, it cannot for that reason be claimed to be any more "value-free" than the history that went before it. It is evident, for example, that a great deal of the newer social history—which has little in common with Trevelyan's "history of the people with the politics left out"[3]—owes a considerable debt to Marx; and we shall see that some of its most active practitioners—including Hobsbawm, Thompson, Labrousse, Demarco, Jean Lhomme, and the Czech and Hungarian historians of 1848—are Marxists, or historians of the Left. British and American economic historians, on the other hand, have tended to go the other way. If David Landes is a liberal, Rostow may perhaps, more properly, be styled a conservative; and this is also the case with the "optimists" of the debate on the English industrial revolution, such as Clapham, Ashton, Chaloner and Hartwell.

Yet it may be objected that such labels are no longer relevant in the case of the "new economic," or "econometric," history that has recently developed in the United States and is increasingly finding a foothold among European historians as well. In particular, it has been argued that the sort of quantitative methods applied by Fogel to the study of railways, North to ocean shipping, or Meyer and Conrad to the economics of slavery (or, say, by Deane and Cole to the English industrial revolution) are as open to Marxists as they are to conserva-

3. G. M. Trevelyan, *English Social History* (New York, 1946), p. vii.

tives or liberals. If it were a matter of *method* alone, there could be no dispute about it—the computer is neutral enough and is as readily available, in the technological age we live in, to any one group of historians or social scientists as it is to any other. But method is only one part, though an important part, of the exercise; and the new economic history is as much indebted to new economic theory as it is to new means of quantification. Indeed, its "methodological hallmarks," Professor Fogel tells us, are a combination of the two.[4] And theory implies evaluation and selection, including the questions historians ask; and these in turn will, irrespective of the neutrality of mechanical aids, reflect his "values" and help to determine the nature of his findings and conclusions. So controversies between historians, even if they assume a more decorous and more muted form, are as liable to continue in the future as they have been in the past. This need not alarm us. Controversy lies at the heart of all historical inquiry, and scholarship would be meaningless without it. Despite their differences, historians lean heavily on one another, and each generation of historians stands on the shoulders of the one that went before it. And the historians whose work is discussed in the following pages are certainly no exception to this rule.

4. R. W. Fogel, "The New Economic History: Its Findings and Methods," *Economic History Review*, 2nd series, XIX, No. 3 (December, 1966): 651.

Chronology of Significant Events

1814–15   Congress of Vienna (Sept.–June)
        Constitutional Charter of Louis XVIII in France
        Restoration governments in France, Germany, Italy, Spain

  1815   Napoleon's "Hundred Days" (March–July)
        Battle of Waterloo and Napoleon's second abdication (June)
        Holy Alliance signed by Russia, Austria, Prussia (Sept.)
        Second Treaty of Paris; Quadruple Alliance (Nov.)

  1816   Renewed Luddite riots in England.

  1817   Independence of Serbia
        "Blanketeers'" March and Pentridge rebellion in England
        Burschenshaft and Wartburg Festival in Germany
        Ricardo's *Principles of Political Economy*

  1818   Congress of Aix-la-Chapelle

  1819   "Peterloo" Massacre in England (Aug.)
        Carlsbad Decrees and early *Zollverein* (customs union) in Germany
        De Maistre's *Du Pape*
        Shelley's *Masque of Anarchy*

  1820   Assassination of Duc de Berri in France (Feb.)
        Revolts and revolutions in Cadiz (Jan.), Naples (July), Portugal (Aug.)
        Congress of Troppau; Austrian intervention in Italy (Oct–Dec.)

1821   Congress of Laibach (Jan.)
        Charbonnerie founded in France
        Liberals crushed in Naples and Piedmont (March–April)
        Greek War of Independence starts (April)
        Hegel's *Philosophy of Law*
        Schubert's Unfinished Symphony

1822   Canning at Foreign Office
        Congress of Verona (Oct–Dec.)

1823   French intervention to restore authority of Bourbon
            dynasty in Spain (April–Aug.)
        Government of Colomardo in Spain, 1823–33
        Beethoven's Ninth Symphony

1824   Death of Louis XVIII and succession of Charles X (Sept.)
        Repeal of Combination Laws (banning trade unions) in
            Britain
        Ranke's *Critique of the Newer Historians*

1825   Decabrist revolt in Russia
        Death of Alexander I of Russia and succession of Nicholas
            I (Dec.)
        Stockton-Darlington railway in England
        Saint-Simon's *New Christianity*
        Pushkin's *Boris Godunov*

1826   Greek capitulation at Missolonghi; Mahomet Ali recon-
            quers Morea (April)

1827   Death of Canning
        Treaty of London (Aug.)
        Naval battle of Navarino (Oct.)
        Heine's *Buch der Lieder*

1828–30 Russo-Turkish War

1829   Catholic Emancipation in Britain (April)
        Polignac government in France (Aug.)

Treaty of Adrianople; Greek independence (Sept.)
Stephenson's *Rocket*
Balzac's *Comédie humaine*

1830   Convention of London recognizes Greek independence
          (Feb.)
        Anti-clerical riots in France (Feb.)
        French expel Dutch from Belgium (Aug.)
        Polish revolt crushed (Sept.)
        Reform Bill riots in Derby, Nottingham, Bristol (Oct.)
        Workers' revolt in Lyons (Oct.–Nov.)
        Faraday's discovery of electro-magnetic induction

1831–2 Cholera epidemic

1832   Attempted royalist *coup* by Duchesse de Berri in Vendée
          (April–June)
        Paris riots in Cloître St. Merri (June)
        Reform Bill passed in Britain
        German democrats at Hambach castle
        Mazzini's "Young Italy" founded
        Goethe's *Faust,* part II

1833   Russo-Turkish Treaty of Unkiar-Skelessi (July)
        First effective Factory Act and first state aid to education
          in Britain
        Oxford Movement in England
        Owen's Grand National Consolidated Trades Union
        Gauss and Weber's electro-magnetic telegraph

1833–6 *Zollverein* of 25 states in Germany

1833–40 Carlist War in Spain

1834   Mazzini's "Young Europe" founded
        Workers' revolts in Lyons and Paris (April)
        Abortive liberal *putsches* in Naples and Piedmont
        German radicals assemble at Badenburg (July)
        New Poor Law in England

Jacobi's electric motor
Lammenais's *Paroles d'un croyant*
Ranke's *History of the Popes,* vol. I.

1835   Fieschi bomb plot in Paris
        Municipal Reform Act in Britain

1836   Molé government in France (Sept.)
        Louis Bonaparte's abortive *coup* at Strasbourg (Oct.)
        Dickens' *Pickwick Papers*

1837   Accession of Queen Victoria
        First draft of People's Charter in London
        Reaction in Germany: Hanover's liberal constitution
          revoked
        Reaction in Italy: Sicily's municipal autonomy revoked
        Carlyle's *French Revolution*

1838   Chartism (first phase) in Britain
        Anti-Corn Law League founded at Manchester
        The screw-propeller

1839   Treaty of London guarantees Belgian neutrality
        Paris insurrection led by Barbès and Blanqui (May)
        Louis Blanc's *Organisation du travail* published in Paris
        Daguerrotype photography

1840   Frederick William IV succeeds to throne of Prussia
        Convention of London and Mahomet Ali crisis (July)
        Louis Bonaparte's abortive *coup* at Boulogne (Aug.)
        Guizot government in France (Oct.)
        Kossuth founds *Pest Gazette* in Hungary
        Napoleon's ashes brought to Paris (Dec.)
        Liebig's *Chemistry in Relation to Agriculture*
        Proudhon's *Qu'est-ce que la propriété?*

1841   Straits Convention signed by Great Powers
        Peel's 2nd government in Britain
        Mazzinian insurrection at Aquila (Naples)

French Republican constitution (Nov.)

The Turning Tide: collapse of Neapolitan revolution (May); capitulation of Prague; defeat of workers' insurrection in Paris (June); Austrians defeat Piedmontese at Custozza (July) and recapture Milan (Aug.); collapse of revolution in Vienna (October); Louis Napoleon elected President of French Republic (Dec.)

Prussian War with Denmark over Schleswig-Holstein (May–Aug.)

Francis Joseph (1848–1916) becomes Austrian Emperor (Oct.)

Marx and Engels' *Communist Manifesto* (Jan.)

Mill's *Principles of Political Economy*

Macaulay's *History of England,* vols. I and II

Pasteur's discovery of yeast as a living organism

1849   Proclamation of Roman Republic (Feb.); crushed by French troops (July)

Hungary's declaration of independence (April); crushed by Austro-Russians (Aug.)

Abortive "Montagnard" rising in Paris (June)

Piedmontese defeated by Austrians at Novara; abdication of Charles-Albert (March)

Frederick William IV refuses Imperial Crown offered by Frankfurt Parliament (April), which is dispersed (June)

People's Congress in Baden (May); dispersed (July)

Venetian Republic destroyed by Austrians (July–Aug.)

Hungarian, Italian, Austrian, German revolutionary movements crushed (Aug.)

British Navigation Acts repealed

Krupp's first steel gun

1850   Cavour becomes Minister in Piedmont (Jan.)

Falloux's education laws in France (March)

Prussia's "capitulation" to Austria by Convention of Olmütz (Nov.)

1851   Louis Napoleon's *coup d'état* (Dec.)
        Austria's liberal constitution revoked (Dec.)
        Great Exhibition at Crystal Palace in London

I

The Settlement of Europe
after the Napoleonic Wars

This chapter is concerned, broadly, with the period between Napoleon's second abdication and banishment to St. Helena in 1815 and the revolutions of 1830. It is sometimes loosely termed the period of the Congress System, the Concert of Europe, the Restoration, or the Holy Alliance. Yet this is both to oversimplify the picture and to confuse the issues. The settlement of 1815 was really made up of four distinctive elements: the territorial settlement mainly associated with the Vienna Congress; the political-constitutional settlement in a number of countries, usually termed the Restoration; and the political-ideological settlement, which is often associated with the Holy Alliance (though the Alliance took other forms as well) and was accompanied by the conservative or counter-revolutionary writings of men like Gentz, Bonald and Joseph de Maistre. In addition, there was the system of alliances between the four victor powers—who were shortly joined by France—mainly centered on the Quadruple Alliance (November 1815), which bound the signatories to a twenty-year agreement termed the "Concert of Europe," whereby they would hold periodic meetings "for the purpose of consulting upon their common interest and for the consideration of the measures most salutary for the maintenance of the peace of Europe." It was due to these provisions that the system has sometimes been known as the Congress System.

The new territorial settlement was mainly, though not exclusively, the work of the Congress of Vienna; in fact, the Vienna Peace Treaty was only one of several treaties that imposed a post-war settlement on France. When Napoleon abdicated for the first time in April 1814, the four allied powers—Austria, Prussia, Russia and the United Kingdom—agreed in the first Treaty of Paris (30 May 1814) that France's boundaries should be pushed back to those of 1792; that she should give up Belgium and the left bank of the Rhine; but she was not to be disarmed or occupied or made to pay any reparations. It was already conceded that France, having once more become a legitimate monarchy, with Louis XVIII as king and Talleyrand as foreign minister, should be represented at subsequent congresses to negotiate a more general settlement. Such plans were delayed by Napoleon's surprise return to France from his first exile in Elba and the new military measures called for on the part of his opponents. But even before their final victory at Waterloo, the five powers decided by the Treaty of Vienna (9 June 1815) on the main lines of the territorial resettlement of Europe. These were supplemented after Waterloo and Napoleon's dispatch to St. Helena by the second Treaty of Paris (20 November 1815), which pushed France's frontiers back further to where they had been in 1790 and subjected her to a three-year military occupation and to the payment of a large indemnity.

For the rest, it was the Treaty of Vienna which redrew the map of Europe. By its provisions, the Austrian Netherlands (Belgium) and the Duchy of Luxembourg were joined to Holland to form a united Kingdom of the Netherlands as a buffer against France in the North; Prussia acquired the Rhineland and a part of Saxony; a Confederation of thirty-nine states was formed in Germany under the presidency of Austria; Lombardy was restored to Austria, which was also given Venetia and the overlordship of Parma, Modena and Tuscany; while the Spanish Bourbons were restored to Naples and Sicily and the Pope to Rome and the Papal States. Meanwhile, the Grand Duchy of Warsaw was entrusted to Russia; Norway was transferred from Denmark to Sweden and Finland from Sweden to Russia; and Britain enlarged her colonial empire at the expense of France, Holland and the Knights of St. John.

It was to maintain this settlement that the victor powers signed the Quadruple Alliance in November 1815 and, on Castlereagh's initiative, pledged themselves to the peace-keeping notion of the Concert of Europe, which France was also invited to join. But, before this, Alexander I of Russia had proposed to his fellow-Christian rulers to bind themselves, by a solemn declaration, to conduct their mutual relations "according to the sublime truths which the holy religion of Christ our Saviour teaches." This declaration—the famous (or notorious) Holy Alliance—was issued in September and signed by the rulers of Russia, Prussia and Austria; it was later signed by France, but not by Britain. The Holy Alliance soon acquired wider implications, but this was not the stated intention, at least, of its signatories and chief promoter.

Meanwhile, as part of the Vienna agreement, most of the old rulers of Europe who had been displaced by Napoleon or the Revolution were restored to their thrones: King William (the former Stadtholder) to the Netherlands, Ferdinand VII to Spain, Louis XVIII to France, Ferdinand IV to Naples, the Pope to Rome; and those of the German princes who had not been made redundant by the new Confederation were restored to their ancestral domains. This, in brief, was the Restoration, which, like the Congress System and the Concert of Europe, is generally held to have remained more or less intact until the next round of revolutions in 1830.

So much for the bare facts of the case—though the discerning reader will note that even so dispassionate a presentation is not entirely free from bias and careful selection. How much more must this be the case with the long succession of historians, the product of different countries and different generations, who have not only selected and recorded the facts but commented on their significance and on the motives and behavior of the principal actors involved! Here it is proposed to treat the successive and varying opinions of historians under four main heads: the Concert of Europe, the Holy Alliance, the Congress Statesmen and the Restoration.

1. The Concert of Europe

We note, in the first place, a considerable confusion of terms. What some historians have termed the "Concert of Europe," others have termed, more or less without discrimination, the Vienna "Settlement," the "Confederation of Europe," or even the "Holy Alliance." Yet, out of the confusion, certain trends have unmistakably emerged:

the tendency of historians to rewrite the events of 1815 in the light of the experience of 1919 or 1945; the tendency of French and Continental historians to take a different view from that of the British or Americans; and the inclination of Marxists (and this is of course not surprising) to see the past in a different light from liberals or conservatives.

In one of the most recent books written on this period, Mr. René Albrecht-Carrié, an American historian, observes:

Much has been written about the Charter that the Congress of Vienna wrote for the future of Europe, and appraisals of it have varied, reflecting the circumstances of the time when they were made.

And he goes on to contrast the attitudes of historians writing in the late nineteenth century, when "the shortcomings of Vienna" were underlined by the "nationalistic triumphs" of the Italians and Germans, with the more charitable estimates made by historians in the light of their experience of the First World War.[1]

In general, this point is sound enough; though it may be doubted whether the hostile view of the 1815 settlement was any more prevalent in the late nineteenth century than it was nearer to the event; further, it would be unwise to assume that such a change in outlook overcame historians as a whole, regardless of their national or political affiliations. It is hardly surprising, for example, that the victims of the Vienna Congress and of the peace that followed were scarcely enthusiastic about its terms; and this was an attitude that continued well beyond the immediate period of the settlement or Restoration and colored judgments of these events for years to come. This may explain why Frenchmen have been less willing to revise their views of the Vienna Congress and its aftermath than Englishmen or Americans. I shall return to this point in a moment.

But first let us consider those critics who, at various points of time, have adopted an unmitigatedly hostile attitude to the Congress and the settlement and all that followed in their train; and, in the first place, hostile contemporary opinion. This was of two kinds. First, there were the vanquished, whose opinion, we may assume, was over-

---

1. René Albrecht-Carrié, *A Diplomatic History of Europe since the Congress of Vienna* (New York, 1958), pp. 15–16.

whelmingly hostile and needs no elaboration here. Then there were the victors, among whom hostility was generally confined to those who had hoped that, after the defeat of Napoleon, the victorious powers would impose a more generous settlement on the French, or at least take some account of the "rights" and national aspirations of the peoples of Europe. In this respect, an unusual view was that put forward in February 1815, before Napoleon's escape from Elba, by the conservative apologist, Theodor von Gentz, who, in drafting a memorandum on the achievement of the Congress of Vienna for Metternich, defined its real purpose as "the division among the Conquerors of the spoil taken from the Conquered."[2] But this was perhaps merely the expression of a temporary bout of cynicism on Gentz's part; and more typical is the view put forward in a radical opposition pamphlet, entitled *The Declaration of England against the Acts and Projects of the Holy Alliance* and printed in London in 1821. After Napoleon's defeat, it runs, "we saw with satisfaction the opportunity return to Europe of repairing its many losses, and of regaining the liberties of which its People had for long been deprived." But, it continues, "these hopes were disappointed. Treaties indeed were made, with more or less regard to an imaginary standard, by which the territorial possessions of certain great states were to be balanced against each other; . . . but neither in settling the treaties of 1814 or 1815, nor at the subsequent congresses at Aix-la-Chapelle and Carlsbad, does it appear that any regard was to be had to the only basis on which, in the present condition of the world, the Peace could be consolidated, to the solemn promises of the Sovereigns in the hour of their necessity, nor to the Rights which the People of Europe had acquired for themselves at the expense of so many sacrifices and sufferings. . . . Public opinion was disregarded. National feeling was despised, and the expression of it harshly repulsed. Whole countries were transferred from one Prince to another, without any consideration for the wishes or habits, or the ancient prejudices under which they had lived happy and become great".[3]

2. Quoted by E. L. Woodward, *War and Peace in Europe 1815–1870* (London, 1931), p. 1.
3. *The Declaration of England against the Acts and Projects of the Holy Alliance* (London, 1821), pp. 2–3.

This theme of an alliance of Kings, imposing their will on the conquered in their own selfish interests while ignoring the national and democratic aspirations of the people, has, of course, passed into the liberal-radical historiography of the settlement in general; and it was certainly not limited to the radical critics of 1821. We find it repeated, seventy years later, in a late nineteenth-century history of European diplomacy written by the French historian Debidour in 1891. This time it was by no means an expression of purely radical opinion; Debidour, in addition to being an academic historian of some note (he was a former dean of the Faculty of Letters at Nancy), was a general inspector of public education under the Third Republic. He writes:

At that time, the people were demanding free institutions, while the nations were clamouring for independence and their natural frontiers. No satisfaction was given to these aspirations by the conquerors of Napoleon. Democracy was outlawed, and the rulers formed a sort of mutual alliance to combat and contain it. Thus, they thought, a *moral* equilibrium would be established, essential to the maintenance of a general peace. As for the *material* equilibrium, this they founded on arbitrary territorial divisions. And to achieve it, they consulted only their own convenience and interest and took no account of the aspirations of the people.[4]

Among French historians, and among Marxists whether East or West, broadly similar views are held today. Félix Ponteil, in the Preface to his volume in the "Peuples et Civilisations" series (published in 1960), defines the year 1815 as marking "the triumph of reaction, which attempts to impose its standards, its traditions and its political and military institutions."[5] Jacques Droz, author of the corresponding volume in the rival "Clio" series (1953) sums up the situation in roughtly similar terms.[6] The views of Soviet historians are not so very different. So we find Professor Jefimow, in a textbook

4. A. Debidour, *L'Histoire diplomatique de l'Europe depuis l'ouverture au congrès de Vienne jusqu'à la fermeture du congrès de Berlin (1814–1878)*, 2 vols. (Paris, 1891), I: viii–ix. (My translation, as in all similar cases.)
5. F. Ponteil, *L'Eveil des nationalités et le mouvement libéral (1815–1848)* (Paris, 1960), p. 1.
6. Jacques Droz, *L'Epoque contemporaine, I: Restaurations et révolutions (1815–1871)* (Paris, 1955), pp. 1, 576.

written a few years after the last war and intended for senior high school students in East Germany and the Soviet Union, relating the post-Napoleonic settlement as follows:

After the fall of Napoleon, the European princes and statesmen assembled in Vienna in 1814 in order to work out the conditions for a peace and to re-draw the map of Europe for the benefit of the victors . . . The monarchs re-divided Europe in their own interests and without any consideration for the rights and aspirations of the people.[7]

But, meanwhile, some historians in the West, particularly in Britain and the United States, had begun to reinterpret these events in somewhat different terms. Broadly, this new direction is that noted by Mr. Albrecht-Carrié when he writes of a turn from an attitude of general hostility to the "shortcomings of Vienna" to one of greater sympathy for a settlement which had "served Europe for a century"; and he continues: "The contrast is certainly arresting between the mere twenty-year truce that followed the 1919 settlements and the story enclosed by the years 1815 to 1914."[8] Mr. E. H. Dance, writing a few years earlier in *History Today,* is a little more specific when he distinguishes, in this respect, between French and British historians. "Whereas French books", he observes, "tend to regard the Peace of Vienna as a main cause of the revolutions of 1830 and 1848, we treat it as a peaceful settlement which lasted for the century during which we ourselves fought no major war."[9]

Of course, the "great divide" between the earlier and the later interpretation, or between the French and the British, was not always as sharp as all that. Even earlier historians, while generally hostile to the Vienna Settlement for the reasons we have noted, often conceded that the Concert of Europe that followed had two sides to it: one the attempt to "turn the clock back" or to impose the will of the victors on the vanquished; the other to create machinery for the maintenance of peace. These historians had, as we have seen, tended to stress the first aspect at the expense of the second. Now Anglo-Saxon historians,

7. A. Jefimow, *Geschichte der Neuzeit 1640–1870* (Berlin-Leipzig, 1951), pp. 139–40.
8. Albrecht-Carrié, *Diplomatic History,* pp. 15–16.
9. E. H. Dance, "English Textbooks and Foreign Complaints," *History Today* (September, 1956): 635.

both liberals and conservatives, began to reverse the process and, fresh from their experience of the First World War (and later of the Second), to give the victors of 1815 the credit for having tried to devise some means of peacefully settling international disputes. Thus the Vienna Settlement and the Concert of Europe changed their image and began to be seen as the forerunners of the League of Nations of 1920 and the United Nations of 1945.[10]

Actually, the first academic historian to give this new twist to the study of the Concert of Europe, Walter Alison Phillips, produced the first edition of his book before the First World War started, in the spring of 1914. Its full title is eloquent expression of what Phillips was attempting to put over. He called it *The Confederation of Europe: a Study of the European Alliance 1813–1823 as an Experiment in the International Organization of Peace.*[11] Like many other historians since his day, the author believed that "the chief value of history lies precisely in the light which it can throw on the problems of the present"; and the immediate problem that concerned him was not so much the current discussion on the peaceful settlement of disputes that was going on in Europe (though this also played a part in his thinking) as "the series of questions involved in recent developments of the Monroe Doctrine, about which so much is now being heard in connection with the relations of the United States with the Republics of Latin America." Of course, the experience of the war and the spate of peacemaking projects that it engendered gave an entirely new relevance to Phillips's book when it reappeared, in a second edition, in 1920. Yet he decided that, in spite of the immensity of the changes that had taken place in the intervening years, the central message of the book and the lessons he had drawn were still perfectly valid and could be restated without any fundamental alteration to his original text. However, he did take account of the more recent work of English scholars like Harold Temperley and Charles Webster, based on Foreign Office records that had just been opened; and, above all, he

10. See René Albrecht-Carrié (ed.), *The Concert of Europe 1815–1914* (New York, 1968), pp. 8–9.
11. Walter Alison Phillips, *The Confederation of Europe* (London, 1914; second edition, 1920).

rewrote his concluding section on the organization of peace and attuned it to the heated debates that were then going on about the League of Nations.[12]

However, Phillips was a somewhat lightweight historian, whose work, pioneering though it was, has now a distinctly outmoded and archaic flavor. It is unlikely, therefore, that his book has had anything like the same influence on the work of subsequent historians as the researches of Harold Temperley and C. K. (now Sir Charles) Webster. Webster, a moderate conservative, was commissioned by the Foreign Office in 1918 to write a short history of the Congress of Vienna. It is a slim volume of little more than 150 pages; yet it firmly established the "new look" that Anglo-Saxon historians were beginning to give to the whole Congress System. Webster was clearly influenced by the experiences and aftermath of the First World War when he wrote that "the primary need of Europe, once the Napoleonic tyranny was overthrown, was a period of peace; and this the statesmen of Vienna undoubtedly secured in a far greater degree than the most sanguine of the publicists of the time dared to hope." And he went on to condone "the failure of the Congress to give any adequate expression to the nobler ideals of universal peace"; above all, "in inventing the 'Concert', they undoubtedly contributed in a very marked degree to the security of Europe, for it cannot be doubted that, in spite of its failures, that system did much for the nineteenth century."[13]

English historians between the two wars, while exploring the problems further, were generally inclined to adopt this view. Being conscious of the failings of the peace settlement of 1919, they tended to see the achievements of the men of 1815 in a more favorable light. R. B. Mowat, a liberal Oxford historian, concludes a chapter that he wrote on the Concert of Europe in 1922 with the words:

If . . . the Settlement of 1815 be compared with that of 1919 in its effects on the vanquished, the comparison is still more favourable; for in France in 1815 the Treaty of Paris was carried out to the letter, and within three years the

12. Phillips, *Confederation*, pp. i–xii, 279–304.
13. C. K. Webster, *The Congress of Vienna 1814–1815* (New York, 1963), pp. 145–8.

conquered State had been rehabilitated and accepted as a regular working member of the European States-system.[14]

In another book, published in 1930 (that is, after the defeated Germans had been admitted to the fold), Mowat has a further friendly word to say for the "Concert of the Powers of Europe," which, under Metternich's guidance, maintained peace "by concerted action, peaceful and precautionary, of the governments of Europe, meeting together and exchanging views whenever the general peace seemed to be threatened." And he contrasts the "period of European peace, 1815–1848" with "the period of wars, 1848–1871" that followed.[15] E.L. (now Sir Llewellyn) Woodward, too, in his book *War and Peace in Europe 1815–1870* (1931), wrote of this period as of an "age of European Peace";[16] and Grant and Temperley, the authors of a textbook that is still in use after forty years, sum up the work of the peacemakers of 1815 in the following words:

It has been customary to denounce the peacemakers of Vienna as reactionary and illiberal in the extreme. It is indeed true that they represented the old regime and were, to a large extent, untouched by the new ideas. But they represented the best and not the worst of the old regime, and their settlement averted any major war in Europe for forty years. According to their lights the settlement was a fair one.[17]

On the whole, historians writing after the Second World War, though similarly struck by significant parallels between the needs of the statesmen of 1945 and those of 1815, have not been prepared to accept such easy generalizations without question. The first work of any consequence to appear on the subject in English after the war was Harold Nicolson's *Congress of Vienna* (1947). Like his predecessors, he stresses the analogies between the two postwar sets of events when he writes:

Then as now Great Britain . . . had destroyed a totalitarian system which threatened to engulf the world. Then as now the common purpose which had united the Nations in the hour of danger ceased, once victory had been

---

14. R. B. Mowat, *A History of European Diplomacy 1815–1914* (London, 1922) p. 27.
15. R. B. Mowat, *The Concert of Europe* (London, 1930), pp. 1–3.
16. Woodward, *War and Peace,* p. 1.
17. A. J. Grant and Harold Temperley, *Europe in the Nineteenth and Twentieth Centuries (1789–1950),* sixth edition, (London, 1933), p. 138.

achieved, to compel solidarity. . . . Then as now there were those who felt that in destroying one menace to the peace and independence of nations they had succeeded only in erecting another and greater menace in its place.

But he went on to warn his readers that "we can learn little from history unless we first realise that she does not, in fact, repeat herself."[18]

Yet Nicolson's is a conventional piece which, in other respects, adds little to the liberal-conservative presentation of the theme by Temperley or Webster. Of greater originality and interest are three books published by non-British authors in the middle-1950s—one by a Frenchman and two by Americans. Pierre Renouvin, one of the veterans of present-day French historical writing, treats "the European system of 1815" as part of a six-volume work entitled *Histoire des relations internationales,* published between 1953 and 1955. His narration of events does not differ significantly from that of earlier writers, nor does he advance a new theory of his own; but, being a Frenchman of this century as well as being a social and a diplomatic historian, he adds an entirely new dimension: he sketches out, before he comes to the relations between the powers, the social, economic and cultural background against which these relations developed. "The rivalries between the states," he writes, "in this period 1815 to 1840, can only be reasonably explained within the framework of a general outline of their social and economic setting and of the trends of contemporary political thought." These are what he calls "les forces profondes," which comprise the social classes in the various states of Europe, their interrelations, their interests and aims and the intellectual and political movements through which they found expression.[19] Thus diplomatic history, long treated in isolation, becomes part of the history of the nation and of society as a whole.

Renouvin's work, like that of his contemporary, Jacques Droz, is typical of the new French school of social-political history. The con-

18. Harold Nicolson, *The Congress of Vienna: A Study in Allied Unity, 1812–1822* (New York, 1970), pp. xi–xii.
19. Pierre Renouvin (ed.), *Histoire des relations internationales,* 6. vols. (Paris, 1953–5). Vol. 5, *Le XIXe siècle (1): L'Europe des nationalités et l'éveil des nouveaux mondes* (Paris, 1954), pp. 9–27.

tribution made by the two Americans is somewhat different. Where Renouvin is concerned with diplomatic relations as the reflection of a nation's social and economic life, the Americans are concerned with essentially political relationships, with power, equilibrium and stability. The more original of their two books, though by no means the more eloquent, is perhaps Edward Gulick's *Europe's Classical Balance of Power,* first published in 1955. To Gulick the settlement of 1815 is a case study in territorial equilibrium, in the restoration of the balance of power after the Revolutionary and Napoleonic interlude, in the interests of the victor-nations. The whole idea is neatly summed up toward the end of the book:

With the crystallization of the Quadruple Alliance and the signing of the various documents of the Second Peace of Paris . . . the great peace settlement of 1814–1815 was rounded out, incomplete in many details, unfortunate in many respects, destined to endless revision in the coming decades, and yet markedly consistent, in major outlines, with the conception of a Europe in balance. It represented the last great European settlement which could be consciously, and with relative consistency, based on the principles of the balance of power. Equipped with a refined system for preserving the European equilibrium, states could turn their faces happily towards the future.

Nor, he argues, is there any sharp historical break between the "balance" system of 1815 and the later "collective security" systems devised after the two world wars. For, he concludes, "at bottom, the collective security of 1919 or 1945 was merely an elaboration and refinement of the coalition equilibrium of 1815, just as the latter was an elaboration and refinement of the [earlier] alliance balance."[20]

Henry Kissinger's *A World Restored* appeared two years later. The theme and presentation are quite different from Gulick's; yet basically they have much in common. Both are conservatives who, in the light of the dangerous imbalance of the 1950s, write with a certain cool and detached respect for the relatively successful efforts of the Congress statesmen to restore a balanced and orderly *status quo.* Where Gulick sees this restoration in terms of an equilibrium in international rela-

---

20. Edward Vose Gulick, *Europe's Classical Balance of Power: A Case History of the Theory and Practice of the Great Concepts of European Statecraft* (Ithaca, New York, 1955), pp. 291, 308.

tions, Kissinger sees it in terms of what he calls "stability." This stability, which was the central goal of conservative statesmanship, had little to do with any conscious quest for peace. It resulted rather (in his view) from "a generally accepted legitimacy," which, he explains, "means no more than an international agreement about the nature of workable arrangements and about the permissible aims and methods of foreign policy." So Kissinger's book, presented in the form of a study of the conservative statesmanship of 1812–1822, is really an essay in "the art of the possible" and a cautionary tale addressed to the peaceseekers of our times. It is not the conscious quest for peace, he is saying, that will restore a balanced harmony between the nations; for "those ages which in retrospect seem most peaceful were least in search of peace"; and "those whose quest for it seems unending appear least able to achieve tranquility."[21]

2. *The Holy Alliance*

If historians have been at loggerheads over their interpretations of the Vienna Congress or the Concert of Europe, they have at least been fairly clear, once they had chosen their ground, as to what they have been talking about. The same cannot always be said of their treatment of the Holy Alliance, which to say the least, is often quite confusing. Is the alliance merely a declaration signed by certain powers; and, if so, is it the original version of the document presented by Alexander or the final draft after it had been doctored by Metternich? Or is it an omnibus term to cover the policies of the three central or Eastern powers, or even broadly synonymous with the "spirit" of the Vienna settlement in general? These questions are of some importance, as the views of historians towards the Holy Alliance has been considerably influenced by the precise meaning they have attached to it. In this case, therefore, we shall not expect historians to divide so neatly along national and political lines as they did over their attitudes towards the Vienna Congress or the Concert of Europe.

21. Henry A. Kissinger, *A World Restored: Metternich, Castlereagh and the Problem of Peace 1812–1822* (New York, 1964), pp. 1–3

Broadly, we may perhaps divide them into the following main groups: those who have damned the Holy Alliance and all its works; those who have viewed it with mild amusement, contempt or indifference; those who have seen it as a noble endeavor to build a durable peace or a better world; and those to whom it has mainly appeared as an instrument in the power struggle between Russia and Britain and the other Congress powers.

The first group are mainly those who adopted a consistently hostile attitude to the Congress system as a whole. To them the alliance, as it took shape, had the single purpose of erecting a barrier against all national and democratic aspirations; it was its spirit that animated the succession of congresses between 1818 and 1822 that mobilized armies to crush revolutions in Italy and Spain. So, if we return to the London pamphlet of 1821, we find the Holy Alliance denounced as "a new compact" whereby the rulers of Europe "proceeded to institute a Council, or Court of High Sovereignty, arrogating to themselves a jurisdiction over the peoples of all countries . . . while they professed to be themselves governed in their decisions by no law, other than their will, measured out according to a new arbitrary and capricious rule of their own invention, and called by them 'THE MONARCHICAL PRINCIPLE.' " Debidour, the French historian of the Third Republic, wrote that the Holy Alliance, whatever the original intentions of Alexander, inaugurated a policy "whose chief object was to stifle the principle of the Revolution"; while to the Soviet historian Jefimow it was "a league of the rulers against the peoples," whose purpose was to suppress revolutions wherever they might arise "in the name of religion." Moreover, it was "a mask for the hegemony of the Tsar over all European governments"; yet it was Metternich that took over the practical direction of affairs, and it was under his guidance that the Alliance assumed a policeman's role in suppressing revolutions in Italy and Spain.[22]

To such historians, the Holy Alliance was, for all practical pur-

22. *The Declaration of England,* pp. 3–4; Debidour, *Histoire diplomatique,* p. 92; Jefimow, *Geschichte der Neuzeit,* p. 142.

poses, an instrument of blind reaction; and it is a matter of relatively minor consequence how far Alexander's original scheme differed from that of Metternich. With subtle variations, this has also been the general view of French liberal and radical historians nurtured on the revolutionary principles of 1789 or 1848. Their British counterparts (whether liberal or conservative) had, of course, no such traditions to uphold and they have tended in consequence to see the Alliance in a somewhat different light. More emphasis has been placed on the origins and purpose of the draft that Alexander presented to Metternich and Castlereagh for their approval, and it has been possible, therefore, to draw a sharper line of distinction between the Alliance as conceived by Alexander and the eventual policies and activities of the Congress powers.

Seeing the problem in this way, these historians have tended to contrast the futile and impractical efforts of the Tsar with the more practical and hard-headed wisdom of Castlereagh as expressed in the alternative policy of the Quadruple Alliance. In this they have followed the example set by Castlereagh himself when he dismissed the Holy Alliance, as presented by the Tsar to his fellow-rulers, as a "sublime piece of mysticism and nonsense," advised the Prince Regent not to sign it, and told Parliament that "this country cannot and will not act upon abstract and speculative principles of precaution." In relating these events, Sir Charles Petrie, a conservative British historian, wrote that "time soon proved that the British government was, from its own point of view, wise to hold aloof"; and added that "the Holy Alliance was, as has so often been pointed out, not very holy nor much of an alliance, but in its origins it was inspired by some not ignoble motives." To Sir John Marriott the Alliance was a piece of "officious benevolence," which, luckily, was saved from having any dire effects by the practical realism of Castlereagh. R. B. Mowat termed it a vague sort of "understanding" that "really committed the signing Parties to nothing at all"; and Temperley, who was also writing in the early 1920s, described it as "merely a vague and romantic piece of sentiment." More recently, Mr. Albrecht-Carrié has gone even further and has dismissed it in a few lines as a "vague declaration" that had "little influence on the future course of events."[23]

Sir Charles Webster, the real progenitor of the more recent Anglo-Saxon thinking on the whole Congress System, wrote, a generation earlier, in almost identical terms that the Holy Alliance "had no influence on affairs"; yet he conceded that it did "produce in the minds of the people the suggestion that the sovereigns were leagued together against them." Harold Nicolson (writing in 1947) develops this idea and has been one of the few British historians to argue, much as the French have done, that the Alliance was perhaps not so silly or so innocuous after all. "For," he asks, "against what or whom could these potentates be allying themselves unless it were against the liberal movement and the spirit of the age?" And he continues:

It may well be that Alexander did not at first intend that his Alliance should become a formula of repression; it only became so when Metternich, playing adroitly upon the Tsar's increasing repudiation of his former liberal senti-ments, used it as an agent of repression. And as such it rapidly cast a blight upon the Quadruple Alliance and brought the whole Conference system, on which Castlereagh had staked so much, into universal suspicion and disre-pute.[24]

Other writers—and these, too, have been mainly Anglo-Saxons—have taken a more generous view of the Holy Alliance, and particu-larly of what they have believed to have been Alexander's original intentions; it is a view shared by both liberal and conservative histori-ans. Walter Alison Phillips, in his *Confederation of Europe,* saw the Holy Alliance as a serious attempt made by the victors of 1815 to establish a workable system for the maintenance of peace; and the centralized model they imposed on the European states was "not primarily in the interests of despotism, but in the supposed interests of the general peace of society." And, in relating the birth of the League of Nations, he writes that "the new age has been born; the new

23. Sir Charles Petrie, *Diplomatic History 1713–1933* (London, 1946), pp. 130–31; J. A. R. Marriott, *A History of European Diplomacy* (London, 1931), p. 144; Mowat, *European Diplomacy,* p. 26; H. V. W. Temperley, "Attempts at International Govern-ment in Europe: 1814–25; 1919–22," in W. N. Medlicott (ed.), *From Metternich to Hitler* (New York, 1963), p. 15; Albrecht-Carrié, *Diplomatic History,* p. 23.
24. Webster, *Congress of Vienna,* p. 145; Nicolson, *Congress of Vienna,* p. 253.

Holy Alliance is in existence"![25] An even greater enthusiast was Elizabeth York, an English writer, who, hot on the heels of the peace settlement of 1919, produced a book entitled *Leagues of Nations,* which included a study of Alexander I and the Holy Alliance. Here Alexander's intentions are described as being purely idealistic and his proposals to have foreshadowed, to a remarkable degree, the most advanced nineteenth-century liberal thinking on European unity, nationalism and democracy. It was only, she argues, the conservatism, duplicity and obstinate hostility of the other Congress leaders that brought these plans to nought. And, she insists, it was not the Holy Alliance, but the other alliances, that were responsible for the succession of repressive congresses that brought the whole system into odium and disrepute. "In 1815," she concludes, "the Monarchs of Europe signed the Holy Alliance. They then had their chance, but, as autocrats, they lost it for ever. In this century there must be a Holy Alliance of Democracy."[26]

No other historian, perhaps, has been quite so uncritically eulogistic of the alliance as Miss York; it has been more customary to draw a line of distinction between the intention and the performance and to concede that the alliance, as conceived by Alexander, went astray, not because it was buried altogether but because it was put to uses that Alexander had never intended. Among those holding, or appearing to hold, this view was W. P. Cresson, an American scholar of the 1920s, who presented the Holy Alliance as a part of the European background to the Monroe Doctrine. To Cresson it appeared that Alexander's "cherished scheme for a Christian League of Peace" was thwarted by the bad reception it was given by his confederates. James Brown Scott, who wrote a preface to the volume, went perhaps rather further than the author himself when he observed that the Holy Alliance lay in the tradition of the Abbé de Saint-Pierre's *Projet de paix perpetuelle* of a hundred years before, and was "conceived in the same generous spirit" as the League of Nations.[27]

25. Phillips, *Confederation of Europe,* second edition, pp. 281–2.
26. Elizabeth York, *Leagues of Nations* (London, 1919), pp. 294–319.
27. W. P. Cresson, *The Holy Alliance: The European Background of the Monroe Doctrine* (New York, 1922), p. iv.

A somewhat different slant is given to these arguments by H. G. Schenk in his *Aftermath of the Napoleonic Wars* (1947). Other writers, in tracing the origins of Alexander's "sublime piece of nonsense," had tended to see it as a gradual development of the Tsar's own political thought, to which the mysterious and fanatical Madame de Krüdener had made a greater or lesser contribution.[28] Schenk saw it, rather, as the outcome of two opposing trends, both of them partly religious. One was a conservative trend, drawing on Edmund Burke's *Reflections* and the political-Catholic ideas of Bonald and de Maistre; the other was a radical trend, variously nurtured by the mysticism of Novalis, Baader, Novikov and de Krüdener, and the spirit of the eighteenth-century Enlightenment. And of the two it was the latter, Schenk argues, that had the greater influence on Alexander. This explains why his project caused alarm as much to the Catholic Church as to Europe's temporal rulers. "In this way," he concludes, "was once more manifested the essentially radical character of Alexander's scheme."[29]

Other writers, as we have seen, while conceding that Alexander may have had some such radical intention, insisted that what eventually emerged had a different purpose altogether. In Harold Nicolson's words, the alliance "became a formula of repression"; and Maurice Bourquin, the Swiss author of an *Histoire de la Sainte Alliance,* concluded that "its story was that of a dream which became degraded in contact with reality."[30] Kissinger is more precise. He shows that Metternich, alarmed at what he considered to be the revolutionary implications of the Tsar's original draft, persuaded its author to accept a number of apparently minor, but in fact significant alterations before recommending it to his Emperor for signature. And so, where "the Tsar had conceived the Holy Alliance as programmatic, as the proclamation of a new era transcending the pettiness of history, Metternich used it to announce the end of a revolutionary period and the

28. See York, *Leagues of Nations,* pp. 294 ff.; and E. J. Knapton, *The Lady of the Holy Alliance: The Life of Julie de Krüdener* (New York, 1939).
29. H. G. Schenk, *The Aftermath of the Napoleonic Wars: The Concert of Europe—An Experiment* (London, 1947), pp. 1–43.
30. Maurice Bourquin, *Histoire de la Sainte Alliance* (Geneva, 1954), p. 471.

re-entry into history." And so it was this amended document, and not the Tsar's original draft, that formed, with the Quadruple Alliance, one "of the two instruments which guided Europe for the next decade." "Thus," he adds, "with misgivings and hesitations, with an exalted vision and a sober calculation, was born the Holy Alliance, the symbol of an era."[31]

Such historians, then, whether English, American or Swiss, have been prepared to allow Alexander, if not unstinted praise, at least the benefit of the doubt; and they have seen the Holy Alliance, if not entirely through rose-tinted spectacles, perhaps somewhat like the traditional curate's egg. But there has been a further group of historians, whose attitude has been far more severe and for whom the alliance has appeared to have been little more than a maneuver (or a series of maneuvers) in a struggle for the mastery of Europe or the world. Few British historians (and possibly none) belong to this group; and A. J. P. Taylor may come as near to them as any when he writes on the second page of his *Struggle for Mastery in Europe*, which was written shortly after the end of the last war:

The nearest thing to a formal alliance was the association of the three conservative monarchies—Russia, Prussia and Austria—or, as they were strangely called, the 'three Northern Courts'. More loosely still, this was 'the Holy Alliance', though it had nothing but the name in common with the declaration of high Christian principles devised by Tsar Alexander I in 1815. The Holy Alliance was conservative in a double sense. It was a *status quo* alliance, opposed to changes of frontier; and it was a political alliance, opposed to political concessions within states.[32]

Though it is distinctive among British historians, there is nothing particularly original about this view of Taylor's; it is one he shares with several French historians, including Ponteil, Renouvin and Droz. Nor is it particularly "tough" if we compare it with the opinions already quoted from the radical *Declaration* of 1821 or the more recent histories of Debidour and Jefimow. A far more uncompromising, and a far more original, treatment is that given to the subject by

31. Kissinger, *World Restored*, pp. 188–90.
32. A. J. P. Taylor, *The Struggle for Mastery in Europe 1848–1918* (New York, 1954), p. 2.

Jacques-Henri Pirenne, a son of Henri Pirenne, the great Belgian historian of the early years of the century. The younger Pirenne's book on the Holy Alliance first appeared in 1946.[33] Strictly speaking, it is not so much a history of the Holy Alliance as a history of the relations between the powers during the post-Napoleonic period. But its originality lies precisely in the new dimensions and the new significance that he gives to the alliance. It is not sufficient, he argues in his Introduction, to limit a discussion of its field of operations to Europe, as has been done by so many other historians. This must be extended to include the wider world, for Britain and Russia were great maritime powers whose interests clashed all over the globe; and why else should the Tsar have been so anxious to have his declaration signed by all the maritime powers and by the President of the United States? And, more important for our present purpose, the Holy Alliance is presented by no means as an airy-fairy mystical piece of nonsense or as a well-intentioned, though impractical, scheme for universal peace, as it has so often been by British historians. Far from it. To Pirenne the Tsar was fully conscious of where his interests lay. These were to promote the claims of the Russian Empire at the expense of Austria and, above all, of the United Kingdom which, since the defeat of Napoleon, had replaced France as Russia's most dangerous rival. So the Tsar's "mystical" document, with its high-sounding phrases and its appeal to the peoples, was really a political manifesto, which aimed to weld all the powers into a single alliance for the purpose of isolating Austria in Europe and of undermining the growing world authority of Britain. And, argues Pirenne, if Castlereagh refused to sign the Holy Alliance, it was not because he thought it too vague or for the "constitutional" objections that he adduced, but for the very sound practical reason that he wished to dodge the Tsar's trap and to promote a plan of his own—the Quadruple Alliance—which promoted the British imperial interest at the expense of the Russian. In the event, it was the Tsar who turned out to be the loser. The Quadruple Alliance survived—though France was soon brought in as a junior

33. J.-H. Pirenne, *La Sainte-Alliance: organisation européenne de la paix mondiale* (Neuchâtel, 1946; second edition, 1951).

partner—and Alexander's own creation, the Holy Alliance, was taken over by Metternich, limited to Europe, and made an instrument of Austrian rather than of Russian domination.

This, in brief, is the new "Pirenne thesis"; it is a theme he repeated, a few years later, in his *Grands courants de l'histoire universelle*.[34] It has influenced the thinking of other Swiss and French historians, such as Bourquin and Jacques Droz, though not that of the more recent work done by Mr. Albrecht-Carrié.[35] Its interest lies not only in the new interpretation given to a much-discussed event, but also in the circumstances under which it was put forward. It was the time of the final defeat of Hitler, when the former allies—the Soviet Union and the Western Powers—fell out, as the allies of 1813–15 fell out after the defeat and abdication of Napoleon. It is not always possible to probe into the mind of the historian; but did Pirenne see the "Truman Doctrine," and the Atlantic Alliance that followed, as another Holy Alliance—this time directed against Soviet Russia and with its controls not surrendered to others, but firmly held and guided by its original promoter?

3. Congress Statesmen: Metternich and Castlereagh

To contemporaries, the Congress statesmen—Metternich, Castlereagh and Alexander of Russia—all appeared in a common light: as conquerors of Napoleon, peacemakers and the settlers of Restoration Europe. To liberals, like the authors of the London pamphlet of 1821, they were all equally reactionary and tarred with the same brush, as spokesmen for the "armed doctrine of Legitimacy" or the "'Rights of Thrones." To conservatives, on the other hand, they appeared as the joint saviours of Europe from wars and revolutions, and their thanks were due as much to Alexander as to Castlereagh or Metternich. In fact, for many, Alexander, with his particular plans for peace, held

---

34. J.-H. Pirenne, *Les grands courants de l'histoire universelle, IV: de la Révolution française aux révolutions de 1830* (Neuchâtel, 1951), pp. 338–43.
35. See Bourquin's preface to Pirenne's *Sainte-Alliance*, pp. xiii–xiv; and Jacques Droz, *Histoire diplomatique de 1648 à 1919* (Paris, 1959), pp. 292–5.

an ascendency over his colleagues. This was certainly the case at Vienna, and even in 1822, at the Congress of Verona, it was Alexander's favors that Châteaubriand courted before the Fench intervened in Spain.[36]

However, in retrospect, for all that has been written about Alexander and the Holy Alliance, his role has appeared to diminish as that of his partners has become inflated. And today it seems established that the real architects of the Vienna settlement and peace were Castlereagh and Metternich. In the words of a recent conservative writer: "That Europe rescued stability from chaos was primarily the result of the work of two great men: of Castlereagh, the British Foreign Secretary, who negotiated the international settlement, and of Austria's minister, Metternich, who legitimized it."[37] Besides, no serious effort has been made to dispel the "mystery" that still enshrouds the character and activities of Alexander, whereas the reputations of Metternich and Castlereagh have undergone something of a sea change.

Let us look at this process more closely. To begin with Metternich, who, of all the Congress statesmen, has made the most powerful impression on contemporaries and posterity. It was he, after all, who gave his name to the system they jointly created, who assumed the leadership of the Holy (or Neo-Holy) Alliance, and left his personal stamp on the whole period covered by this book. This was partly because he was the minister of the European state with the largest stake in conservatism and the lowest possible stake in change and revolution. It was partly because he lived so long—Castlereagh died in 1822, Alexander in 1825, Talleyrand in 1835; and Metternich, long outliving his former colleagues, died in 1859. It was also because he not only presented but actively promoted an image of undeviating conservatism, as a die-hard reactionary and the inveterate opponent of all the awakening forces of liberalism, nationalism and democracy. Grillparzer, the Austrian poet and dramatist, writing a quarter of a century after Vienna, called him "the Don Quixote of Legitimacy";

36. *Oeuvres complètes de Châteaubriand,* 12 vols. (Paris, 1931), XII: 105–7.
37. Kissinger, *World Restored,* p. 11.

and it was not a title he would have resented. In 1831, he wrote to a friend: "My principles, my dear Prince, have not changed, and they will never change . . . That which I wish in 1831, I wished in 1813 and in all the period in between"; and, twenty-eight years later, a few weeks before he died, he described himself to a visitor as having always been "a Rock of Order." Though he said it with pride, it was not a record to recommend him to the liberals of the Congress period any more than to those of 1848; nor did it endear him to a more flexible and less conservative statesman like Canning, who described him as "the greatest rogue and liar in Europe, perhaps in the civilized world." Yet he was optimistic about his future reputation; and in 1819, he wrote to Countess Lieven that "in a hundred years writers will judge me quite differently from the way those do who are concerned with me today."[38] And, although the image of the conservative statesman has remained virtually unchanged, it has in some quarters found warm admirers; and Mr. Albrecht-Carrié has written, with some justice, that "Metternich's stock has risen" as a consequence of the wars and peace settlements of the present century.[39]

During the greater part of the nineteenth century, Metternich's reputation, as may be imagined, was consistently low with liberals; but it was not only liberals to whom his name was anathema. For the "coachman of Europe" had been as stern an opponent of the nationalists of his day—even of the conservative, German kind—as he had been of liberals and democrats. So it is not surprising that Heinrich von Treitschke, the arch-conservative advocate of the *kleindeutsch* solution to the German problem, should have written of him with particular venom in his *History of Germany in the Nineteenth Century.* Metternich's "system," he wrote, was a

system of spiritual narrowness, the offspring of a mind empty of ideas, which did not to the slightest extent feel the dynamic forces of history; but this policy met the immediate needs of the Austrian monarchy; it answered the universal desire for repose felt by an exhausted world, and it was put into execution with practiced cunning; with a thorough knowledge of all the mean motiva-

38. Nicolson, *Congress of Vienna,* p. 274; Henry F. Schwarz (ed.), *Metternich, the "Coachman of Europe": Statesman or Evil Genius?* (Boston, 1962), p. vii.
39. Albrecht-Carrié, *Diplomatic History,* pp. 15–16.

tions of human nature, it understood perfectly those little arts of pleasantly smiling prevarication, which since ancient times have been the strength of Habsburg statesmanship.[40]

Albert Sorel, a Frenchman, in an essay written at about the same time, found it easier to be charitable. Besides, as a historian of diplomacy, he admired Metternich's technical dexterity. For the rest, he found him somewhat obtuse, pig-headed and resistant to all change; and, as a liberal-minded Frenchman, he deplored his attitude to the French Revolution. "Hatred of the French Revolution," he wrote, "was Metternich's dominant thought: the war which he waged against this revolution constitutes his whole role in history." And he sums up his faults and qualities as follows:

A man of expedients rather than a man of principles, he was unable to understand or to combat the French Revolution in its human foundations or in its national outburst; but when the Revolution became incarnate in a man [Napoleon], he comprehended it marvellously and entangled it in an inextricable net . . . It is there that one must see him at work, and that it will be possible to study the diplomat and statesman.[41]

In England, liberal hostility to Metternich was maintained longer than in France. The first biography in English, published in the 1880s, describes him as a Jesuit and petty intriguer, who overthrew Napoleon, the soldier, and enslaved Europe for a generation. G. A. C. Sandeman's *Metternich* (1911) was the first English study to abandon the old liberal caricature, to paint a relatively sympathetic picture and attempt a balanced judgment.[42] But none of these works, not even Treitschke's or Sorel's, was based on solid scholarly research in the Vienna archives. The first work of this kind was Heinrich von Srbik's monumental (and conservative) *Metternich, der Staatsmann und der Mensch*, published at Munich in 1925. Srbik held the Chair of History at the University of Vienna, and it may well be that he was moved to view Metternich more favorably than his liberal predecessors by his experience of what had so recently befallen the Austrian Empire. Like

40. Quoted (and translated) by Schwarz, *Metternich,* p. 52.
41. Schwarz, *Metternich,* pp. 4, 7.
42. C. B. Malleson, *Life of Prince Metternich* (Philadelphia, 1888); G. A. C. Sandeman, *Metternich* (New York, 1911); see Kissinger, *World Restored,* p. 339.

Sorel, Srbik presents Metternich as the arch-opponent of the French Revolution and all its works; but he also portrays him as a European statesman, intent on maintaining a balance of power in the Austrian interest, which a unified Germany and Italy would have inevitably destroyed. The effort failed but, in the author's view, it did not lack a certain grandeur. "However much room," he writes, "his political thought gave for criticism, it was a thought in the grand manner and as such is worthy of historical preservation: the idea of rebuilding Europe anew on the basis of a federation of states and of organizing the center of the Continent in two great federative unions, led in the ultra-conservative sense by the historical power of Austria."[43]

Following Srbik, English liberal and conservative historians of the interwar years have revised the old hostile liberal view of Metternich and accorded him varying degrees of respect. R. B. Mowat, a liberal, offered an evenly balanced judgment: on the one hand, he thought Metternich had "made a mistake" in so stubbornly opposing the constitutional and national movements of his day; on the other hand, he thought he was "right" to have made such strenuous efforts to maintain the peace.[44] E. L. Woodward, also a liberal, found him not unsympathetic, but considered his conservative principles too "doctrinaire" to meet the needs of the nineteenth century. "Metternich was fighting against the dead, the one battle in which the living must always be the loser."[45] Algernon Cecil, a conservative, was far more warmly enthusiastic. Metternich, in his view, was "the greatest statesman that the Austrian Empire ever possessed"; he rose to his eminence "by capacity of understanding"; above all, he was "a great European"; for "more than any man of his period, he stood for that international solidarity which is admitted on all hands to be our own urgent need, and, in this respect, if in no other, he looked beyond his own age into ours."[46]

---

43. Schwarz, *Metternich*, p. 15.
44. Mowat, *Concert of Europe*, p. 2.
45. E. L. Woodward, *Three Studies in European Conservatism* (London, 1929; second edition, 1960), pp. 42–43.
46. Algernon Cecil, *Metternich 1773–1859: A Study of his Period and Personality* (London, 1933), pp. 1–11.

But one, at least, of Srbik's countrymen was not impressed. Viktor Bibl, like Srbik, was professor of history at the University of Vienna in the interwar years; but, unlike Srbik, he was a liberal whose judgment on Metternich, which he expressed in three considerable works between 1922 and 1936, was entirely different from his. In Bibl's pages, Metternich, far from emerging as a rock of stability and a great European, appears as a liar, a traitor, a coward and a fool, an "evil genius," and a disruptive force which led both Austria and Europe close to disaster. "Metternich," he wrote (in flat contradiction of nearly everything his colleague had said of him) "was not the conservative principal: everywhere he acted as a disintegrating force on the authority of the state, sowed mistrust and dissension between prince and people, prince and ministers, and finally in Austria himself put the ax to the structure of the state . . . He was also not the preserver of the peace of Europe: everywhere he caused unrest, and the armed peace which existed after the Vienna Congress hindered the work of reconstruction no less than would have a number of wars. Above all, however, the artificially repressed forces and problems burst upon Europe with devastating violence. The ruin which the collapse of November 1918 left behind, is in the last analysis the work of Prince Metternich."[47]

Since the last war, Metternich has again come in for praise: somewhat whimsical and muted in Sir Lewis Namier's brief piece on him in *Vanished Supremacies* (1958) and in Bertier de Sauvigny's *Metternich et son temps* (1959).[48] But to Kissinger, Metternich shares with Castlereagh the honor of being one of the two "statesmen of repose" who gave Europe stability and saved her from the chaos left by the Napoleonic Wars. They divided the task: Castlereagh negotiated the peace settlement and Metternich "legitimized it." He was a superb diplomat and manipulator; but he lacked creativity and confessed his inability "to erect a new structure in our Empire . . . and for this

47. Viktor Bibl, *Metternich, der Dämon Oesterreichs* (Vienna, 1936), pp. 378 ff., quoted (and translated) by Schwarz, *Metternich,* p. 28.
48. L. B. Namier, *Vanished Supremacies* (London, 1958), p. 13–16; G. de Bertier de Sauvigny, *Metternich et son temps* (Paris, 1959; English translation: London, 1962).

reason all my care was directed to conserving that which existed."
That statement, argues Kissinger, "marks the limits of Metternich's
abilities." "For statesmen must be judged not only by their actions but
also by their conception of alternatives. Those statesmen who have
achieved final greatness did not do so through resignation, however
well founded. It was given to them not only to maintain the perfection
of order, but to have the strength to contemplate chaos, there to find
material for creation." Yet, he adds, "a man who came to dominate
every coalition in which he participated, who was considered by two
foreign monarchs more trustworthy than their own ministers, who for
three years was in effect Prime Minister of Europe, such a man could
not be of mean consequence."[49]

But the most fulsome eulogist of them all, in the postwar years, has
been Peter Viereck, a German-American, whose *Conservatism Re-
visited* was published in New York in 1949. Where Treitschke, eighty
years before, denounced Metternich as the arch-enemy of German
nationalism, Viereck, looking back from the German experience of
the 1930s and forties, praised him for the very qualities that
Treitschke had condemned. Metternich's conservative internationalism, he argues, erected a salutary barrier against the chauvinist agitation of Fichte, Arndt and Jahn and the student patriots of his day; for
these, together with men like Kleist and Wagner, he sees as the
forerunners of modern anti-Semitism and of the Hitler movement in
Germany. So Metternich, who would have no truck with similar
"demagogues," nationalists and anti-Semites, becomes in retrospect
the farsighted opponent of the most destructive and illiberal forces of
the present century. Moreover, the author extends his argument to a
wider field and, "in the light of two World Wars of nationalism," faces
his readers with the choice: "is western man's 'native country' to be
an ever broadening community of humanity—as Metternich's was
'Europe'—or is it to be some narrowly and meanly provincial 'nation'?" And he concludes: "The Metternichian demand for a universal
law above private force is the best hope not only of internationalism,

49. Kissinger, *World Restored*, pp. 11, 192–213.

not only of peace, but perhaps—since Hiroshima—of the survival of man."[50]

So nationalism and internationalism, conservatism and liberalism have been important counters in the century-long debate on Metternich's vices and virtues. Yet although it is true that his stock has generally risen, there are still many with ample reservations; and so the argument goes on. In the case of Castlereagh, the issue has been simpler; in fact, for liberal and conservative historians (though hardly so for socialists and Marxists), it has been largely a matter of rehabilitation. In his own day, Castlereagh certainly enjoyed a most unenviable reputation and, when he died by his own hand in 1822, he was accompanied to his grave by the jubilant shouts of his opponents. For he had enemies in plenty. His cold and reserved manner, for one thing, was forbidding and repellant and induced Bulwer Lytton to describe him as "stately in quiet, high-bred self-esteem." As Lord Lieutenant of Ireland, he incurred odium for his part in the Act of Union of 1801; and Daniel O'Connell regarded him as "the assassin of his country." As the associate of Metternich and Alexander in the post-war settlement of Europe, he attracted the hatred of liberals everywhere. Moreover, as Lord Sidmouth's fellow-minister, he was deeply implicated in the "Massacre of Peterloo" at Manchester in 1819 and spoke in support of the notorious Six Acts, which muzzled liberal opinions, that followed. It was the Six Acts that prompted Shelley to write his famous lines in *The Masque of Anarchy:*

> I met Murder on his way,
> He had a mask like Castlereagh.

And Byron, who derived his radical ideas from Moore and Hobhouse, was no less hostile, referring at various times to Castlereagh as "a wretch never named but with curses and jeers," as an "intellectual eunuch," a "cold-blooded, smooth-faced, placid miscreant," a "tinkering slave-maker" and "that long spout of blood and water—Castlereagh."[51]

50. Schwarz, *Metternich,* pp. 77–92.
51. Nicolson, *Congress of Vienna,* pp. 297–8.

To add to all this, Castlereagh had the misfortune to be followed at the Foreign Office by Canning, whose style and flair for public relations and willingness to appeal for support beyond the House of Commons won him the popularity that Castlereagh had always lacked, and professed to despise. Moreover, as Britain's national interest weakened her association with the three Eastern powers—over Italy, Greece, Spain and the Spanish colonies—Canning was credited with the sole responsibility for the change and was believed to be a "liberal" statesman promoting policies totally at variance and sharply contrasted with those of his reactionary and conservative predecessor.

As long as this legend (or part legend) persisted, Castlereagh naturally continued to be seen by the "Whig" school of historians, who held the field for a large part of the nineteenth century, as an inveterate Tory, the close ally of Metternich and a main bulwark of the Holy Alliance. Tories alone were willing to say a kind word for him: as, for example, the Marquess of Londonderry in his *Memoirs and Correspondence of Viscount Castlereagh* (1848–53) and Sir Archibald Alison in *The Lives of Lord Castlereagh and Sir C. Stewart* (1861). But as these were works of partisan hagiography, they did little to redeem the minister's reputation. It was only in France that reputable historians paid him tribute, as in the general histories of Capefigue (1839–41) and Thiers (1845–62).[52]

Meanwhile, in England, liberal opinion continued to be hostile; and even after the First World War, Elizabeth York's *Leagues of Nations* associated Castlereagh's "coercionist policy in Britain" with Metternich's "treatment of Italy" and contrasted them, to the evident discredit of both, with Alexander's liberal policies in Poland.[53] But, long before this, the work of serious rehabilitation had begun. It proceeded in three main stages. In the 1880s, as the records of the Foreign Office were opened up to the time of the Vienna Congress, Fyffe published the second volume of his *History of Modern Europe,* which gave credit to Castlereagh for his substantial contribution to the postwar settle-

---

52. C. K. Webster, *The Foreign Policy of Castlereagh, 1815–1822: Britain and the European Alliance* (New York, 1970), p. 495.
53. York, *Leagues of Nations,* p. 303.

ment of 1815. The second stage came twenty-five years later, on the eve of the First World War, when Alison Phillips's researches into the "Confederation of Europe" revealed Castlereagh to have been a diplomatist of vision and talent. But the real turning-point in the process of rehabilitation came with the publication, after the war, of Webster's two volumes on the foreign policy of Castlereagh and Temperley's parallel volume on Canning.[54]

Once more, it was not only access to new records that prompted historians to ask new questions, but also a new "climate of opinion," in this case provoked by the experiences and problems of another world war. The new records certainly played an important part; Webster had fresh Foreign Office documents at his disposal, and he was able to make effective use of the Windsor and Londonderry archives, both of which had been made available for the first time. And, in addition, as Webster himself noted, there was the new situation in Europe. "The result," he wrote, "has been a great revulsion of feeling, which has been intensified by the new interest aroused by recent events in the history of the last European settlement"; and "for the first time," he added, "the difficulty and the danger which Castlereagh had to face, have been realised."[55] The outcome has been, largely, two-fold. In the first place, Castlereagh has been firmly established as a diplomatist "of the very highest class" and as a statesman of vision and purpose who created the Quadruple Alliance—though, admittedly, he failed dismally to impress this constructive image on the Britons of his day! And even more significant perhaps for Castlereagh's reputation, the "great divide" separating his own from Canning's policies has been largely bridged. In this respect, an important discovery has been that of Castlereagh's State Paper of May 1820 and of his circular of January 1821, which clearly showed his opposition to the attempts being made by the Eastern powers to use the Holy Alliance and the Concert of Europe as instruments for intervening in the internal affairs of other states. This was already an important step

---

54. Webster, *The Foreign Policy of Castlereagh 1815–1822; The Foreign Policy of Castlereagh, 1812–1815: Britain and the Reconstruction of Europe* (New York, 1970); Howard Temperley, *The Foreign Policy of Canning, 1822–1827* (Hamden, Connecticut, 1966).
55. Webster, *Foreign Policy of Castlereagh 1815–1822*, p. 492.

towards that more positive breach with the whole Conference system for which Canning was responsible after Castlereagh's death.

Webster, who was mainly responsible for this new judgment on Castlereagh, warned, in the passage from which we have just quoted, that the pendulum might have swung too far; for "the result has been, perhaps, to exalt unduly some of his achievements." Yet, by and large, the new image presented by Webster and Temperley has been accepted, with minor qualifications, by liberal and conservative historians alike; and Castlereagh's reputation has not, since Webster wrote, gone through the same gyrations as Metternich's since Srbik first gave him his scholarly accolade. The new image was adopted, without question, by Sir John Marriott, a one-time bitter critic, in his *History of Europe from 1815 to 1823* (1931). Federick Artz, an American liberal historian, commended his practical statesmanship in *Reaction and Revolution* (1934). R. W. Seton-Watson, in his *Britain in Europe* (1938), went further and claimed that "no-one today will seriously deny that Castlereagh was one of the very greatest, and most constructive of British Foreign Secretaries."[56] After the last war, there has perhaps been a tendency to swing back the pendulum a little and to emphasize Castlereagh's failings as well as his achievements. Harold Nicolson, for example, writes that "the essential fallacy of Castlereagh's political philosophy was that by exaggerating the general need for 'repose' he sought to enforce static principles upon a dynamic world."[57] This sounds remarkably like some of the more recent criticisms of Metternich and opens up the gap again between Castlereagh and Canning. Kissinger, in his *World Restored,* returns to Webster's and Temperley's view and claims that the difference between the two "was largely a matter of emphasis." He also commends Castlereagh for bringing about "a peace of equilibrium and not of vengeance, a reconciled and not an impotent France"; and for bringing England, almost single-handed, into the "concert" of Europe. "It was," he argues, "the measure of Castlereagh's statesmanship that he recognized the precedence of integration over retribution in the construc-

---

56. Marriott, *History of Europe,* p. 18; Frederick B. Artz, *Reaction and Revolution 1814–1832* (New York and London, 1934), p. 112; R. W. Seton-Watson, *Britain in Europe 1789–1914* (Cambridge, England, 1938), p. 65.
57. Nicolson, *Congress of Vienna,* p. 260.

tion of a legitimate order." Yet he thought that, like Metternich, he overshot his mark; for "they set themselves tasks beyond the capacity of their material: Castlereagh through a vision beyond the conception of his domestic structure, Metternich through an effort unattainable in a century of materialism."[58]

So, by and large, Webster's "new look" has survived, without serious challenge, for forty years. But, of course, it does not take account of the other image, presented by Byron and Shelley, of the hero of "Peterloo"!

4. The Restoration

Even more hotly debated than the Settlement and the records of the statesmen have been the nature and merits of the Restoration in the various countries of Europe. Sometimes the debate has been waged over the European scene as a whole; more frequently, it has taken a more limited, national form. In either case, the questions posed have been broadly the same. Did the Restoration, with its alliance of Throne and Altar, turn back the clock on the new era opened up by the French Revolution? Was it, in fact, a reactionary interlude between the revolutions of 1789 and the new wave of liberal revolutions of 1830 and 1848? Or, alternately, did it provide a welcome respite and a salutary corrective to the excesses and commotions of the revolutionary years, allowing society to advance peacefully and gradually under conditions of stability and orderly government? Liberals have, of course, tended to adopt the former view and conservatives the second; though we shall see that the debate may have lost some of its sting and vigor in recent years.

On the European scale, the debate may perhaps have been a little one-sided and, up to the 1930s at least, it seems to have been the Whig or liberal view that has generally held the field. To take three examples from the interwar years. The first is from F. J. C. Hearnshaw, an English "Whiggish" professor who lectured on the history of modern Europe at King's College, London, in the early 1920s. To Hearnshaw,

58. Kissinger, *World Restored,* pp. 325–6.

the Restoration was almost total reaction. In France, it began with a moderate interlude, with Louis XVIII and the Charter; but the franchise in 1820 "prepared the way for the complete triumph of reactionaries over moderates in 1821." In England, the Liverpool ministry, dominated by Castlereagh, suspended Habeas Corpus, imposed a more rigorous censorship over all liberal publications and arrested all attempts at reform. Meanwhile, "in the Latin countries of southern Europe—countries where political moderation is unknown and where no thought of compromise or concession ever mitigates the insensate determination of each extremist to get his own way—a veritable royalist reign of terror was instituted; espionage, inquisition, treachery, imprisonment, assassination, execution, all played their part in an orgy of religious persecution and veiled war of extermination."[59] The great Italian liberal and idealist philosopher, Benedetto Croce, presents a less lurid and highly-charged picture. To him the issue was not so much one of black reaction and brutal persecution as of a battle of ideas between the forces of absolutism and the "religion of liberty"; and "in these fifteen years [between 1815 and 1830] the liberal ideal resisted the absolutist ideal, fought it without giving truce, and in the end won over it a victory that was permanent because it was substantial."[60] But, in English at least, it was probably an American, Frederick Artz, who formulated most distinctly and characteristically what may be considered the moderate liberal view of the Restoration years in Europe. Artz frankly told his readers of his own liberal commitment: "Among these [assumptions] is my Liberal point of view, which I have tried to minimize but which I have not attempted to conceal." Nevertheless, he puts forward a view with which many more conservative historians would not quarrel when he sums up his picture of "European Society after the Napoleonic Wars" as follows:

The monarchs and the aristocracies of Europe were more in agreement than they had been in earlier centuries. Years of disaster had brought them together, and by 1815 both had joined the clergy to combat the ravages of

59. F. J. C. Hearnshaw, *Main Currents of European History 1815–1915* (London, 1925), pp. 133–4.
60. Benedetto Croce, *History of Europe in the Nineteenth Century* (New York, 1933), p. 58.

revolutionary change. The old struggles between the monarchy and the aristocracy, like the Fronde in France and the old differences between the monarchy and the church . . . were now forgotten in a new alliance of the throne and the altar. For good or for ill, Europe in 1815 was in the control of King, nobles and priests as it had not been since the Age of Louis XIV.[61]

If the argument, then, on the European plane, has been somewhat muted and one-sided, the same cannot be said of the battle of words around the Restoration among historians of the various countries, whether of France, Germany, Italy or Spain. Let us take France as our example. The choice is perhaps justified, if for no other reason than that it is in France, as the progenitor ŏf revolution, that the issue has been most clear-cut, with the champions of the "principles of 1789" (or of 1793) being engaged with those who have always, in substance if not in detail, rejected the long revolutionary tradition which has exerted so powerful an influence on France's national life. So here, at least, Restoration has quite simply appeared as the antithesis of Revolution and has been largely debated in such terms. But two points need to be noted at the outset. One is that though the Restoration presents, as it were, the other side of the coin to the Revolution of 1789, it has received nothing like the same attention from historians. It has been noted, for example, by Professor Lynn M. Case of the University of Pennsylvania that while the *Guide to Historical Literature* of 1961, published in the U.S.A., lists 229 works on the Revolution and Empire, it lists a mere twenty-four on the Restoration.[62] The other point worth noting is that during the nineteenth century and the early years of the twentieth, the debate has been conducted in almost exclusively political and ideological terms. This is natural enough in a century which witnessed such a rapid succession of political experiments, from Empire to Restoration, from the July Monarchy of Louis-Philippe to the Second Republic of 1848, and from Louis-Napoleon's Second Empire to the short-lived Paris Commune and the Third Republic of the half-century leading up to the First World War. One result of this has been to make for a continuous and variegated

61. Artz, *Reaction and Revolution,* pp. 1–10.
62. Lynn M. Case, Preface to G. de Bertier de Sauvigny, *The Bourbon Restoration* (Philadelphia, 1966).

duel, in which moderate Royalists have battled with "ultras," liberals and Republicans with moderates, and liberals with Radicals or socialists; and this, in turn, has meant that the verbal duel has been maintained at a fairly high pitch of political polemic. In fact, it has been only in the past forty years that other factors—social, economic, cultural and institutional—have been thrown into the scales and, in consequence, taken some of the heat out of the polemic and imposed new perspectives and a certain consensus among the contestants as to what the Restoration was all about.

The duel began during the Restoration itself, when moderate Royalist historians (among them Mignet, Thiers, Guizot and Madame de Staël) sought to defend and extend the operation of Louis XVIII's liberal Charter by extolling the virtues of the "principles of 1789." These writers deliberately used history to wage their current political disputes with their conservative opponents; and Augustin Thierry, one of them, wrote that, "preoccupied with a strong desire to contribute to the triumph of Constitutional opinions, I began to look into works of history for proofs and arguments which would support my political beliefs." This first round proved to be a little one-sided, as the conservatives (with the possible exception of the unpredictable Châteaubriand) were easily out-classed by their liberal opponents.[63]

During the next phase, conservative historians were still at a discount. In the 1830s, when Thiers, Guizot and Mignet still flourished, the only Royalist historian of repute was J. B. Capefigue (we have already noted him as an early apologist for Castlereagh), who wrote a rather pedestrian ten-volume history of the Restoration and the fall of Charles X.[64] More interesting is the case of four eminent survivors of the Restoration—three of them were survivors of 1848 as well—who, looking back on these events from the 1840s and 1850s, recorded their impressions. The first is Mignet, who, in 1844, published a new edition of his *History of the French Revolution* with a brief postscript devoted to the Restoration. To him the revolution of 1830, which

---

63. See Stanley Mellor, *The Political Uses of History: A Study of Historians in the French Revolution* (Stanford, California, 1958).
64. J. B. H. R. Capefigue, *Histoire de la Restauration et des causes qui ont amené la chute de la branche aînée des Bourbons,* 10 vols. (Paris, 1831–3.)

toppled Charles X, was both just and inevitable. "In looking back on the sixteen years of the Restoration [he wrote], any impartial and unbiased observer will perceive that France, during most of that period, was in a state of crisis from which, regrettably, the only escape was by means of a new revolution." But Mignet, as a moderate Royalist, was not partial to mass movements and revolutions and he rallied loyally to the Orleanist throne.[65] Another Orleanist-supporter, who had also been a liberal historian under the Restoration, was Guizot; but he had more cause than Mignet to take a jaundiced view of revolutions and it was perhaps in consequence that he looked back on the Restoration, when he published his Memoirs in 1858, with something akin to nostalgia. From the outset, he tells us that he "felt no bitterness towards the old Government of France," and he did not feel "called upon to consider the House of Bourbon, the aristocracy of France, and the Catholic clergy, in the light of enemies." What he prized most was "just policy and liberty restrained by law" and, having despaired of both under Napoleon, he "hoped for them from the Restoration." Moreover, "true peace and liberty," after the wars, "returned with the accession of Louis XVIII." France, he writes, had (like himself) "no desire for a new revolution"; and if only Charles X had taken sensible advice, there would almost certainly have been none.[66] We shall find that the eulogy of Louis XVIII and the censure of Charles X is a constant theme among moderate Royalist (or ex-liberal) historians. This is, of course, similar to the distinction so frequently drawn between the practical good sense of Charles II and the blind obduracy of James II of England.

Guizot's old enemy, Lamartine, a Republican of 1848, looked back on the Restoration with even greater nostalgia, or (to use his own terms) with "tenderness" and "weakness of mind." Like Guizot, he had lived through a long succession of political experiments since 1789; and it is not surprising that he cherished happy memories of a

65. F. A. Mignet, *Histoire de la Révolution française depuis 1789 jusqu'à 1814, augmentée de l'histoire de la Restauration jusqu'à l'avénement de Louis Philippe 1er* (Paris, 1844), pp. 657–60.
66. F. Guizot, *Memoirs to Illustrate the History of My Time,* 2 vols. (New York, n.d.), I: 27–31, 356–7.

time when he had himself risen to literary fame. So to him the Restoration, sandwiched as it was between the "tyranny" of Napoleon and the "vulgar utility" of Louis-Philippe, was "an epoch of regeneration, pacific, intellectual and liberal for France"; and one where "poetry, literature and arts, forgotten, enslaved, or disciplined under the police of the Empire, seemed to spring from the soil under the feet of the Bourbons." Compared with this, the July Monarchy was a vulgar fraud commanding little respect: "Nothing was true in that royalty, but a throne and a people equally defrauded . . . Between hereditary right, which it had banished, and national election, which it had eluded, what could it do? Manoeuvre, negotiate, compound, unduly influence, or corrupt. It was a government with two faces, neither of which spoke the truth."[67]

Finally, in this quartet, there was the utopian socialist, Louis Blanc, advocate of "social" workshops and, like Lamartine, a minister (though a junior and short-lived one) in 1848. Unlike the other three, Blanc's approach is strictly clinical and impersonal, and, having little use for any of the systems that succeeded one another since the fall of Robespierre, he shows no more distaste (and no more affection) for the Restoration than for any other. All these régimes, he considered, had risen in response to the prevailing needs and interest of the *bourgeoisie:* the Restoration specifically, was, in his view, "essentially a *bourgeois* transaction"; and it was only when Charles X, with his priests and *émigrés* and reactionary advisers, ceased to serve their interests that he was removed in the July revolution with the aid of the streets.[68]

With the Second Empire and Third Republic we return to the political polemic, with Royalists and Republicans taking turns in commending or criticizing the work of the Restoration. Of the older works, Vaulabelle's *Histoire des deux Restaurations*[69] was liberal, while Nettement's *Histoire de la Restauration* (1860) was Royalist.

---

67. A. De Lamartine, *The History of the Restoration of Monarchy in France,* 4 vols. (London, 1851) I: ix–xv.
68. Louis Blanc, *The History of Ten Years, 1830–1840,* 2 vols. (New York, 1969), I: 18–19, 32–3.
69. Vaulabelle, *Histoire des deux Restaurations,* 8 vols., third edition, (Paris, 1857).

There followed two liberal studies: the first by Duvergier de Haranne (in 10 vols.) in 1857–71, the second by Viel-Castel (20 vols.) in 1860–78; and, in 1879, a shorter Royalist work (2 vols.) by Dareste de la Chavanne. Dareste, like other Royalists, defends the Restoration against the "unjust legend which, since 1830, had distorted the deeds and memories of the elder Bourbon branch"; and he praises the French army and the generals for their intervention against the Spanish Liberals in 1823. But, like Mignet and Guizot, he is a moderate, who condemns the "ultras" almost as much as he condemns the liberal opposition. It was these two extremes, he argues, whose "blind passions," compounded with the follies of Charles X, brought the dynasty to disaster.[70]

The same type of narrowly political history, more often conservative than liberal, persisted into the twentieth century. An early example is the work of an English historian, John R. Hall, whose *The Bourbon Restoration* was published in 1903. Hall, like so many Frenchmen, draws a clear distinction between the "wisdom" of Louis XVIII and the "folly" of Charles X; the latter, he maintains, "was by temperament unsuited to the part of a Constitutional Sovereign." He antagonized the middle classes and, "in the hour of distress the best elements of the nation stood aloof and allowed the Monarchy to fall to the ground." But Hall comes down strongly on the side of the Restoration and dismisses the charge that the Bourbons were oppressive as a "legend" sedulously propagated by their successors. In fact, he concludes: "under the Restoration the people enjoyed a greater degree of liberty than under any régime which preceded it, and fully as much as under the one which followed it."[71] A similar picture is presented, twenty years later, by J. Lucas-Dubreton, whose *La Restauration et la Monarchie de Juillet* appeared in English translation in 1929. We have the same eulogy of the Restoration as "a period of originality and power," as "the golden age of parliamentarism," when "honesty was almost universal, there were no scandalous trials, no corruption or embezzlement"—a clear allusion to the shoddy political

---

70. M. C. Dareste, *Histoire de la Restauration*, 2 vols., (Paris, 1879) I: i–iv, II: 130–3.
71. John R. Hall, *The Bourbon Restoration* (Boston, 1903), pp. 492–6.

horse-trading and "corruption" of the Third Republic. Once more, to establish the cause of the catastrophe that followed, a contrast is made between the two royal brothers: Louis "with his subtle intellect and his rigid good sense" and Charles, "a slave to cliques, narrowminded and chivalrous," who allowed himself to be trapped by Polignac into a *coup de force*, badly conceived and badly carried out.[72]

But, from the 1920s, there is a move away from the narrow framework of this older-style history with its emphasis on personalities and on the political issues largely to the exclusion of all others. The first decisive step in the new direction is taken by S. Charléty's *La Restauration* (1921) in Ernest Lavisse's series in the History of Contemporary France.[73] Charléty's book is still staunchly partisan: it is, in fact, a classical example of the radical-socialist point of view. There is no equivocation about the author's involvement on the liberal and revolutionary side: the Bourbons, though subtly distinguished, are an anachronism and an outdated survival from the past, while the future lies with their liberal opponents and (even more) with the Parisian democrats and participants in "les trois Glorieuses." But it is far more than a political polemic or party manifesto. A serious attempt is made to present a comprehensive and rounded picture of the Restoration from within and, for the first time, due weight is given to social, economic and intellectual affairs. This has the effect of reducing the temperature of the political debate and, in particular, of turning the heat off the wretched Charles X, the *bête noire* of all previous liberal, Republican and moderate-Royalist historians, and reducing him to something like life-size.

This turn to the twentieth century and to a less strident type of polemic is also evident in Frederick Artz's book, *France under the Bourbon Restoration*, first published in New York in 1931. As in his *Reaction and Revolution*, Artz once more proclaims his "middle-class Liberalism" to his readers, and he makes no bones about where his real sympathies lie. "To the great mass of the population," he writes,

72. J. Lucas-Dubreton, *The Restoration and the July Monarchy* (New York, 1925), pp. 171–2.
73. E. Lavisse (ed.), *Histoire de France contemporaine*, vol. 4; S. Charléty, *La Restauration* (Paris, 1921).

"the Restoration seemed only to have profited the clergy and the nobility. One can only conclude that the majority of Frenchmen from 1815 to 1830 were either hostile or indifferent to the political régime under which they lived." But the "political régime," imperfect as it was, is only a part of the picture. The Restoration, he writes further, was a highly significant period for the internal development of France, as it afforded the French their first extended experience of self-government. He notes, too, the growth of the industrial *bourgeoisie*, which henceforth, irrespective of the government in power, would continue on its irresistable forward and upward march. Intellectually, it was one of the richest periods in the history of France: literature and the arts flourished; in social and economic thought she was supreme; and, in many other respects, she dominated the whole political and economic life of the Continent.[74]

Finally, to return to French historians, we have a work similar to Artz's, though from a Royalist point of view, in Bertier de Sauvigny's *The Bourbon Restoration*, which first appeared in French in 1952 and in English in 1966. De Sauvigny is a Roman Catholic clerical historian, who holds chairs at both the University of Notre Dame in the United States and at the Institut Catholique in Paris; he also had an ancestor, Ferdinand de Bertier, who played a prominent part, on the "ultra"-Royalist side, in the Restoration. So it is perhaps not surprising that his sympathies should lie as decidedly with the Royalists as Charléty's with the liberals; his work has, in fact, been called "a kind of restrained rehabilitation of the Bourbon régime."[75] It is most certainly a *rehabilitation:* France (he writes) had never been so justly and honestly governed; she had her first taste of a genuinely parliamentary régime; she was preeminent in science, letters and the arts; her economy flourished; and, for good measure, in foreign affairs (as over Spain, Greece and Algiers), "the government of the Bourbons committed almost no mistakes." Even the unhappy Charles X is made to appear in a generally favorable light and his detractors, both past and

74. F. B. Artz, *France under the Bourbon Restoration 1814–1830* (New York, 1963), pp. 3–7, 96–8.
75. Gordon Wright, *France in Modern Times. 1760 to the Present* (Chicago, 1960), p. 283.

present, are gently taken to task. But most strikingly significant of the author's persisting Royalist sympathies is his eloquent peroration after the expulsion of the King:

Who was the real loser—the nation, which at that hour thought it was victorious; or the obstinate old man who was leaving these shores for good? The latter was giving up the most glorious throne of the finest kingdom in Europe; the former was depriving itself of a principle of political authority, of national unity, and of social stability, the equivalent of which it was never again to recapture. After a hundred and thirty years of revolutions and wars, of dictatorial or anarchical governments, France can today estimate the irreparable seriousness of the wound which she inflicted upon herself by her eviction of Charles X, and she beholds with nostalgic envy her great neighbor across the Channel who had the wisdom to reconcile monarchical tradition with the inevitable democratic evolution.[76]

So Bertier de Sauvigny's is a clear conservative challenge, which throws down the gauntlet without equivocation and with no holds barred. But, so far, there appears to have been no response from the liberal or radical side. Is it because of the author's restraint and urbanity, the elegance of his style, the comprehensiveness of the picture he paints, or the excellence and modernity of his scholarship? Or is it, more simply, that, with all that has happened to France since the 1930s, the Restoration has lost its appeal and relevance as a subject for political discussion? This has not been so, as we have seen, with the Vienna Congress and Settlement, the Holy Alliance and the Congress statesmen, but, in their case, modern experience has brought old issues into sharper relief and, thereby, lent a new edge to a century-old debate. But it seems unlikely that we may expect any similar shots in the arm to revive the debate on the Restoration in France.

76. de Sauvigny, *Bourbon Restoration,* pp. 454–60.

II

Industrial Revolution

The period we are concerned with was one of a rapid growth of population and industrial expansion. Yet it can only within closely defined limits be described as an age (let alone *the* age) of industrial revolution. It is true enough that such a "revolution" had begun, but it was one-sided and partial and had as yet been largely confined to Britain. It was only Britain that had, by the time of the Congress of Vienna, been through what W. W. Rostow has called the "take-off" stage of an industrial revolution; France and Belgium were to follow in the 1830s, Germany a dozen or fifteen years later, and Russia only in the 1890s. So, even by 1850, Britain alone was set firmly on a course of sustained industrial expansion and consolidation, while her rivals lagged far behind. The extent of this lead may perhaps be most simply measured in terms of capital goods and railway mileage. Between 1813 and 1850, the number of power-looms in England multiplied nearly a hundred times—from 2,400 to 224,000. Prussia had no steam engines in 1815, 419 in 1837, and 1,444 in 1849. Belgium had 354 engines in 1830 and 2,282 in 1850; and France had 15 in 1815, 625 in 1830, 2,500 in 1840, and over 5,000 in 1848. In railway-building, Britain was again the pioneer, though she had not so long a start. The first railways were built in England in 1823, in France in 1828, in Germany in 1835, and in Russia in 1838. But Britain's greater industrial capacity soon assured her of a substantial lead: in 1842, she had 2,260 miles of railways where Germany had 1,750, France (a slow developer) 528, and Belgium 388; by 1850, she had 6,500 miles, Germany had 3,250, and France only 1,875.[1] In all, with the solitary

1. Figures from E. J. Hobsbawm, *Industry and Empire* (Baltimore, 1970), p. 47; W. O. Henderson, *The Industrial Revolution on the Continent 1800–1914* (London, 1961), p. 21; Rondo E. Cameron, *France and the Economic Development of Europe 1800–1914* (Princeton, 1961), pp. 334, 347; E. J. Knapton and T. K. Derry, *Europe 1815–1914* (New York, 1965), p. 227; F. Ponteil, *L'éveil des nationalités,* pp. 668, 689.

exception of Britain, Europe's economy was still what the French economic historian Edouard Labrousse has called an "economy of the old régime"; that is one in which agriculture predominated over industry, transport was as yet poorly developed, and industry was still largely geared to the production of consumers' goods.[2]

Meanwhile, there had been a general growth of population, which had by no means been limited to countries undergoing an industrial revolution. Between 1800 and 1850, it has been claimed, Europe's total population rose by approximately one-third: from 180 to 266 million. The largest share in the increase went to Britain and Russia —that is, to an "industrial" country on the one hand and a "non-industrial" country on the other—in both of which the population almost doubled. Next, of the larger countries, came Germany with 56 percent, Spain with 50, and Italy with 39; while France, with her notoriously falling birth rate, merely kept pace with the European average and lagged behind with 34.[3] So there would appear, at first sight, to be no concordance whatever between an expanding industry and an expanding population (except perhaps in the case of Germany and Britain); why else should Russia, an obviously slow developer, expand so rapidly, while France, next to Britain the most industrialized country in Europe, lag so patently behind the rest? Yet such a conclusion would be quite misleading; for the figures quoted are overall figures, which take no account of regional variations in either industry or population. In fact, students of population are agreed that there is a close connection between the two "explosions"—the demographic and the industrial—even though the relationship varies greatly as between one country and another and it is not always possible to determine which of the two came first and how the one reacted on the other. This peculiar relationship is noted by Miss

2. C.-E. Labrousse, *Le mouvement ouvrier et les théories sociales en France de 1815 à 1848*, Cours de Sorbonne, (Paris, 1948), pp. 19–20.
3. D. Thomson, *Europe since Napoleon* (New York, 1962), p. 92; F. Ponteil, *L'éveil*, pp. 657–60. For a parallel growth in population densities, see W. Bowden, M. Karpovitch and A. P. Usher, *An Economic History of Europe since 1750* (New York, 1937) p. 3.

Phyllis Deane in a recent study on Britain, entitled *The First Industrial Revolution;* she writes:

Associated with the industrial revolution in time, and in a complex relationship of cause and effect, was a demographic revolution the mechanics of which are still not fully understood. One thing is clear however. One of the features that distinguishes the modern industrial (or industrializing) economy from its predecessors in the chain of economic development is that it involves sustained long-term growth in *both* population *and* output.[4]

5. The New Demography

Our period, then, is one of a "demographic revolution," associated with, though not necessarily coincident with, an industrial revolution which was as yet developing in only a handful of the European countries. But there has also been, in quite recent times, a demographic revolution in a different sense from that intended by Miss Deane: in the scholarly study of population and in the emergence of the new social science of historical demography. The study of population is in itself nothing new. Such study, Professor David Glass reminds us,[5] goes back to John Graunt's *Observations* of 1662; these were followed by eighteenth-century speculations (by men like Price and Hume in Britain and Massance and Montesquieu in France) about the causes of expansion and decline and, more spectacularly, by Malthus's famous *Essay on the Principles of Population* (1798). Malthus's thesis, with its gloomy prophecy that nations would face starvation without the rigorous control of population, has been hotly debated ever since; but it was not until after the last war that the study of population has been systematically pursued in Britain, France and the United States and developed into a social science in its own right. Here again, as in the case of so much historical investigation, current problems have prompted new questions and speculation about the past. So, on the eve of the last war, there was considerable concern about the appar-

4. Phyllis Deane, *The First Industrial Revolution* (New York, 1966), p. 20.
5. In his Introduction to *Population in History: Essays in Historical Demography,* D. V. Glass and D. E. C. Eversley (eds.) (Chicago, 1965), p. 1.

ently chronic decline in fertility in certain countries of the West; France was a notable example. The interest has persisted; but, since the war, the main problem has appeared to be one of a population "explosion" rather than one of decline, and attention has shifted to the developing countries of Africa, Asia and Latin America with their pressing need to feed and clothe their multiplying millions. So demography has become a vital public service and the demographers have sharpened their tools and, in search of long-term patterns, have turned to new sources of inquiry—the decennial census, parish registers, records of prices and wages and business profits, to notarial records, inventories and taxation rolls; and, generally, to such sources as are amenable to some degree of quantitative analysis. With such materials at their disposal, demographers and historians have looked more closely behind the sort of "global" statistics we quoted in an earlier paragraph; they have asked new questions and broken down the old questions to allow for a greater degree of subtlety and precision. "At each point of development," writes Dr. Eversley, "the historian wants to know:

How many (people) were there, and where did they live? How were their households organized? At what age did they marry, how many children did they have, what was their expectation of life? What was the proportion of children and of old people, and how many mothers worked? How frequently did they move, and over what distance? How easily did they change their occupations, what was the degree of social mobility? How far do these movements differ between town and country, between industrial and food-producing villages, between different occupations and social classes, between people of various religious persuasions and degrees of education? . . . What were their principal diseases, the causes of death and, perhaps even more important, disability? What was the length of their effective working life? . . . What contribution did medical and scientific advances (some of them related to industrial technology) make to health and survival?[6]

With such questions as these in mind, the new generation of historical demographers has set to work, and they have already achieved some notable results. Much of their work has been related to periods

6. D. E. C. Eversley, "Population, Economy and Society," in *Population in History,* p. 25.

in the history of Europe earlier than the one with which we are immediately concerned. Pierre Goubert, for example, has made a study-in-depth of the Beauvaisis in seventeenth-century France. Similarly, Louis Henry's studies on fertility and the size of families, Labrousse's on prices and wages, E. A. Wrigley's on London, Glass's and Habbakuk's on English population and mobility, and McKeown's and Brown's study of the medical evidence relating to the growth of population have, generally speaking, been largely focused on the eighteenth century. Yet some of this work has a particular relevance for the earlier nineteenth century as well. McKeown and Brown, for example, have argued that for lack of adequate statistics relating to births, deaths and marriages little could be known of the actual causes of death (the key to an understanding of the general rise in population) before registration was introduced in Britain in 1838; and that it is what happened *after* 1838 that provides the clue to what is likely to have happened before. Adopting this "forward-looking" technique, they have shown that even as late as the third quarter of the nineteenth century, medical treatment and sanitation played only a minor part in preventing disease and in lowering mortality, and thus in stimulating population growth. From this they have argued further that the most likely cause of the rise of pupulation and the fall in mortality in the whole period between about 1760 and 1860 lay in an improved environment or rising living standards, largely brought about by an improved diet and better supplies of food.[8] Such a view, if it can be sustained, considerably modifies the views of other scholars who have argued that the decline in mortality or the rise in the birth rate, towards the end of the eighteenth century, may be explained in terms of rising fertility, the cultivation of the potato, the disappearance of the plague, improved sanitation, inoculation against smallpox, or other medical measures to combat disease.

7. Glass and Eversley (eds.), *Population in History,* pp. 147–58, 221–46, 269–307, 434–73.
8. T. McKeown and R. G. Brown, "Medical Evidence Related to English Population Changes in the Eighteenth Century," *Population Studies,* IX, 1955, 119–41. See also, by the same authors, "The Interpretation of the Rise of Population in England and Wales," *Central African Journal of Medicine,* XV, 1969, 187–90.

Equally apposite for our purpose has been the work of two French demographers regarding the relative stagnation of France's nineteenth-century population. M. Charles Pouthas, for many years the holder of a chair in history at the Sorbonne and a remarkably versatile scholar, has, among numerous other works, written a book on the population of France in the first half of the nineteenth century. Like others before him, he points to the astonishing relative decline of France's population during these hundred years, when an increase of 31 percent between 1800 and 1850 fell to one of 9 percent between 1850 and 1900, while as a proportion of the European population as a whole, France's population fell from 15.7 percent in 1800 to 9.7 percent a century later. Why this phenomenal decline? M. Pouthas attributes it largely to the persistently heavy fall in the birth rate which set in during the last years of Louis-Philippe's reign and the first two years of the Second Republic (though why this happened is not clear). "The crisis of 1847–1850," he writes, "dug a veritable chasm between two demographic periods, for it wiped out, as it were, the demographic prosperity which began in the middle of the eighteenth century."[9] It was a crisis that lasted, with brief intermissions, until the end of the Second World War.

M. Louis Chevalier's work is, like M. Pouthas's, the product of the *Institut national d'études démographiques* in Paris, but it is confined to a study of the capital, and largely to its growth through immigration. Unlike other French cities, Paris drew its heaviest influx of migrants during the second quarter of the century; and, inversely, the proportion of Paris immigrants declined after the 1850s, just at the moment when migration was at its height in the rest of France. It was in the last decades of the century that the two streams of migration flowed in more or less equal proportions; and by this time it had changed its complexion and Paris, from recruiting its migrants largely from the departments adjoining the capital, now drew them, in balanced numbers, from all over France. Parallel with this transformation in the provenance of migrants came a gradual transformation of the city as a whole, which only now, for the first time, assumed the

9. Charles H. Pouthas, *La population française pendant la première moitié du XIXe siècle* (Paris, 1956), p. 29.

appearance of a centralized and integrated modern capital city. And so, Chevalier concludes, "one can hardly fail to believe that, notwithstanding the demographic explosion, in spite of the economic expansion, in spite, too, of the extending horizon of factories, the population of Paris, right up to the end of the nineteenth century, in many respects more closely resembled the population of the late eighteenth century than it did that of the twentieth."[10] In short—and this is of some significance for the history of France during the July Monarchy and the revolutions of 1830 and 1848—Paris remained remarkably unchanged, during the period covered by this volume, from what it had been at the time of the great Revolution and the Napoleonic Empire.

6. *The Debate on the Industrial Revolution*

The reader will have noticed that, in this chapter, we have so far recorded the discoveries and achievements of historians rather than their differing interpretations and disagreements. This is mainly because historical demography, as a comparatively recent science, has as yet had little time to divide itself into rival schools and because all its practitioners have, by and large, come from a common radical-liberal stable sharing broadly common views. (An exception should perhaps be made of Chevalier, who in the last ten years has returned to the use of literary and impressionistic records and cast doubts on the value of the quantitative-analytical methods of his old associates.) With the long succession of historians and economists who have written about the industrial revolution—particularly of the "revolution" in England—the case is somewhat different. Here, too, there has been a perceptible break with the past and a new school of writers has developed since the war, a new generation of scholars who have leaned more heavily than their predecessors on economic theory and abandoned the old descriptive-narrative methods for quantitative analysis and the use of "models." Yet, in this case, the break with the past has not been as sharp as in the case of demography and the writers of

10. Louis Chevalier, *La formation de la population parisienne au XIXe siècle* (Paris, 1950), pp. 280–82.

economic history, even if their methods have been new, have, essentially, been continuing a tradition that had already been well established.

The tradition really goes back to the first volume of Marx's *Capital* (1867), which was the first serious attempt made to relate and analyze the emergence of the new capitalist-industrial society in England. Marx was followed by Arnold Toynbee, whose *Lectures on the Industrial Revolution in England* (published in 1884) for the first time stimulated a continuous public interest in Britain's industrial history. Twelve years after Toynbee's *Lectures* came another popular work, H. de B. Gibbins's *Industry in England,* which went into five editions by 1907. Yet the most influential, if not the most popular, product of these earlier years was the work of a Frenchman, Paul Mantoux, whose great book *The Industrial Revolution in the Eighteenth Century* was written in 1906 and first appeared in English translation in 1928. To Mantoux the essence of the industrial revolution was not so much the rise in output or technical advance (as stressed by Toynbee and Gibbins) as the emergence of the modern factory system, which began in England between 1760 and 1800. Yet, though this was its main achievement, the new industrial system had other important features besides. It had its peculiar technical aspect, which lay in the succession of inventions and innovations—the work of men like Hargreaves, Crompton, Darby, Cort and Watt, which "made it possible to speed up and constantly to increase production." More broadly, it had an economic aspect, whose substance was "the concentration of capital and the growth of large undertakings, the existence and workings of which, from being only exceptional, came to be the normal condition of industry." And lastly, it had a social (and an implied political) aspect, in that it tended to polarize society into industrial employers on the one hand and industrial workers on the other; for the industrial revolution (in Mantoux's phrase) "gave birth to social classes whose progress and mutual opposition fill the history of our times."[11]

11. Paul Mantoux, *The Industrial Revolution in the eighteenth century: an Outline of the Beginnings of the Modern Factory System in England* (New York, 1962), pp. 25–9, 486–9.

One feature that these late-nineteenth century and early-twentieth century writers had in common was their conviction that the countries concerned were really going through a "revolution" and not simply a gradual and protracted, though intensified, process of industrial advance. Toynbee, in fact, had first given the term "industrial revolution" (though it had been used earlier by Engels) scholarly respectabilty; to him the old industrial system "was suddenly broken in pieces by the mighty blows of the steam engine and the power loom." Gibbins, another "revolutionist," also saw the revolution in essentially technical terms. "The change [he wrote] was sudden and violent. The great inventions were all made in a comparatively short space of time . . . In little more than twenty years all the great inventions of Watt, Arkwright, and Boulton had been completed . . . and the modern factory system had fairly begun."[12] Mantoux's emphasis is somewhat different. While not denying "the continuity of the historical process underlying even the most rapid changes," he nevertheless insisted that the consequence of the factory system and its attendant social implications marked a "revolutionary," if not a sudden change. "We know," he wrote

that there were machines before the era of machinery, 'manufacture' before factories, combinations and strikes before the formation of industrial capitalism and the 'factory proletariat'. But in the slow-moving mass of society, a new element does not make itself felt immediately. And we have not only to note its presence, but its relation to its environment and, as it were, the space it occupies in history. The industrial revolution is precisely the expansion of industrial forces, the sudden growth and blossoming of seeds which had for many years lain hidden or asleep.[13]

This "revolutionist" view was generally challenged by the next generation of economic historians. J. H. Clapham, in the first volume of his *Economic History of Modern Britain* (1926), showed that "no single British industry had passed through a complete technical revolution before 1830"; and, following a similar line of thought, H. Heaton (writing in 1933) argued that "a revolution which continued

12. H. de B. Gibbins, *Industry in England: Historical Outlines* (London, 1897), p. 341.
13. Mantoux, pp. 488–9.

for 150 years and had been in preparation for at least another 150 years may well seem to need a new label."[14] This new gradualist view received powerful support, a dozen years later, from the work of T. S. Ashton, the author of the most widely-read of all the histories of the industrial revolution that have appeared in England since the war. Ashton was struck by the fact that "early observers" had "tended to regard the technical innovations as the hinge on which all else turned" (this was an obvious reference to Toynbee and Gibbins), and he supposed that it was for this reason that they had lain such emphasis on a sudden revolutionary change. But, he argued in *The Industrial Revolution* (1948), "the word 'revolution' implies a suddenness of change that is not, in fact, characteristic of economic processes"; yet, though showing such an evident distaste for the term, he had to confess that it "has become so firmly embodied in common speech that it would be pedantic to offer a substitute."[15]

Much of Ashton's criticism was that of a new-style conservative tilting at the views of his radical and "Whiggish" predecessors; but he was also an innovator who opened up new perspectives in the study of the industrial revolution. He laid greater emphasis on causes and analysis and he stressed the wider economic, rather than the more narrowly technical, changes that the "revolution" brought about. In these respects, he stands half-way between the older descriptive-historical school and the newer analytical school that developed in the 1950s. These writers have seen themselves as economists or social scientists rather than as pure historians, they have been strongly influenced by economic theory and methodology; they have, like the new school of historical demographers, resorted more freely than their predecessors to quantitative analysis; and they have seen the industrial revolution more in terms of sustained economic "growth" (of output, in particular) than of technical, industrial and social change. This "new look" has, as in the case of the new demography,

14. H. Heaton, "Industrial Revolution" (1933), in *The Causes of the Industrial Revolution*, R. M. Hartwell (ed.) (New York, 1967), p. 35.
15. T. S. Ashton, "Some Statistics of the Industrial Revolution in Britain" (1948), in *Essays in Economic History*, ed. E. M. Carus-Wilson, 3 vols. (New York, 1954–1962), III, p. 237; *The Industrial Revolution 1760–1830* (New York, 1957), p. 2.

partly been the result of a preoccupation with new problems that have arisen since the war—such problems as the role of the state in economic planning (both in the East and the West) and the particular difficulties facing the developing nations of Asia and Africa as they seek to industrialize and modernize their economy. This new emphasis on "growth" is brought out in Dr. R. M. Hartwell's view of what the industrial revolution is really all about. "The obvious and essential character of the industrial revolution," he writes, "was the sustained increase in the rate of growth of total and per capita output at a rate which was revolutionary compared with what went before."[16]

But apart from their common concern with "growth"[17] and their general agreement on the nature of the "revolution," the new historians and economists have held widely differing views on how, why and when the "revolution" came about. Such differences are partly due to the economist's tendency to look for blueprints and prescriptions for the future, while the historian's natural inclination is to record and analyze the past; or, as Pierre Vilar, a French historian, told a conference at Stockholm in 1960, it is the historian's natural bent to probe the question *how* and the economist's to probe the question *why*.[18] This may be true, but there are other differences that leap across professional boundaries. To take the starting-point of the English "revolution," for example. The older view centered firmly around 1760; among more recent writers, Deane and Cole have favored 1740, and Ashton, Hartwell and Rostow the 1780s; while Charles Wilson and J. U. Nef (who are hardly "revolutionists") have pushed their "turning-point" (or prelude to a later and bigger revolution) back to 1660 and even to 1540.[19]

A larger question is why the "revolution" ever came about. Ashton,

16. Introduction to *The Causes of the Industrial Revolution*, p. 8.
17. See, e.g., E. J. Hobsbawm's figures for the rate of growth of U.K. industrial production, 1800–1850:

1800s–1810s:	22.9%	1830s–1840s:	37.4%
1810s–1820s:	38.6%	1840s–1850s:	39.3%
1820s–1830s:	47.2%		

(*Industry and Empire*, p. 51).
18. Jean Lhomme, *Economie et Histoire* (Geneva, 1967), p. 44.
19. Hartwell, pp. 11–13, 68–70.

who was one of the first historians to attempt a methodical formulation of its causes, traced its origins in England to a combination of exceptional and favorable factors:

> The conjuncture of growing supplies of land, labour and capital made possible the expansion of industry; coal and steam provided the fuel and power for large-scale manufacture; low rates of interest, rising prices, and high expectations of profit offered the incentive. But behind and beyond these material economic factors lay something more. Trade with foreign parts had widened men's views of the world, and science their conception of the universe: the industrial revolution was also a revolution of ideas.[20]

All subsequent writers have made their own lists of causes and rearranged, amended and juggled with Ashton's order of priorities. Hartwell summarizes the "forces making for economic growth" as follows: 1. *Capital accumulation.* 2. *Innovations,* or changes in technology and organization. 3. *Fortunate factor endowments* (minerals, a skilled labor force, entrepreneurial talent). 4. *Laissez-faire* (intellectual and ideological factors; social mobility). 5. *Market expansion,* both at home and abroad. 6. *Miscellaneous,* including favorable Continental wars and "the English genius." But, as he points out, not only does every writer have his own list and his own order of priorities, but he also tends to have his own favorite single cause, or to stress *one* force above all others. We saw, for example, that, among the older historians, Toynbee and Gibbins favored technological change; while Ashton, writing in the 1940s, had a *penchant* for the falling interest rate. More recently, H. J. Habbakuk and Phyllis Deane have plumped for international trade, A. H. John for changes in agriculture, J. D. Chambers for a growth in population, and W. W. Rostow and Arthur Lewis for a rising rate of annual investment. Lewis has even argued (and here he has encountered considerable opposition) that the rate of investment, or capital accumulation, is the only factor that really counts: "All countries," he has written, "which are now relatively developed have at some time in the past gone through a period of rapid acceleration, in the course of which the rate of annual net investment has moved from 5 percent or less to 12 percent or more.

20. Ashton, *The Industrial Revolution,* p. 44.

This is what we mean by an Industrial revolution.[21]

Other questions have centred round the actual *process* of industrial growth. Did it develop first in one industry (for example, textiles or mining) or in one region (such as Lancashire in England)? Did the "revolution" take place all of one piece, equally spread over a shorter or longer period of time, or did it proceed in short spurts, or in phases or stages of greater or lesser duration? In recent years, it has been the "phase"-theory that has generally held the field after being popularized in the work of two distinguished writers of the 1950s. One of these, W. G. Hoffmann, a German, has argued in his *Growth of Industrial Economies* (translated into English in 1958) that the process of industrialization always follows the same pattern and passes through three phases: a first phase of high output of consumers' goods (textiles or processed foods) and a relatively low output of capital goods; a second phase, in which heavy industry begins to catch up, but consumers' goods still predominate; and a third phase, in which the output of consumers' and capital goods is more or less evenly balanced.[22]

But far more influential has been the model that Professor Rostow first outlined in an article in the *Economic Journal* in 1956 and later elaborated in his book, *The Stages of Economic Growth* (1960).[23] Rostow's model, like Hoffman's, is composed of three phases. First, a preparatory phase of a hundred years or more, during which the economical, technical, social and political conditions evolve, which make possible the transition from a predominantly agrarian to a predominantly industrial economy. Secondly, a shorter period of perhaps thirty years, during which the rate of investment rises from 5 to over 10 percent and advances take place in productive techniques. This is what Rostow calls the "take-off" period and which he sees as having occurred in Britain in 1783 to 1802, in France and Belgium in 1830 to 1860, and in Germany in 1850 to 1873. And finally,

21. Hartwell, pp. 58–65; W. A. Lewis, *The Theory of Economic Growth* (New York, 1970), p. 208.
22. Cit. W. O. Henderson, *The Industrial Revolution on the Continent*, pp. 3–4.
23. W. W. Rostow, "The Take-off into Self Sustained Growth," *Economic Journal*, LXVI, 1956; and *The Stages of Economic Growth* (New York, 1960).

following the crucial "take-off" phase, is a long period of industrial expansion, interrupted by sharp fluctuations in the nation's economy, but during which the new rate of savings is maintained and the productive potentialities become more fully exploited.

One consequence of this preoccupation with "growth" and "take-off" has been the new attention paid to the spread of industrial revolution from its initial starting-point in England, first to the continent of Europe, and subsequently to other countries in the world. In this process, Britain's role has not surprisingly been seen as quite unique. In David Landes's phrase, the industrial revolution became "a chase," in which "there was one leader, Britain, and all the rest were pursuers." The "chase" might take different forms; but purely internal developments were generally accompanied by the importation of British capital, techniques, trained manpower and managerial skills. In his book, *Britain and Industrial Europe*, W. O. Henderson has shown how, in this way, Britain contributed to the industrialization of France, Germany and Belgium in the course of the nineteenth century.[24] But Britain was unique in other ways as well. She was the one country in which the crucial years of industrial revolution took place before the advent of railways; and railways, according to Rostow, have been "historically the most powerful initiator of take-offs." Again, Britain's industrialization was promoted by private enterprise and a philosophy of *laissez-faire*, whereas Europe's developed under the protective mantle of tariff barriers and government controls. This has become even more of a feature in recent times; and Professor Gerschenkron has argued, in *Economic Backwardness in Historical Perspective* (1962), that "the more backward a country—the bigger the gap between its economic performance and possibilities—the more necessary the intervention of authority in promoting growth."[25] But such problems as these had, of course, only begun to impinge on

24. W. O. Henderson, *Britain and Industrial Europe 1750–1870* (Liverpool, 1954). For similar proselytization by France, see Rondo E. Cameron, *France and the Economic Development of Europe 1800–1914* (Princeton, 1961).
25. Quoted by David Landes, "Technological Change and Industrial Development in Western Europe, 1750–1914," in *The Cambridge Economic History of Europe*, Habbakuk and Postan (eds.) (Cambridge, England, 1965) VI: 595.

the relations between states—even within Europe—by the middle of the nineteenth century and, therefore, need not concern us further here.

7. Industrial Revolution and Society

In the passage just quoted, Professor Landes notes that "economic development, particularly when it takes the form of industrialization, affects all aspects of social life and is affected in turn by them." He adds that this may appear to be a truism; yet it is a truism that the recent school of economic historians, with their overriding concern for output and "growth," have, unlike their predecessors, shown a disposition to neglect. Hartwell himself, though a "modern," quotes with evident approval H. L. Beales, a British economic historian of the older school, as saying that "the analysis of industrial revolution is still too much in economic terms."[26] Of course, the non-economic or social aspect of the "revolution" can be tackled in one of two ways. On the one hand, there is the society out of which industrialization develops, and on the other the society which it creates, or what Eric Hobsbawm calls "the human results" of industrial revolution. In his recent book, *The Origins of Modern English Society,* Harold Perkin, professor of Social History at the University of Lancaster, has, as his title suggests, been concerned with the first. He concedes that Arthur Lewis and W. W. Rostow, in tracing the origins of economic growth, "rapidly move beyond the economic causes to the social and political factors underlying them." The state of society, in fact, is seen as an essential pre-condition for "development" or "take-off." Yet, he insists, with these writers it remains an abstraction and, in the case of the pioneer country, Britain, which had no opportunity of adopting the blueprints or learning from the example of others, it is insufficiently explored. In her case, he argues, "the causes of the Industrial Revolution are so complex and manifold as at first sight to constitute almost the whole antecedent history of Britain." But one factor, he adds, eclipses all others and gives cohesion to the rest: "that central,

26. Hartwell, p. 73.

integrating cause was the nature of and structure of English society";
for "the only spontaneous industrial revolution in history occurred in
Britain because Britain alone amongst the nations with the full com-
plement of economic resources and psychological attitudes had the
right kind of society to generate a spontaneous industrial revolution."[27]

As far as Britain is concerned, a similar exploration would take us
back to the century before Waterloo and so far back beyond the scope
of the present volume. For our purpose the more appropriate question
is, what sort of society grew out of, rather than *into,* the industrial
revolution—and, specifically, in Britain? To this the earlier writers,
being social as well as economic historians and being more concerned
with Hobsbawm's "human values," had often quite specific answers.
Mantoux, as we saw, stated quite simply that the "revolution" led to
the emergence of two new social classes of manufacturers and factory
workers; but he added (and this was far more controversial) that, in
so doing, "it gave birth to social classes whose progress and mutual
opposition fill the history of our times." But social historians, as well
as contemporary observers, have gone much further, delved more
deeply into that new society, applied moral values, and damned it or
praised it according to their own social attitudes or political affiliations.

Thus, the early socialists and Tory radicals in England, who saw
the new society developing around them, tended to portray it in
almost uniformly gloomy and unflattering terms. Engels's *Condition
of the Working Class in England* (1845) and Benjamin Disraeli's *Sybil*
(1845), with its portrayal of two mutually antagonistic "nations," are
obvious cases in point. In the present century, the main protagonists
of this "catastrophic" school have been J. L. and Barbara Hammond.
Their great "Labourer" trilogy appeared with *The Village Labourer*
in 1911 and was completed with *The Skilled Labourer* in 1919; other
studies, including *The Age of the Chartists* and *The Bleak Age* carried
on the tradition to the eve of the last war. For the Hammonds, it was
not just that the industrial revolution reduced or threatened the peo-

27. Harold Perkin, *The Origins of Modern English Society 1780–1880* (Toronto, 1968),
pp. 1–16.

ple's living standards (we shall come to this aspect later), but that it created a thoroughly evil and immoral society, which uprooted and degraded the masses and drove them to riot or despair. In their preface to the second edition of *The Town Labourer* (1925), they wrote:

A civilization is the use to which an age puts its resources of wealth, knowledge, and power, in order to create a social life. These resources vary widely from age to age. The Industrial Revolution brought a great extension of material power and of the opportunities that such power bestows. The first result, so this book contends, was deplorable, for instead of creating a happier, wiser, and a more self-respecting society, this revolution led to the degradation of large masses of people and the rapid growth of a town life in which everything was sacrificed to profit.

It was an age, too, they argued elsewhere, that robbed men of freedom, leisure, entertainment and all means of cultural expression; for "the age that regarded men, women and children as hands for feeding the machines of the new society had no use for libraries, galleries, playgrounds, or any of the forms in which space and beauty can bring comfort or nourishment to the human mind." And to them the history of England from the accession of George III to the Reform Act of 1832 reads "like the history of a civil war."[28]

Today, it would be widely admitted that the Hammonds drew their picture in too stark and lurid colors and generally overstated their case; and they have consequently found critics, among historians, on both the Right and the Left. This is partly due to their evidently Fabian (or moderate-socialist) affiliation, but also to the occasional naïveté of their writing at a time when historians had been largely untouched by the experience of other social scientists. Yet it is hardly surprising that, given their predilections, the revision of their judgments should have largely been undertaken by conservative rather than by liberal or socialist historians. Among such critics from the Right is Dr. George Kitson Clark, the Cambridge scholar and author of *The Making of Victorian England*. Dr. Clark takes the Hammonds to task for allowing their emotions to run away with them. He pays

---

28. J. L. and B. Hammond, *The Town Labourer* (New York, 1968), p. 1; *The Skilled Labourer* (New York, 1970), pp. 1–11.

them the customary tribute paid to the work of pioneers: "No one interested in nineteenth-century studies should refuse to be grateful to them. They uncovered much, and the strong emotions which inspired their work were in many ways appropriate, for there is material which ought not to be considered in cold blood. But those emotions were not always good servants"; and (he adds) "indignation, however honest, is a dangerous passion for historians." Above all, he considers the authors to have been unjust to the "Upper Classes" and to have disregarded "the very difficult problems of what a man of a different era could be reasonably expected to understand or to do."[29] T. S. Ashton has also re-drawn the Hammonds's picture, though in his case it is less of a frontal assault. To Ashton, the industrial revolution, far from being catastrophic, was an age of outstanding achievement, in which such disasters as occurred were far outweighed by the benefits that it brought to the nation at large. Had England had no industrial revolution, he insists, she would have suffered the fate of Ireland. "She was delivered, not by her rulers, but by those who, seeking no doubt their own narrow ends, had the wit and resource to devise new instruments of production and new methods of administering industry." And he concludes his book with a stirring eulogy of the age of the machine:

There are to-day on the plains of India and China men and women, plague-ridden and hungry, living lives little better, to outward appearance, than those of the cattle that toil with them by day and share their places of sleep by night. Such Asiatic standards, and such unmechanized horrors, are the lot of those who increase their numbers without passing through an industrial revolution.[30]

8. *The Standard-of-Living Controversy*

One aspect of the industrial revolution in Britain that has been more heatedly and more continuously debated than any other is the effect that it had on the standard-of-living during the early decades

---

29. G. Kitson Clark, *The Making of Victorian England* (London, 1962), pp. 11–14.
30. T. S. Ashton, *The Industrial Revolution*, p. 61.

of the nineteenth century. Did it fall, as claimed by the "pessimists"; or did it rise, as claimed by the "optimists"? The debate has gone on for a considerable time, going well back beyond the Hammonds and even before Engels, and was first engaged in by the eyewitnesses of the newly emerging industrial society.

In the first phase of the debate (roughly the 1830s to 1840s), though the "pessimists" could muster the larger battalions, the honors were fairly evenly shared. On the "optimists" ' side there were Andrew Ure, author of a *Philosophy of Manufactures* (1835), and G. R. Porter, a classical economist whose *The Progress of the Nation* (second edition) appeared in 1847. Among the "pessimists" were the economists Malthus and Ricardo, and Thomas Carlyle and Frederick Engels. Ure wrote enthusiastically of the factory children as "lively elves" at play; and Porter, in comparing the living standards of the 1840s with those at the beginning of the century, thought it "hardly possible to doubt that here, in England at least, the elements of social improvement have been successfully at work, and that they have been and are producing an increasing amount of comfort to the bulk of the people"; and, surprisingly perhaps, his views were shared by Edwin Chadwick, the gloomy architect of the first Public Health Act and the New Poor Law of 1834. On the other hand, Carlyle raised his stentorian voice to denounce the new factory system as "but a dingy prison-house, of rebellious unthrift, rebellion, rancour, indignation against themselves and against all men"; while Engels, fresh from his study of the Blue Books of the early factory inspectors, wrote, in *The Condition of the Working Class in England,* that, before the industrial revolution, "the workers enjoyed a comfortable and peaceful existence . . . their standard of life was much better than that of the factory worker today."

It was perhaps natural that, during the more prosperous years of the 1850s to 1870s, the debate should have lost its vigor or, at least, become a little one-sided; and no one on the "pessimist" side was ready to challenge the statistics brought forward by Leone Levi and Sir Robert Giffen, which tended to show that the working classes were enjoying a perceptibly higher standard in 1875 than they had been a quarter of a century before. However, the next prolonged economic crisis (though after some delay) brought new grist to the "pessi-

mists' " case: from Thorold Rogers, the economist, and Arnold Toynbee, the industrial historian. To Rogers the years of rapid industrialization were a "dismal period" for the working classes, and the
twenty-five years following 1790 were "the worst time in the whole
history of English labor." Toynbee wrote in a similar strain: "We now
approach a darker period—a period as disastrous and as terrible as
any through which a nation ever passed; disastrous and terrible because side by side with a great increase of wealth was seen an enormous increase of pauperism."[31]

A generation later, on the eve of the first world war, the "immizera-
tion theory" (as R. M. Hartwell has called it) received a further lease
of life. H. de B. Gibbins, in his *Industry in England* (1907), wrote that
"the condition of the mass of the people in the first half of this [the
nineteenth] century was one of the deepest depression," and that "the
lowest depth of poverty was reached about the beginning of the reign
of Queen Victoria." The voice of the social reformer was joined to that
of the economist and industrial historian in the work of the Hammonds and the Webbs, who both took a gloomy view. Sidney Webb
had already written in a Fabian tract of the 1890s: "If the Chartists
in 1837 had called for a comparison of their time with 1787, and had
obtained a fair account of the social life of the working-men at the two
periods, it is almost certain that they would have recorded a positive
decline in the standard of life of large classes of the population."[32] The
Hammonds, for their part, in their "Labourer" series, accompanied
their general denunciation of the new industrial society with particular charges concerning the workers' wages and conditions. Specifically, they pointed to the growing disparity between the wealth of the
employers and the persisting poverty of the working classes.

If [they wrote] a traveller had moved among the employers and had been
shown the brimming life of mills, mines, canals, and docks, he would have

---

31. For the preceding paragraphs (including quotations), see A. J. Taylor, "Progress
and Poverty in Britain, 1780–1850. A Reappraisal," *History,* XLV, Feb. 1961, pp.
16–31.
32. For the above, see R. M. Hartwell, "Interpretations of the Industrial Revolution
in England: a Methodological Inquiry," *Journal of Economic History,* XIX, 1959, pp.
229–31.

said that England as an industrial nation was making an advance unprecedented in the history of trade. If he had moved among the working classes, learned what wages they were receiving, how they lived, he would have concluded that the industries in which they were employed were either stagnant or declining.[33]

At last, after a half-century of virtual silence, the "optimists" found two new champions in the 1920s. Mrs. Dorothy George, in her *London Life in the Eighteenth Century* (1925), argued, largely on the basis of a declining mortality, that the standard of life of a London worker had improved considerably during the half-century preceding Waterloo. Her thesis was confined to London, but it received a more general confirmation from the evidence published a year later by Buer and Talbot Griffiths of a nationwide decline in the death-rate between 1750 and 1850. More impressive, however, was the statistical evidence relating to wages and commodity prices put forward by Sir John Clapham in the first volume of his economic history of Britain in 1926. He wrote in his preface, in a direct allusion to the "pessimists," that "the legend that everything was getting worse for the working-men, down to some unspecified date between the drafting of the People's Charter [1836] and the Great Exhibition [1851], dies hard" and that "after the price-fall of 1820–21, the purchasing power of wages in general . . . was definitely greater than it had been just before the revolutionary and Napoleonic wars." More specifically, he added:

For every class of urban or industrial labourer about which information is available, except—a grave exception—such dying trades as common handloom cotton weaving, wages had risen markedly during the intervening years [since 1790]. For fortunate classes, such as London bricklayers or compositors, they had risen well over 40 per cent, and for urban and industrial workers in the mass, perhaps about 40 per cent."[34]

Clapham's authority was such as to tip the balance firmly in favor of the "optimists"; other writers (W. H. Hutt, T. E. Gregory and Mrs. George among them) rallied in support; and the Hammonds were

33. Hammonds, *The Town Labourer*, pp. 102–3.
34. M. D. George, *London Life in the Eighteenth Century* (New York, 1965); J. H. Clapham, *An Economic History of Modern Britain. The Early Railway Age 1820–1850* (Cambridge, England, 1959), pp. vii, 561.

generous enough to make concessions. Like others, they were impressed by Clapham's use of statistical sources; and J. L. Hammond
conceded in the *Economic History Review* (1930)—and both Hammonds in *The Age of the Chartists*—that total earnings were probably
rising during the period under review. But, while surrendering this
comparatively minor position, they clung resolutely to the major part
of their case: even if wages went up, hours had generally become
longer; more members of the family, including children, were at work;
workers were losing their old freedom of when and how to work; and
no amount of statistics relating to wages, prices and the sales of meat
could explain away the general indictment of contemporaries (they
cited Crabbe, Cobbett and Bamford, in particular) that the period was
one of increasing spirtual suffering and moral degradation. "For all
these classes," they wrote, as they looked back to a would-be happier
age, "it is true that they were more their own masters, that they had
a wider range of initiative, that their homes and their children were
happier in 1760 than they were in 1830."[35]

And this is roughly where the argument stood on the eve of the last
war, with the balance—as far as the statistical evidence went, at least
—tipped towards the "optimists' " side. But the debate opened up
again in the immediate post-war years and, with occasional lulls, has
filled many columns in the economic history journals ever since. Once
more, the "optimists", this time in the person of T. S. Ashton, set the
pace. Ashton, as we saw, presented a distinctly rosy picture of early
nineteenth-century England in his book, *The Industrial Revolution*.
The book was closely followed by two articles on the standard-of-
living of the English workers between 1790 and 1830.[36] He agreed
with Clapham that the period of the French wars and its aftermath
were years of hardship, and probably of a declining economic status,
for the mass of the people; he agreed, too, that by the early 1820s, "the
economic climate had become more genial" and conditions had begun

35. Hammonds, *The Skilled Labourer*, p. 2.
36. T. S. Ashton, "The Standard of Life of the Workers in England, 1790–1830",
Journal of Economic History, Supplement IX, 1949, 19–38; "Some Statistics of the
Industrial Revolution in Britain" (1948), in *Essays in Economic History*, III, pp.
237–51.

to improve. Yet he rejected much of Clapham's evidence and found new arguments to support his view. Above all, he cast doubts on the validity of Norman Silberding's cost-of-living index for 1799–1850, and he dismissed as unreliable the data assembled on wages and prices covering different groups of people "separated widely in time and place." He pleaded for more caution, less generalization and for greater statistical precision. "We require not a single index but many, each derived from retail prices, each confined to a short run of years, each relating to a single area, perhaps even to a single social or occupational group within an area." Having perused such evidence for the Manchester area during the 1820s, he noted that the price of cloth was falling and the factory workers were extending the range of their personal consumption: "boots began to take the place of clogs, hats replaced shawls, at least for wear on Sundays . . . and after 1820 such things as tea and coffee and sugar fell in price substantially." He admitted that masses of unskilled or poorly skilled workers (seasonal agricultural workers and handloom weavers, in particular) were probably still living on the borderline of bare subsistence; but (he concluded) "my guess would be that the number of those who were able to share in the benefits of economic progress was larger than the number of those who were shut out from these benefits and that it was steadily growing."[37]

Other "optimists" took over where Ashton left off. W. H. Chaloner, a Manchester economic historian, has attempted to explode the "legend" of the so-called "Hungry Forties." Like Ashton, he turned to local indices of wholesale and retail prices, noted that the average consumption of sugar, tea, tobacco and rum steadily increased between 1842 and 1848, and concluded that "the period from the end of 1842 until 1847 was marked by a general prosperity and trade revival."[38] R. M. Hartwell, after conducting a "methodological inquiry" into the whole debate in the *Journal of Economic History* for 1959, came down firmly on the side of the "optimists" in a contribution on "the rising standard of living" to *The Economic History Re-*

37. Ashton, "Standard of life . . . ," pp. 28–38.
38. W. H. Chaloner, *The Hungry Forties* (London, Historical Association, 1957).

view in 1961. He chose the period 1800 to 1850 and argued from a wide range of data: from national incomes, wages and prices, births and mortality, new "social and economic opportunities," and (of considerable importance to his case) from comparisons with the eighteenth century. From all this Hartwell concluded in terms far more confident and self-assured than Clapham's and Ashton's and which he was to repeat elsewhere:

> Briefly the argument is that, since the average per capita income increased, since there was no trend in distribution against the workers, since (after 1815) prices fell while money wages remained constant, since per capita consumption of food and other consumer goods increased, and since government increasingly intervened in economic life to protect or raise living standards, then the real wages of the majority of English workers were rising in the years 1800 to 1850.[39]

A few years later, Hartwell was to claim that the "pessimists" had been virtually routed and that the new arguments adduced by Clapham and Ashton had "converted most historians to the view that the industrial revolution in England benefited the workers, not only in the long run, but also in the short run." Quite literally, this may indeed have been so; but there was life in the "pessimists" yet. During the last dozen years, they have found new advocates, notably in the socialist historians, E. J. Hobsbawm and E. P. Thompson. Hobsbawm, in particular, has been as active in the (mainly) "pessimists'" cause as Hartwell has been among its opponents; but, like Ashton, he has shown a larger measure of caution and restraint. His first contribution to the debate appeared in *The Economic History Review* in August 1957. His argument was not so much that the "pessimists'" case was strong as that the "optimists' " case was weak: once they had had to abandon Clapham's cost-of-living figures, they had (as in the case of Ashton) been compelled to draw on few and scattered data, largely relating to consumption, from which no general conclusions could reasonably be drawn. In their place he considered the evidence

---

39. R. M. Hartwell, "The Rising Standard of Living in England, 1800–1850," *Econ. Hist. Rev.*, 2nd series, X111, 1961, pp. 397–416. For the same conclusions, projected back to 1780, see his *The Industrial Revolution in England* (London, Hist. Assoc., 1965).

bearing on mortality and health and unemployment, and, returning to the consumption argument, he looked again at the sales of meat at Smithfield and a wide variety of items (sugar, tea, bread, jam, butter) entering into the poor man's diet. And he concluded that the "optimists' " case was, beyond certain limits, extremely "slim" and that "the plausibility of, and the evidence for deterioration was not to be lightly dismissed." He summed up his argument as follows:

It is altogether likely that living standards improved over much of the eighteenth century. It is not improbable that, sometime soon after the onset of the Industrial Revolution—which is perhaps better placed in the 1780s than in the 1760s—they ceased to improve and declined. Perhaps the middle 1790s, the period of Speenhamland and shortage, mark the turning-point. At the other end, the middle 1840s certainly mark a turning-point.[40]

E. P. Thompson's point is a somewhat different one. In his bestselling book, *The Making of the English Working Class* (1963), he takes frequent swipes at both parties in the debate; and where Hobsbawm writes (in his *Industry and Empire,* published in 1968) that "there may or may not have been deterioration between the middle 1790s and the middle 1840s," he decides that "over the period 1790–1840 there was a slight improvement in average material standards." So, as far as the purely *material* conditions of the workers (as measured in wages or articles of consumption) are concerned, Thompson leans towards the "optimists' " view. But, he argues, this is only a part of the case and a standard-of-living can as readily be measured in terms of homes, health, family life, leisure, work-discipline, intensity of labor, education and play—in short, in terms of those further "imponderables" on whose deterioration the Hammonds continued to insist even after they had yielded to Clapham over wages and incomes. And, basically, Thompson shares their view. "Over the same period [1790–1840]", he writes, "there was intensified exploitation, greater insecurity, and increasing human misery. By 1840 most people were 'better off' than their forerunners had been fifty years before, but they

40. E. J. Hobsbawm, "The British Standard of Living, 1790–1850," *Econ. Hist. Rev.,* 2nd series, X, 1957, pp. 46–68; reproduced (with a Postscript) in *Labouring Men. Studies in the History of Labour* (New York, 1965), pp. 64–104, 120–25.

had suffered and continued to suffer this slight improvement as a catastrophic experience."[41]

The debate has continued, sometimes involving a head-on collision between the two opposing sides, as when Hartwell and Hobsbawm met on common ground in *The Economic History Review* in August 1963. But more often it has taken the form of a more muted commentary by the relatively uncommitted who were willing to see some virtue in both parties to the dispute. One of the most objective, and helpful, contributions of this kind was that offered by Professor A. J. Taylor in *History* in February 1960. In presenting a report on the debate up to that time, Taylor decided that the "ultimate question" was still an open one, though he brought into play arguments that could help to strengthen the "pessimists' " case. One was that a diminution of consumption was likely to arise in all countries (whether capitalist or socialist) undergoing rapid industrialization: the point was equally valid for France, Germany and Russia (though Japan had proved a notable exception).[42] Another was that even if there was in England no *absolute* decline in the workers' standard-of-living, "it lagged increasingly behind that of the nation at large."

Had working-class incomes [he wrote] kept pace with the growth of the national income, the average worker could have expected to find himself some 50 per cent better off in real terms in 1840 than thirty years earlier. Even the most sanguine of optimists would hardly claim that such was in fact the case.[43]

Similarly, R. S. Neale, in a recent regional study, found, after constructing an index of real wages related to the City of Bath, "that it confirms the impression that the rise in real wages after the Napoleonic Wars did not permanently restore the labourer to the real wages obtaining between 1780 and 1890 until the early 1840s, even though the real wage was then double what it had been in 1812."[44]

---

41. E. P. Thompson, *The Making of the English Working Class* (London, 1968 edn.), pp. 230–31.
42. The point was made earlier by S. Pollard, "Investment, Consumption and the Industrial Revolution," *Econ. Hist. Rev.*, 2nd series, XI, 1958.
43. A. J. Taylor, "Progress and Poverty in Britain, 1780–1850," pp. 25, 30.
44. R. S. Neale, "The Standard of Living, 1780–1844; A Regional and Class Study," *Econ. Hist. Rev.*, 2nd series, XIX, 1966, pp. 590–606.

What lessons and conclusions may we draw from this long-drawn debate which, even at present, shows no signs of grinding to a halt? One is that the whole controversy has been shot through with political undertones and that the main protagonists are as much concerned with the vices or virtues of early capitalist society as they are with the social effects of the industrial revolution. This, broadly speaking, has been true of each of the major phases in the dispute. In the 1830s and forties, as we saw, Tory radicals and socialists, though holding widely different views, tended to take the "pessimist" side; and we find Disraeli and Carlyle uneasily allied with Engels against "optimistic" Whigs or Whig-radicals like Andrew Ure, Edwin Chadwick and G. R. Porter, who, looking at the new industrial world around them, found that, substantially, it was good. By the late nineteenth century, the Tories had moved over to the "optimist" camp, while the Fabian and "Whiggish" sympathies of Toynbee, the Hammonds and the Webbs are equally in evidence among the "pessimists." In the most recent stage of the debate, there have been new alignments along broadly political lines; and liberals and conservatives (Mrs. George, J. H. Clapham, Ashton, Chaloner and Hartwell) have manned the "optimistic" barricades against the mainly "pessimistic" onslaught of socialist or Marxist historians like Eric Hobsbawm and Edward Thompson.

Related to these alignments and to the stage reached in the debate have been the diverse choice of records by historians and the type of questions asked. It was natural that the Webbs and Hammonds, being social reformers as well as social historians, should have turned to Home Office reports and local government records for the evidence they wished to find. Equally, the sort of new evidence brought forward by Sir John Clapham in the 1920s had to wait on the preliminary researches carried out by Bowley, Wood and Silberding in the earlier years of the century. When Silberding proved to be a weak reed, it was natural, too, that Ashton, as Clapham's ally, should turn to other sources of this kind, such as the sales of meat at Smithfield Market and the indices of consumption goods in the Manchester region; also that Hobsbawm, wishing to debate with Ashton on his own ground, should have felt the need to explore some of these sources (such as the meat-sales at Smithfield) at greater depth and for different times. Similarly, Hartwell, to widen the debate, looked to other records, such as per capita incomes, further lists of food-prices, and figures of births, deaths and marriages; while Thompson, being a social rather than an economic historian and convinced that the battle of statistics had reached a dead end, turned for evidence of his "imponderables" to literary rather than to purely statistical sources.

The same diversity has characterized the historians' choice of dates and the area and social classes over which their enquiry has ranged. Where Clapham chose the period 1820–1850 and Ashton 1790–1830, the Hammonds chose 1760–1832, Hobsbawm 1790–1850 (or 1842), Thompson 1790–1840, A. J. Taylor 1780–1850, and Hartwell 1800–1850; and the divergence was in each case of some significance to the varying conclusions reached. With regard to the geographical scope of their enquiries, the differences have been nominal rather than real. Where Ashton and Hartwell are concerned only with England, Hobsbawm purports to be studying the condition of the people in Britain as a whole; but Scotland and Ireland play no more part in his treatment than in that of his opponents. It would, of course, have made a significant difference to his case if in fact they (Ireland, in particular) had. For the Irish certainly had their "hungry forties" even if England had not; and the Irish population, through famine and exodus fell from a little over 8 million in 1841 to 6½ million ten years later. And these figures, writes the historian of "the Great Hunger," are probably an understatement; for "vital statistics are unobtainable, no record was kept of deaths, and very many persons must have died and been buried unknown, as the fever victims died and were buried in west Cork, as bodies, found lying dead on the road, were buried in ditches, and as the timid people of Erris perished unrecorded."[45] So it is evident, to say the least, that the inclusion of Ireland would have added solid substance to the "pessimists' " case.

But, even within England, a great deal would depend on whether the regions examined lay in the new industrial Midlands and north or in the older urban and agrarian west or south; and Ashton may

45. Cecil Woodham Smith, *The Great Hunger. Ireland 1845–9* (London, 1962), pp. 408–10.

have done the "optimists'" cause some service by paying specific attention to the Lancashire towns. Equally significant has been the attention paid to certain types of worker rather than to others: were they old-style craftsmen, f ctory workers, domestic workers, or hand-loom weavers; were they town or country dwellers, men and women regularly employed, seasonal workers, or the chronically unemployed? For several of these groups (the unskilled and unemployed, in particular) statistics have been hard to come by and have defeated all attempts to make convincing generalizations: no wonder Ashton was compelled to fall back on a *guess* to sustain his belief in a generally rising standard! No wonder, too, such being the dearth of reliable statistical records—covering all the working people all over England during the whole period under review—that historians have sought their evidence where they could find it and have, consequently, often argued about conflicting and unrelated sets of facts.[46]

So there has been a considerable confusion of evidence and, not surprisingly, the outcome has been inconclusive. Yet there have been some positive results. For one thing, the period in dispute has, in the course of argument, been narrowed down. Both "optimists" and "pessimists" are generally agreed that conditions deteriorated from about 1790 to the end of the Napoleonic wars, if not to 1821. Hobsbawm, for his part, has conceded that things probably began to improve after 1842. (Here he differs from another "pessimist," the German Marxist-labor historian, Jürgen Kuczinski, who considered that "the low point of real wages was reached in England at the end of the 'forties—taking losses through unemployment, etc., into account.")[47]

There still remains, therefore, a disputed period of some twenty years between 1821 and 1842, which will no doubt be the subject of further spirited discussion. This would appear to be a comparatively minor problem, were it not for the fact that regional differences,

46. See. E. P. Thompson, pp. 228–31; also A. J. Taylor, pp. 28–31; and J. E. Williams, "The British Standard of Living 1750–1850," *Econ. Hist. Rev.*, 2nd series, XIX, 1966, pp. 581–2.

47. J. Kuczinski, *Labour Conditions in Western Europe 1820–1935* (London, 1937), p. 83. For a similar "pessimistic" appraisal of conditions in France and Germany in the early decades of industrial capitalism, see pp. 110–12. See also Kuczinski's *A Short History of Labour Conditions under Industrial Capitalism*, I. *Great Britain and the Empire, 1750 to the Present Day* (London, 1942).

though recognized as being important, have as yet been only marginally explored. Moreover, there are also the Hammonds' (and Thompson's) "imponderables," which, being even less susceptible to statistical calculation, are more "open-ended" and contentious and may, as such, be expected to promote further debate (not only in England) for many years to come.

9. The Growth of Cities

Parallel with the growth in national population went a growth in the size of cities. There were several reasons for this, not all of them connected in any way with an industrial revolution. In all European countries, capital cities grew larger in response to the developing needs of the Court or administration or as part of the general movement into the towns from the countryside. Growth might be stimulated by the development of new agricultural methods or changes in the organization of the food supply. In some cities, such as Marseilles, Hamburg, Barcelona, and even London, trade might be as great a stimulus as any other. But the industrial, as well as the agrarian, administrative and commercial, "revolution" also clearly played a part, though in some countrie, (in England for example), conspicuously more so, and earlier, than in others. After the 1830s, a new stimulant to urban growth was provided by the railways and now for the first time towns grew up (like Crewe in the north of England), whose purpose it was to build and repair the new railways or to act as junctions between one railway network and another. The general influence of railways on urban growth was already noted, with extraordinary prescience, by Robert Vaughan, who wrote in *The Age of Great Cities* in 1843:

The new and speedy communication, which will soon be completed between all great cities in every nation of Europe, will necessarily tend to swell the larger towns into still greater magnitude and to diminish the weight of many smaller places, as well as the rural population generally in social affairs. Everywhere we trace this disposition to converge upon great points.[48]

48. Quoted by Asa Briggs in Foreword to *The Study of Urban History,* H. J. Dyoss (ed.) (New York, 1968), p. x.

Of the largest cities, London grew from about a million in 1801 to 1½ million in 1830 and 2¼ million in 1846; and Paris from a little under 550,000 in 1801 to 750,000 in 1830 and over a million in 1846 (although then, for reasons we have already noted, the population fell slightly until 1852). In addition to these giants, there were by 1850 40 towns of a population of 100,000 or more (of which ten were in Britain and five in France), where there had been only twenty fifty years before. Of these the largest may have been Constantinople (with a half-million since 1830), followed by Berlin, Vienna and Naples (over 400,000), St. Petersburg (300,000), and Moscow, Amsterdam and Dublin with populations of 200,000 or more apiece.[49]

So there was a general movement from villages to towns, and a tendency for towns to become cities and cities—particularly capital cities—to grow larger and more quickly. But once more, within this general pattern, the situation of Britain was quite unique. Where in all other European countries the great majority still continued to live in villages and small market towns, in England and Wales by the middle of the century the population was already evenly divided between towns and countryside.* Moreover, where in other European states, cities and large towns were scattered islands dotted almost haphazardly over the map, by the 1830s in England alone there were concentrated areas of urban development (the forerunners of today's "conurbations"), as in the industrial triangle formed by Birmingham, Liverpool and Hull. Engels, writing in 1845, noted that the population of the great woolen region of the West Riding had nearly doubled in thirty years, while the population of Birmingham and Sheffield had almost trebled between 1801 and 1844. He also noted the peculiar quality of London, "where a man may wander for hours together without reaching the beginning of the end, without meeting the slightest hint which could lead to the inference that there is open country

49. Pouthas, p. 98; R. W. Hartwell, "Economic Changes in England and Europe," in *New Cambridge Modern History*, X (1965), pp. 31–2; A. Briggs, *Historians and the Study of Cities* (Sydney, 1960), p. 6.
*That is, towns of 2,000 or more inhabitants (Bowden, Karpovitch and Usher, *op. cit.*, p. 8).

within reach."[50] London had in fact, for over a century at least, girdled itself with a ring of suburbs that only gradually merged with the surrounding countryside; Paris, with its encircling *barrières*, or customs-wall, sharply dividing city from country, offered a remarkable contrast. The point was specifically noted by another observer, J. F. Murray, who, two years before Engels, wrote in *The World of London:*

The vastness of suburban London distinguishes that city eminently from continental cities. A mile beyond Paris you are in a wilderness of bond hills, gypsum quarries, sterile rocks and windmills; beyond the walls of Rome there is literally an expanse of desert; whereas London . . . surrounds itself, suburb clinging to suburb, like onions fifty on a rope.[51]

It is not surprising that this increasing urbanization should, like the growth of industry, have made a deep impression on contemporaries and stimulated conflicting reactions. Some were filled with awe and admiration (as Engels was, in part, by what he saw in London) or at least disposed to view the new developments with quiet detachment or philosophical calm. Robert Vaughan, for example, observed that "it avails nothing to complain of this tendency as novel, inconsiderate, hazardous; the pressure towards such an issue is irresistible, nor do we see the slightest prospect of its ceasing to be so". Francis Place, looking back in old age from the 1820s and thirties, thought London infinitely preferable to the city he had known in his youth a half-century before.[52] Other observers, however, took a gloomier view and were often appalled by what they saw. A notable case was William Cobbett, to whom London was a "Great Wen," or human ant-heap, draining old England of its wealth and vitality. Engels also tempered his enthusiasm with the remark that "the very turmoil of the streets has something repulsive, something against which human nature rebels." The growth of Paris, which took place within a far more restricted area then London's and was accompanied by far more misery and turbulence, provoked even louder protests and cries of lamenta-

50 Engels, *Condition of the English Working Class,* pp. 9, 12, 23.
51. Quoted by D. A. Reeder, "A Theatre of Suburbs: Some Patterns of Development in West London, 1801–1911," in *The Study of Urban History,* p. 253.
52. M. D. George, *London Life in the Eighteenth Century,* pp. 4, 59–61, 104–5, 209–13, 321–2.

tion. French literature of the period abounds with lurid descriptions of Paris as a den of iniquity, of crime, prostitution, poverty, wretchedness and despair. Joseph Proudhon wrote of it as a "vast sewer, a place of masters and lackeys, thieves and prostitutes"; and where Dickens wrote almost light-heartedly of the antics of Fagin and the Artful Dodger in the streets and alleys of London, the picture of Paris painted by Eugène Sue in *Les Mystères de Paris* and Hugo in *Les Misérables* strikes a far more sinister and despairing note.[53] And, of course, something of this cataclysmic view of the city has continued up to the present day. Its most notable exponent over the past thirty years has been Lewis Mumford, with his eloquent denunciation of the "urban hive," "Necropolis" and the "paleotechnic paradise" or "Coketown." Of the nineteenth-century city Mumford writes:

Between 1820 and 1900 the destruction and disorder within great cities is like that of a battlefield, proportionate to the very extent of the equipment and the strength of the forces employed . . . Industrialism, the main creative force of the nineteenth century, produced by the most degraded urban environment the world has yet seen; for even the quarters of the ruling classes were befouled and overcrowded.[54]

We shall find a similarly pessimistic view of the city expressed in the work of Louis Chevalier (of which more will be said later).

But, meanwhile, from the earlier casual or literary impressions, the study of the city has, like the study of industry and population, grown into something like a distinctive social discipline with norms and standards of its own. The process reaches back, of course, far beyond the early nineteenth century. The late-sixteenth century had already seen John Stow's *Survey of London* (1598), and there were the eighteenth-century histories of London by John Strype and William Maitland (to name but two), along with William Hutton's Birmingham, John Whitaker's Manchester and William Barrett's Bristol, while Mercier's twelve-volume *Tableau de Paris* appeared in 1782. But these authors (with the exception of Mercier, a shrewd social ob-

53. See L. Chevalier, *Working Classes and Dangerous Classes in Paris during the First Part of the Nineteenth Century,* (New York, 1971), pp. 73–134, 181.
54. Lewis Mumford, *The City in History, Its Origins, its Transformation and its Prospects* (New York, 1961) pp. 3–4, 446–7.

server) were antiquarians or "town-boosters" (as Dr. Dyos calls them) rather than historians; and the same may be said of many of the numerous contributions to commemorative studies of Victorian cities and municipalities during the greater part of the nineteenth century in Britain. It was not, in fact, until the eve of the First World War, under the impact of the newly developing social sciences, that urban history emerged as a serious, though extremely variegated, discipline. It has by no means developed as the speciality of historians. Indeed, among its main features has been a diversity to which geographers, sociologists, economists, anthropologists, cartographers, demographers, social psychologists and town-planners have probably made as important a contribution as the historians themselves, often more so. One of its pioneers in the United States was Robert Ezra Park, a Chicago sociologist, whose paper *Suggestions for the Investigation of Behavior in the City* was published in 1915 and who was one of the founders of the Chicago school of urban studies. Sociology has continued to play a major part in the study of cities in North America —as at Harvard, Berkeley, Toronto—ever since. In France, where history and geography are closely related subjects in both the *lycée* and university, it was the urban geographer rather than the sociologist who took the lead. The pioneering work was Raoul Blanchard's *Grenoble: étude de géographie urbaine,* published in 1912. From this followed a spate of French urban-geographical studies on Paris, Rouen and other cities and the formation of an *Institut d'urbanisme* at the University of Paris, whose Director for many years was Pierre Lavedan, author of a three-volume *Histoire de l'urbanisme* published in 1926–52. Meanwhile, town-planners (*urbanistes*), sociologists, historians and demographers have also entered the field. Historians began to make their contribution after 1929, when Marc Bloch and Lucien Fèvre founded their journal, *Annales d'histoire économique et sociale;* and the demographers set up a center of their own, the *Institut national d'études démographiques,* and launched their own review, *Population,* shortly after the last war.

In Britain, urban studies took longer to get off the ground and there was nothing to compare, in the early years of the century, with the pioneering work of the Americans and French; at best, mention might be made of the social surveys carried out by Charles Booth in London and Seebohm Rowntree in York. But when the "break-through" came in the 1920s, it was historians as much as other social scientists who played the leading role. In 1925, Dorothy George wrote the first rounded social history of the capital in her *London Life in the Eighteenth Century* (which we have noted more than once already); W. H. Chaloner pioneered the study of a modern town in *The Social and Economic Development of Crew, 1780–1923* (published in 1950); and Asa Briggs, wrote the first volume of his *History of Birmingham* in 1952 and his *Victorian Cities,* an early essay in comparative urban history, in 1963. Meanwhile, centers or programs of urban studies have developed at the Universities of London, Glasgow, Leicester and Sussex; and from a recent issue of the *Urban History Newsletter,* edited by Dr. Dyos of Leicester, we learn that over 500 research projects, the great majority related to the nineteenth-century city, are in progress in Britain alone.[55]

Yet, with all this welter of activity, confusion as to common aims and definitions—let alone as to the possibilities of interdisciplinary cooperation—still reigns supreme. What *is* urban history? What should it include? What should it omit? What are the best methods to promote it, the immediate tasks to be undertaken? Is the essence of the city its streets and buildings, its economy, its "culture" or "personality," or the people who live within its walls? Such questions are still being asked and have not been satisfactorily answered. But confusion has at least the virtue of leaving the field open to a wide diversity of talents, approaches and undertakings. In a recent contribution to an urban studies seminar at Leicester, M. François Bédarida, Director of the *Maison française* at Oxford, spoke of the diversity in the theoretical conceptions underlying such studies in France. There is the "organic" (or "organicist") theory, common to geographers and town-planners (and some historians), whereby the city is compared to a living organism, with "arteries," "tissues" and "circulation" and its constituent parts organically linked together.

55. For the above, see *The Study of Urban History,* pp. 1–60; Briggs, *Historians and the Study of Cities,* p. 21; *Urban History Newsletter* Leicester, July, 1969.

Thus social history becomes an adjunct of the natural sciences. There is also a "functionalist" theory, dear to many geographers and economists, which presents the life of a city in terms of its *functions* (whether organic or institutional) by which that life is largely determined. Further, there is the "positivist" (or "neopositivist") school of thought that eschews ideology and claims to confine itself to the objective and scientific description of urban phenomena, which it measures largely in quantitative and mechanical terms. Such a view is shared by many civil servants, civil engineers and town-planners but, tending as it does to eliminate the human element, rarely finds favor with historians. In addition, there is the "socio-cultural" conception of the city, whereby its evolution is presented in terms of its contribution to the history of civilization, whether in the form of its economy, its arts, its culture or its human relationships both communal and individual. The city is presented as an integrated whole, in which material conditions, human relations, psychological attitudes and social values are all closely related. Not surprisingly, such a conception of the city has commended itself to many urban historians.[56]

But this is not all. Included in M. Bédarida's list is another theory, having elements in common with both the organic and the socio-cultural conceptions, yet with distinctive features of its own. This is the so-called biological theory of the city which, up to now, has had as its sole exponent of distinction M. Louis Chevalier, whose earlier demographic study of Paris we have briefly noted. Chevalier's *Classes laborieuses et classes dangereuses* was published in 1958. Like his other book *La formation de la population parisienne* it deals with Paris in the first half of the nineteenth century; but, whereas the earlier book was the work of a historical demographer who drew largely on the census and other demographic materials, the later book is conceived in quite different terms and the sources used are as often literary and impressionistic as they are statistical or demographic. In fact, the former tend to dominate the latter. What M. Chevalier has set out to

56. F. Bédarida, "The Growth of Urban History in France: Some Methodological Trends," in *The Study of Urban History,* pp. 56–60.

do is to present the city in a state of constant human flux in terms of the transformation of its life in the course of a half-century by the constant transfusion brought about by the inflow of a new population, with habits, standards and social values different from, and often alien to, the old city it invades. It is most decidedly a one-sided, pathological, picture of the city, in which great emphasis is placed on crime, violence, overcrowding and disease, factors that become increasingly prevalent with the rising tide of invading "nomads" and "barbarians" from beyond the city's walls. Thus "laboring classes" and "dangerous classes" become virtually indistinguishable and the older inhabitants learn to live in constant terror of the new. The role played by demographic factors is certainly not neglected: figures relating to migration, fertility, ages and occupations, and to births, deaths and marriages are paraded in profusion; but in even greater evidence are those relating to crime, suicide, violent assault, prostitution, beggary, starvation and disease. And at the base of the structure lies what the author calls the "biological foundations"—that is, the deeper impulses and attitudes of human beings, both individual and collective, which Chevalier believes to have as valid a claim to be seen as an "infrastructure" underpinning social habits, public morals, political ideas, parliaments and revolutions as the material and economic factors commonly stressed by Marxists.

The influence [he writes] of economy and society on the evolution of population . . . has been sufficiently demonstrated by others for us not to repeat it here . . . Unless we are endlessly to repeat, on the basis of documents that are readily available, truths that none will now deny, it now appears more appropriate to attempt to use another tool, not out of indifference to the other, but from a desire to search more deeply and to open up further channels of historical enquiry. The need is no longer to probe the influence of economic on demographic factors, but to probe the influence of biological on social factors. We are no longer required to describe the economic and social foundations of the evolution of society, but the biological foundations of social history; . . . [And by this we mean] the influence of the physical characteristics of the population on those different aspects of individual and collective existence, without a knowledge of which there can be no valid study of society whether of the past or present.[57]

57. Chevalier, pp. 557–61.

M. Chevalier's book is highly original and provocative and the ideas he puts forward will no doubt be further discussed and developed by others. Yet his thesis suffers from two major defects. One, as may perhaps be inferred from the passage quoted, is that the "biological foundations" remain singularly vague and ill-defined. The other is that the thesis, as applied to nineteenth-century Paris, is thoroughly emotive and one-sided. Thus we have here not so much a rounded picture of a city's life as an exercise in urban pathology pure and simple; and so unrelieved is the author's use of shade that the Hammonds' England appears, in contrast, to have been a land of perfect bliss!

10. Urbanization and Social Protest

One further aspect of M. Chevalier's biological thesis calls for comment. An important part of his theme, as we saw, is that Paris became progressively invaded by a feckless, "nomad" population, resentful, depressed, uprooted and proletarian, which attempted to impose its standards and way of life on the old settled population; and that the city, in consequence, became more overcrowded, impoverished and ridden with crime, violence and disease. So much is deliberately stated and carefully spelled out. But M. Chevalier goes further. He implies—though he nowhere specifically proclaims—that, parallel with the increase in crime and slums and disease and, like them, as a concomitant of urbanization, went an increase in social protest and rebellion as the new "nomadic" Paris sought to come to grips with the older, settled population. Thus Paris is presented as sharply divided between two warring camps ever ready to jump at each other's throats.

Admittedly, Mr. Chevalier does not deal directly with popular disturbance; in fact, towards the end of his book, he deliberately stops short of it and tells us why. Yet the inference is clear enough. In one passage, for example, he paraphrases Balzac's statement that "crime swelled under the impact of popular revolt, blended with it and took on its shape"; and, looking back on the revolution of 1789, he sees it "in certain respects, as a settlement of accounts between these two groups of the population: the old *bourgeoisie* and the rest, those who in earlier times were termed savages, barbarians, or nomads . . ." Again, the basic conflict of the 1830s and 1840s is presented as "the problem of a population which attempts to find itself a place in a hostile environment and, failing to do so, resorts to every sort of hatred, violence and violation.[58] In short, whatever the author's intentions and whatever his reservations, the book presents a powerful case for what Mr. Charles Tilly has called the "uprooting thesis" of rebellion and revolution.[59]

M. Chevalier is certainly not alone in holding this view. Professor Girard, for example, in a recent course of lectures given at the Sorbonne on the French revolutions of the nineteenth century, writes of Paris as "sick" (Chevalier uses the term *malsaine*) and unbalanced and of the dangerous confrontation of two opposing and totally different "nations," constituting "a chronic imbalance, dangerous for the life of the capital."[60] Mr. David Pinkney, an American scholar who has done excellent, pioneering work on the revolution of 1830 in Paris, goes even further to substantiate M. Chevalier's case.

Paris in 1830 [he writes] had a fourth, perhaps even more, of its population living both physically and morally on the edge of civilized life—thousands were beyond the edge and most passed readily from one side to another. In this mass crime was normal—a kind of settling of accounts between the outcasts and the society that had no place for them. It was only another step to revolution—a mass settling of accounts.

The connection in 1830 between misery, both economic and moral, and rejection by society, on the one hand, and revolution on the other, has not been conclusively proved, but there are a number of significant links. Geographically there is a close correlation between the worst slums where the Parisian savages lived out their miserable lives and the bitterest street fighting

---

58. *Ibid.*, pp. 71, 265, 469, 553.
59. Charles Tilly, "Reflections on the Revolution in Paris. An Essay on Recent Historical Writing," *Social Problems*, XII, 1964, p. 108.
60. M. Girard, *Etude comparée des mouvements révolutionnaires en France en 1830, 1848 et 1870-71*, Cours de Sorbonne (Paris, n.d.), p. 46.

in 1830. A similar correlation exists between the areas of high incidence of cholera in 1832, which attacked the poorest quarters, and the street fighting in June of that year . . .

Here we are face to face with insurrection that sprang not from simple economic distress. It was the protest of the outcast against a society that had no honorable place for him and his children. Perhaps, too, it was the action of the rootless, amoral individual who in existing society could find self-expression only in violence.[61]

Moreover, the view is by no means confined to nineteenth-century Paris; we find a similar stress on the relationship between crime and popular disturbance in Mrs. George's book on eighteenth-century London; and Mr. A. J. P. Taylor, among others, cites urban over-crowding as one of the essential ingredients of the revolutions of 1848.[62] Besides, it is an argument that must appeal to the "man in the street"; for does it not appear to be the simplest commonsense that the larger the numbers in Mumford's "urban hive," the greater the probability of riot and disorder?

So M. Chevalier's theory has a relevance by no means limited to any one city or any one period. However, in this instance, let us confine ourselves to the half-century under review and to the city of the author's own choice. The question is: is there any close concord-ance between the urbanization of Paris at this time, with its attendant overcrowding, slums, crime, prostitution, beggary and disease, and violent popular protest in the form of riot, rebellion or revolution? M. Chevalier and Mr. Pinkney both imply (or state directly) that there is. Others (Mr. Charles Tilly and myself, for example) say (or imply) that there is not. Of course, it is not enough, to prove M. Chevalier right, to show that overcrowding, crime and disease on the one hand and riot and rebellion on the other were both common features of early-nineteenth-century Paris. This is true enough, as everyone knows. But the point is not that such things happened side by side

61. David H. Pinkney, "A New Look at the French Revolution of 1830," *Review of Politics*, XXIII, 1961, pp. 490–501; reproduced in part in *The Shaping of Modern France*, J. Friguglietti and E. Kennedy, (eds.) (New York, 1969), pp. 217–22.
62. M. D. George, *London Life in the Eighteenth Century*, pp. 118–19; A. J. P. Taylor, *The Habsburg Monarchy 1809–1918* (New York, 1965), p. 58.

within the same city over a half-century of time; the point is rather whether the second set of factors was directly related to, or was the direct outcome of, the first. In fact, we have to ask such questions as: did popular disturbance follow, or did it precede, the rapid growth of population? In what forms and in what parts of the city did the disturbances take place? Who took part in them and where did they live? Were they nomads or criminals, laborers or craftsmen, homeless or settled?

It is, broadly speaking, by asking questions such as these that M. Chevalier's critics have tested the validity of his uprooting theory and found it, in their view, to be wanting. Mr. Charles Tilly, of the University of Michigan, has begun work on a long-term inquiry into collective violence and political disturbance in nineteenth-century France. Only a part of his findings have as yet been published.[63] Some of these deal specifically with the temporal relationship between migration to cities and urban riot or revolution. In France as a whole, he shows that the peak years of urban expansion and migration were the late 1850s and late 1870s, whereas the peak periods of disturbance were 1830–34, 1847–48, 1851 and 1871. As regards Paris, he repeats the findings of M. Pouthas and others: that the growth of the city was far more "explosive" and remarkable after Louis Napoleon's seizure of power (December 1851) than it was during the socially turbulent period of 1830 to 1851. In short, it would seem that, both in France as a whole and in Paris in particular, migration and expansion followed rather than preceded rebellion or revolution.

A related question is: what sort of cities were more prone to riot and rebellion—those growing more quickly, or those growing more slowly, or those whose population remained relatively static? M. Chevalier's thesis would clearly favor the first, as it presents population "explosion" and civil commotion as following the one from the other. Mr. Tilly, however, tells us that for the years 1830 to 1851— the period of maximum social unrest—disturbances were just as con-

---

63. For what follows, see Tilly, "Urbanisation and Political Disturbances in Nine-teenth-Century France," paper presented to the Annual Meeting of the Society for French Historical Studies, Ann Arbor, Michigan, April, 1966.

spicuous in slow-growing cities like Nîmes, Grenoble and Auxerre as they were in expanding cities like Bordeaux, Lyons and Paris; and that, conversely, some fast-growing cities, such as Marseilles, Toulouse and St. Etienne, were comparatively immune from any disturbance whatever. And he adds that, up to the 1860s at least, it was the older cities (such as Paris, Lyons, Rouen) that were the typical seedbeds of both political and industrial disturbance, rather than newly developing manufacturing centers like Roubaix, Mulhouse and St. Etienne. In short, the older and the more established the area of settlement, the greater its proneness to riot and rebellion; and this applies as much to the constituent parts of a city—such as the suburbs and *arrondissements* of Paris—as it does to the city as a whole. For, as Mr. Tilly observes: "Cities had their characteristic forms of disturbance; they were indeed training grounds for rebellion, but the training took time and commitment."

So it was the older residents rather than the "uprooted," the newest arrivals or the "nomads," who were the most likely participants in riot and disturbance; and Mr. Tilly notes the continuity in the composition of those taking part in urban riots and revolutions between 1789 and 1848, with its emphasis on the small craftsmen of the old established trades. The detailed studies made by a number of scholars within the field tends to confirm this view. Mr. Pinkney's is an example. Mr. Pinkney, as we have seen, can hardly be counted among M. Chevalier's critics; yet certain of his findings appear to lend support to the critics' rather than to Chevalier's case. He has made an analysis of those taking part in the three "glorious" days of the revolution of July 1830 from the lists of the dead and wounded and of the recipients of rewards and decorations. The 1,538 case studies he has assembled bear little resemblance to M. Chevalier's "dangerous classes." These *combattants de juillet* were, he found, largely composed of skilled workers or craftsmen of the traditional Paris trades and were rarely drawn from the uprooted or poorest of the poor, and they cannot by any stretch of the imagination be classed among criminal elements or the socially dispossessed.[64]

---

64. David Pinkney, "The Crowd in the French Revolution of 1830," *American Historical Review*, October, 1964, pp. 1-17.

The events of July 1830 were followed by successive outbreaks of almost insurrectionary proportions in June and September 1831, June 1832, April 1834 and May 1839. I have myself made a brief study of the most violent and extensive of them: the riots of June 1832, attending the funeral of a popular general in the cloisters of St. Merri's Church in the central market area of Paris. Among the judicial records relating to the affair,[65] I found the names of 230 persons who had been arrested and brought to trial. About half of those for whom sufficient details are given were craftsmen, skilled workers and independent artisans; the rest were a medley of professional people, tradesmen, clerks, shop assistants, laborers and domestic workers; and they were recruited from scattered districts within the capital, but mainly from the old and central areas of residence. So they, roughly, fit the earlier pattern. But, admittedly, the conclusion is based on a somewhat slender sample. The same, however, cannot be said of the far larger number of persons arrested and brought to trial after the great popular upheaval of June 1848. After this event, many thousands of people were brought before military tribunals and firing squads; and when M. Rémi Gossez, a French historian who has been working on the affair for over twenty years, brings his full evidence to light, we shall probably be more fully informed than we are about any equivalent event in the whole history of France. M. Gossez's findings and conclusions, however, are yet to come; meanwhile, we have to depend on the far more limited investigations carried out by others. Mr. Tilly and I have both studied the official records of the origins and occupations of the 11,693 persons who were charged with participation in the affair once the street-battles and preliminary judicial slaughters were over.[66] At first sight, they bear a remarkable resemblance to similar, earlier lists of the *Vainqueurs de la Bastille* and of those killed, or wounded and pensioned, after the assault on the Tuileries in August 1792, with the same prevalence of small employers, workers and craftsmen of the old established Paris trades. On closer inspection, however, it becomes evident that new social forces have come into

---

65. In the Archives Nationales and the Archives of the Prefecture of Police in Paris.
66. *Liste générale en ordre alphabéthique des inculpés de juin 1848*, Arch. Nat., F7 2585–6.

play: mechanics, railwaymen, building workers, not to mention the unemployed from the government's National Workshops. So there is a clear combination here of the old industrial Paris and the new. But, with comparatively few exceptions (the unemployed, for example, are in a relatively small minority), there is no more sign here of M. Chevalier's nomads and dangerous classes than there was among the participants in the earlier revolutions of 1789 and 1830.

All this strongly suggests that M. Chevalier and those who share his views on the relationship between urbanization, crime and social unrest may be mistaken; but it does not, of course, prove that the conclusions drawn by his critics are necessarily correct. Basically, it would seem that Chevalier's prognosis is ill-conceived, not just because it leans too heavily on the impressions of prejudiced contemporary observers, but because it confuses two types of behavior: the antisocial behavior of individuals and the collective action of social groups. The two may occur together, as they often did in nineteenth-century Paris (a study of the police files will establish the point), but they arise from different causes, have their own distinctive histories, and there is no necessary connection between the two. We may grant that Paris, like other cities of the time, had a lopsided growth; that this growth was attended by social evils such as extreme poverty, destitution and beggary, overcrowding and despair; and that these in turn, among the growing numbers of uprooted and socially rejected, bred crime and individual acts of violence. Such elements might also, on occasion, participate in economic protests, such as food riots, and even be drawn by hunger to engage in political actions directed against a Bastille, a City Hall, a Royal Palace or a Chamber of Deputies. But the evidence presented by M. Chevalier's critics suggests that such participation was marginal and seldom on an impressive scale. This need not surprise us, as the social instability and uprooting that were conducive to crime and acts of individual violence were probably not conducive to any but the most elementary forms of collective action. Furthermore, as has been argued, it was neither the "dangerous" districts nor the newly settled towns or quarters that proved the most fertile breeding-ground for social and political protest, but the old areas of settlement with established customs, such as the old cities of Paris, Rouen or Lyons in France, and, for that matter, the old cities of Westminster and London, and old chartered towns like Derby, Bristol and Nottingham, in England. For as Mr. Tilly reminds us, it "took time" to breed rebellion. It took time, too, to build up, through craft and workshop, that *camaraderie* of rebellion that grew out of long association and memories, hopes and hardships shared in common. So we shall end this discussion by turning M. Chevalier's thesis inside out and asking the paradoxical question: was it not rather the *stability* of old social relationships that provided the characteristic seed-bed of protest, and not the *instability* of mass emigration, uprooting and the dissolution of old social ties? But, admittedly, the whole problem requires fuller investigation before we can return a confident affirmative reply.

III

The Battle of Ideas

Every age has its slogans and battle cries, its own type of ideological ferment and battle of ideas; and every historian, whether liberal, conservative or Marxist, recognizes that this conflict is an intrinsic part of the processes of change, comparable with, if not equal to, the social conflict, economic and political revolutions, wars, or the activities of parties, parliaments and governments. It is generally accepted, too, that in the period after the fall of Napoleon, among these activating ideas, or *idées-force*, should be counted nationalism, liberalism, and socialism—and no doubt romanticism and religious ideas as well.

This, then, is fairly common ground. But historians have differed considerably both over the importance to attach to the history of ideas in general and the priority or relative importance to attach to each of these *idées-force*. In the nineteenth and early twentieth centuries, it was perhaps normal for historians, excepting Marxists and those with a social or economic bent, to write the history of Europe in terms of ideas and ideologies rather than of social or economic change. Since the last war, however, this has largely changed, though the change has been more pronounced in some countries than in others. Thus Franco Valsecchi, an Italian historian of distinction, has observed (writing in 1959) that "the spiritual and political climate of the post-war period and the ever-increasing influence of Marxism have led contemporary historians to give pride of place, in their reconstructions of the past, to economic and social factors." But, he adds, "in Italy and Germany, the great schools of history deriving from Hegel and reaching their culmination in Croce and Meinecke, have directed historical enquiry towards *Geistesgeschichte* and *Ideengeschichte,* the history of the internal movements of the European mind, as both an accompaniment and a guideline to *Tatsachengeschichte,* or the history of facts and events."[1] Perhaps, since Valsecchi wrote this passage, the influence of

Croce has lost some of its magic for Italian historiography; but the distinction certainly remains true of West Germany, where *Geistesgeschichte,* or the pure history of ideas, continues to exert a fascination that has been superseded elsewhere.

This may serve as a broad distinction, in their approach to the history of ideas (whether related to the *idées-force* of this or any other period), between the historians of one group of countries and those of another, but this is only a part of the problem. Even if historians agree on the importance to attach to the impact of ideas in general, they may still disagree about priorities and on the precise nature and origins of these ideas and the part they played in history. In respect to the first, we may obtain a rough-and-ready notion of historians' priorities by reading the titles that they give to their books. Where one author, writing of the early nineteenth century, chooses the title an *Age of Nationalism* or *Awakening of Nationality,* a second may prefer such a title as *Age of Revolution,* a third *Age of Progress* or *Age of Transformation,* a fourth *Romantic Age,* and a fifth *Era of Liberal Revolutions.* So where one author appears to accord the palm of all *idées-force* to nationalism, others may accord it to romanticism or liberalism or revolution. Let us take a number of these ideas in turn and see how historians have written about them in their European and early nineteenth-century context.

11. Liberalism

Liberalism, like so many other political creeds, had its origin in the French and American Revolutions. On the Continent of Europe, as in America, it was associated with human rights and liberties—the right to property, freedom of speech, press, worship and assembly, equality before the law, and "the pursuit of happiness"; such rights had been expressly proclaimed in the two great Declarations of the Rights of Man and of Independence. In Britain, where "natural rights" never quite enjoyed the same vogue as they did in Europe and

---

1. Franco Valsecchi, "L'évolution politique," in *L'Europe du XIXe et du XXe siècle (1815-1870). Problèmes et interprétations historiques,* 2 vols. (Milan, 1959), I, p. 258.

America, liberalism had other origins and associations. One was in Jeremy Bentham's Utilitarianism, or the theory of "the greatest happiness of the greatest number"; and another in the free-trading principles of Adam Smith and the classical economists, which were particularly well suited to a country which could claim an industrial lead over all other countries in the world. But all over Europe, whether they were grounded in the principles of the Rights of Man or in those of Bentham and Ricardo, all such persons generally acquired the label of "liberal," pure and simple.

The term first appeared in England about 1816, though it was only with the Spanish liberal revolt of 1820 that it received a wider and more general application. At first used by its enemies as a term of abuse, it acquired a cloak of respectability—at first in England, in France after 1830—as the Congress System and Metternich's Europe gradually fell apart. The earliest manifestations of nineteenth-century liberalism are to be found, within the Vienna Settlement itself, in the peacefully imposed charters and constitutions of the immediate post-Napoleonic years: the French Charter of 1815, the German and Swiss Federal Acts and the Polish Constitution of the same year. But, gradually, it became a battle cry for the armed opponents of the Congress System and it was under its banner that the Spaniards, Neapolitans, Russian Decabrists and Greeks fought for their freedom and independence in the 1820's, that the Belgians revolted against the Dutch and the Poles against the Russians and the French otherthrew the Bourbons in the revolutions of 1830–1831; that Mazzini launched his "Young Italy" and the British rioted for Reform in 1832; and that revolutions were fought out in Paris, Vienna, Prague, Berlin, Milan, Rome, Budapest and Naples in 1848.[2]

So early-nineteenth century liberalism appeared as a common creed, transcending the boundaries of the various European states. Yet it had, clearly and recognizably, its own national characteristics and variations. In France, for example, the Mecca of all revolutionaries of the time, it had quite distinctive revolutionary, nonreformist,

2. See, *int. all.*, Irene Collins, "Liberalism in Nineteenth-Century Europe," in *From Metternich to Hitler*, W. N. Medlicott (ed.) (New York, 1963), pp. 25–46.

associations. In Britain, on the other hand, the land of Corn Law Repeal and the Great Reform Bill, its message and expression were generally, though not exclusively, reformist. In Italy, more than elsewhere, it was almost inseparable from the movement for national independence from Austria and the Spanish Bourbons. In Germany, too, it was linked with nationalism, though nationalism or *Volkstum* of a more aggressive, exclusive and illiberal type; and historians have been generally agreed (though the fact has been deplored by some and counted a virtue by others) on the failure of liberalism to take firm root on German soil. Commonly, this failure has been traced back to the collapse of the reforms, initiated by Hardenberg and Stein in Prussia in 1819, under the dual impact of Metternich's Carlsbad Decrees and a general popular indifference to the aims of a small professional reforming group. Walter Simon, an American historian, in relating this episode, represents it as being of crucial importance for Germany's future history. He writes, "In 1819 Prussia, reverting to the political, social, and military forms of the *ancien régime,* turned her back on the political heritage of western Europe: on the Enlightenment, on English constitutionalism, and on the French Revolution. In this year was confirmed the political cleavage between Germany and the West which was to prove disastrous not only for Germany but for all of Europe."[3] Similar views have been expressed, though with more particular reference to the renewed failure of liberalism in 1848, by British and American historians like A. J. P. Taylor, Sir Lewis Namier, Roy Pascal and T. S. Hamerow, and the German liberal historian, Friedrich Meinecke. Other German historians, reared in a more aggressively nationalist tradition, have recognized the fact without shedding any tears for the loss of liberal experience and ideas. The arch-exponent of the antiliberal and nationalistic view, though himself a former liberal, was Heinrich von Treitschke, who, in his *History of Germany in the Nineteenth Century* (1879), misses few opportunities of castigating liberalism (though not liberalism of the "National," Bismarckian brand) as an alien creed, destructive of the old Teutonic

---

3. Walter M. Simon, *The Failure of the Prussian Reform Movement, 1807–1819* (Ithaca, New York, 1955), pp. 4–5.

ideal and of the military and authoritarian virtues of the Prussian state.[4] Sixty years later, the historians of Nazi Germany took up the refrain. Walter Frank's *Reichsinstitut für Geschichte des neuen Deutchlands* was established in the 1930s to trace the origins of Hitler's Third Reich in Germany's recent past. Among the Institute's sponsored works was Erich Botzenhaft's *Geschichte des Einbruchs der westlichen Ideen in Deutchland 1789–1848*, in which, together with the usual "exposure" of socialists and Jews, liberalism is denounced as an "alien," anti-Germanic culture of the West.[5]

So much, then, is more or less common knowledge and beyond serious dispute. But even among those who have taken a more charitable view of liberalism than German nationalist or National-Socialist historians, it has not always appeared in the same glowing colors or in that guise of a universally beneficent creed ascribed to it by its early theorists and promoters. Even in 1859, when the luster of European liberalism had become considerably dimmed, its main British theoretical exponent, J. S. Mill, presented it in the following all-embracing and unequivocal terms:

No society [he wrote] in which these liberties are not, on the whole, respected, is free, whatever may be its government; and none completely free in which they do not exist absolute and unqualified. The only freedom which deserves the name, is that of pursuing our own good in our own way, so long as we do not attempt to deprive others of theirs, or impede their efforts to obtain it.[6]

The English Whig historians of the nineteenth century, and G. M. Trevelyan in the twentieth, have tended to take such words at their face value and treat these "liberties" as the common heritage of the nation at large and not those of a single group or class. This, broadly, has also been the case of the twentieth-century Italian philosopher and historian, Benedetto Croce. Croce, after toying with Marxism in his

---

4. H. von Treitschke, *History of Germany in the Nineteenth Century*, 7 vols., (New York, 1915–1919).
5. K. F. Werner, "On Some Examples of the National-Socialist View of History," *Journal of Contemporary History*, III, 1968, pp. 193–206.
6. J. S. Mill, "On liberty" (1859), in *Utilitarianism, Liberty and Representative Government* (New York, n.d.), p. 100.

earlier years, ended by rejecting both the Christian-transcendentalist and the Marxist-materialist conception of history and substituting for them a view of history as man's quest for "spiritual liberty." It was an *élitist* vision, for only those were equals who shared in the vision and actively promoted its realization; yet its benefits accrued to the nation as a whole. This idealist picture of "liberty" and "liberalism" is presented by Croce in his *History of Europe in the Nineteenth Century*, which he wrote in his sixties, at the height of Mussolini's Fascism, in 1932. The opening chapter, appropriately entitled "The Religion of Liberty," firmly sets the tone:

When [he begins] the Napoleonic adventure was at an end and that extraordinary despot had disappeared from the stage where he had reigned supreme; while his conquerors were agreeing or trying to agree among themselves . . . then among all the peoples hopes were flaming up and demands were being made for independence and liberty. These demands grew louder and more insistent the more they met repulse and repression; and in disappointment and defeat hopes went on springing up afresh, purposes were strengthened . . . And over all of them [their various demands] rose one word that summed them all up and expressed the spirit which had given them life—the word *liberty*. On every side rang out the cry of a new birth, of a "century that is being born again," like a salutation full of promise to the "third age," the age of the Spirit . . . which now opened out before the human society that had prepared for it and waited for it.

And from this liberal awakening the half-century now proceeds as a continuous battle between liberty on the one hand and "other rival and hostile religions" on the other. Among these rivals he numbers democracy and socialism, but, more particularly, absolutism and "the Catholicism of the Church of Rome, the most direct and logical negation of the liberal idea." Yet, of the two, liberalism's most constant and characteristic struggle was with Absolutism, a struggle in which "the liberal ideal [like Michelet's spirit of Justice in 1789] resisted the absolute ideal, fought it without giving truce, and in the end won over it a victory that was permanent because it was substantial." And, to lend substance to his thought, he instances the struggles, in the 1820s and 1830s, of the Italians, Spaniards, Belgians, Hellenes, French and Germans for constitutions and independence and of the English for parliamentary reform, and the "national-liberal revolu-

tions" of 1848, which "confirmed their own principles, supplied them
with new and better-suited forms, and thus bore them magnificently
forward on the path of actuation."[7]

But, outside Italy, few twentieth-century historians have conceived
of "liberty" and liberalism in quite such fervent, uncritical and abstract terms. They have been inclined to ask such questions as "liberty
for whom, and to do what?" Croce himself repeats the questions
("What is liberty anyway? Liberty of whom or what?"); but he does
not take long to decide that liberty is really all of one piece and "could
not accept adjectives or empirical delimitations because of its intrinsic
infinity" and that "its significance lay solely in the goal at which it
aimed—that human life should draw breath more fully, should grow
deeper and broader."[8] Others, however, have preferred to see liberalism in a fuller historical context, both as a beginning and an end, with
a deeper exploration of its aims and content and its particular associations with any given class or group. Croce's compatriot, and part-
contemporary, Valsecchi adopts a half-way position. He deplores the
modern tendency to identify liberalism too closely with narrow *bourgeois* interests. Yet he concedes that liberalism provided the wealthy
bourgeoisie with a formula that enabled it to share political power
with the aristocracy, while allowing it to retain its preeminence over
other social classes, and that "liberal economic theory responded to
the expansionist needs of nascent capitalism."[9] French and English
historians, however—and Marxists in particular—have gone considerably further and have seen both the economics of *laissez-faire* and
political liberalism, in the forms they assumed in the early nineteenth
century, as direct expressions of the needs of an aggressive and rising
middle class. "The rise of the bourgeoisie," writes Jacques Droz, "was
matched by a certain concept of the world known as liberalism, which
in the last analysis was simply the expression of its economic and
political interests." And far from being all-embracing, its aims were
clearly circumscribed: to restrain the State from interfering with the

7. Benedetto Croce, *History of Europe in the Nineteenth Century,* pp. 3–5, 19–21, 58 ff., 169.
8. Croce, pp. 12–13.
9. Valsecchi, pp. 266–7.

operation of "natural" laws, to end privilege and grant equality before the law, and to extend the franchise to all men of property. As an example of an early-nineteenth century liberal holding similar views, Droz quotes Benjamin Constant, in France, to whom "the great achievement of the French Revolution was to have admitted the middle classes to the administration of political affairs."[10]

Dr. Hobsbawm, while sharing broadly such a view, goes into the matter more deeply in his *Age of Revolution*. It was not all political theorists who were as patently selfish and class-centred as Constant; nor were they all as outspoken as Malthus, with his gloomy prophesies of increasing pauperization and his "devil-take-the-hindermost" philosophy. After all, their contemporary, Jeremy Bentham, had set no limits to "the greatest number" who should share in his "greatest happiness"; nor had the American and French revolutionaries narrowly defined the scope of man's "natural" rights in their Declarations of Independence and of the Rights of Man. Admittedly, even in the two earlier revolutions, things had not quite worked out that way in practice, and qualifications had to be introduced both in France and America. Now the same problem rose again and a balance had to be struck. On the one hand, the unqualified assertion of human rights, without restrictions or apparent equivocation, had the enormous advantage of stimulating working-class and peasant support for liberal demands and the middle-class cause; on the other hand, such assertions proved to be a source of embarrassment when it came to settle accounts once the revolution (like that of July 1830 in Paris) was over. "For," Hobsbawm asks, "if government really were popular, and if the majority really rules (i.e. if minority interests were sacrificed to it, as was logically inevitable), could the actual majority—'the most numerous and poorest classes'—be relied upon to safeguard freedom and to carry out the dictates of reason which coincided, as was obvious, with the programme of middle class liberals?" Moreover, there was the competing lure of democracy which, more specifically, promised votes for all; and with industrialization came working-class movements and the new ideology of socialism, which reformulated

10. J. Droz, *Europe between Revolutions 1815–1848* (New York, 1968), pp. 45–53.

the old eighteenth-century "liberty," "equality" and "fraternity" in new nineteenth-century terms. So, faced with this threat and this dilemma, Hobsbawm argues, the old liberal ideology lost its former "confident swoop"; and, after the last outburst of liberal-inspired revolutions in 1848, pulled in its horns, adopted safeguards in defence of minorities, and adapted itself to a more respectable, socially conformist and more overtly middle-class future.[11]

12. Nationalism

The "nation" was another of the great rallying cries of the early nineteenth century. *"La nationalité,"* writes Valsecchi, *"s'affirme, aux côtés de la liberté, comme la deuxième grande idée-force du siècle."*[12] Nationalism, like liberalism, stemmed from the two earlier revolutions, but notably from the French. It was the French who, in 1792, first clearly formulated the principle of the nation's "natural frontiers" within which the "sovereignty of the people" should properly be exercised. It was the French, too, who, both by their example and by their military conquests under the Directory and Empire, aroused a new sense of nationhood, or nationality, among Italians, Spaniards and Germans; and this awareness became magnified, extended and charged with a new dynamic and emotional content in the period following the Napoleonic wars.

And so, writes Cobban, the nation state "ceased to be a simple historical fact and became the subject of a theory."[13] But, as with liberalism, it took time before men became fully conscious of the new force that had been unleashed and before the term "nationality," or "nationalism," entered into the current vocabulary of politics. This happened in the early 1830s, when the term came into use in England, in Germany (as *Nationalität* or *Volkstum*), in Russia (as *Narodnost*), and among Czechs and Italians. In Paris it was adopted—as a sign of genuine maturity—by the Académie Française in 1835. It was a

11. E. J. Hobsbawm, *The Age of Revolution,* pp. 234–41.
12. Valsecchi, p. 261.
13. A. Cobban, *The Nation State and National Self Determination* (London, 1969), p. 33.

year earlier that a manifesto of Mazzini's "Young Europe" movement proclaimed that "every people has its special mission, which will cooperate towards the fulfilment of the general mission of humanity. That mission constitutes its nationality."[14] This, however, was only one definition among many. To the Mazzinians, as to the French revolutionaries of the 1790s and the Polish rebels of 1831, nationalism still had an international revolutionary significance, whereby it was expected that each nation, while claiming its own separate identity, should contribute to the universal brotherhood of man. But this was only one side of the picture, even at this time. There was also a nationalism of a more exclusive, self-centered and antiliberal kind, which, far from looking to Paris or to Mazzini's Brotherhoods for inspiration, sought it exclusively within a country's own history and folklore and within its own national, political, linguistic or religious tradition. Something of this kind happened with the Spanish and Tyrolean revolts against Napoleon and in the so-called *Befreiungskrieg* of the Germans after Napoleon's retreat from Moscow. It became a distinctive feature of German nationalism (or *Volkstum*) particularly after the failure of Prussia's liberal experiments in 1819; and, in Eastern and Southeastern Europe it took shape in the Slavophil or Panslav movements with their glorification of Holy Russia (or Holy Austria). So nationalism, from the assertion of a nation's right to independence, might, by its very nature or by an almost imperceptible progression, exchange subjection by one Great Power for that of another or serve as a springboard for the suppression of the nationhood of others.

Some of these features, and some of these divisions and ambiguities within nationalism, became more readily apparent and assumed a new significance with the revolutions of 1848. But, for the present, nationalism, whether of the more radical or the more conservative type, generally played a liberating or revolutionary role. Usually (though not commonly with Slavs and Germans), it became the ally of liberalism, and liberals and nationalists were often one or fought side by side for constitutional reform and national independence. This was par-

14. *Cit.* Hobsbawm, p. 132.

ticularly the case with Italy where, as we saw, the two movements tended to become inextricably confused (and continued to be so after 1848); but it was also evident in the revolutions of the 1820s and 1830s among Poles, Serbs, Belgians, Spaniards, Irish and (outside Europe) Latin Americans; and even in Germany, the radicals of the Hambach Festival of 1832 proclaimed their comradeship with the liberal French and refused to publish a proposal, made by one of their speakers, that a united Germany must recover the lost provinces of Alsace and Lorraine.[15]

Nationalism has naturally excited the curiosity of historians and even, on occasion, set them at each other's throats. Once more, as with liberalism, we may note differences among the "ideologists"—those for whom the battle of ideas is paramount—and between the "ideologists" in general and those (mainly twentieth-century) historians who have associated nationalism with certain economic interests and social groups. Of the former, Croce may serve again as an obvious example. To Croce (perhaps because he was an Italian?), nationalism and liberalism are merely two sides of the same coin and may scarcely be distinguished. The quest for nationhood, like the quest for a liberal constitution and the Rights of Man, is a part of the same "religion of liberty," which is the very essence of the history of man. It is therefore a universal phenomenon, and virtually no distinction is made between the differing moods, methods and aspirations of Slavs, Germans, Belgians and Italians. "In Germany," he writes, "in Italy, in Poland, in Belgium, in Greece, and in the distant colonies of Latin America, oppressed nations were beginning to attempt some opposition to foreign rulers and governors." And, as with the more formally liberal movements of the 1820s and 1830s, "the word *liberty* united them all."[16]

With Croce, as with Michelet, history is all black and white—a straight fight between the forces of good and evil; and, in this struggle, the antiliberal, antinational forces (such as absolute monarchy or the

15. See J. P. T. Bury, "Nationalities and Nationalism," in *New Cambridge Modern History,* X, pp. 213–45; Hobsbawm, p. 317; Irene Collins, *The Age of Progress* (New York, 1964), p. 317.
16. Croce, pp. 1–5.

Church of Rome) are wholly black, and their liberal and nationalist opponents are wholly white. Other liberal historians, however, even if equally preoccupied with ideological issues, have seen this contest in entirely different terms. Lord Acton, for example, the British "Whig" historian of the late nineteenth century. As a Whig and an admirer of Tocqueville, Acton had an equally passionate concern for personal "liberties," an equally passionate dislike for socialism, though, as a liberal Catholic, he did not share Croce's aversion for the Church of Rome and saw it as the ally of liberty and nationalism rather than the reverse. But his Whiggish liberalism also led him to take a generally unfavorable view of nationalism, particularly of what he called "the modern theory of nationality," which he saw as a dangerous threat to "liberties" and the rights of minority groups. He set out his views, as a young man, in a paper contributed to the *Home and Foreign Review* in July 1862; and he reproduced them, apparently unchanged, in his *History of Freedom,* published forty-five years later. The time he was writing of was Bismarck's rising ascendancy in Germany, and Acton, who was of German origin himself, must have been strongly influenced by Bismarck's manipulation of German national aspirations in the service of the Prussian state. These aspirations, he considered, were not in themselves harmful or evil, and "the denial of nationality [whether to Germans or anyone else] . . . implies the denial of public liberty"; moreover, he wrote, "the great importance of nationality in the State consists in the fact that it is the basis of political capacity." But in whose interest would this "capacity" be exercised? Undoubtedly in the interest and to the greater glory of the nation-state. Thus the "theory of nationality," harnessed to the service of the State, had become both the most seductive of the subversive theories of the time and "the richest in promise of future power"; and the right of nationality (which in itself was good and just) was being sacrificed to the very system of State power which it had itself so enthusiastically helped to create. He expounds the apparent paradox as follows:

The greatest adversary of the rights of nationality is the modern theory of nationality. By making the State and the nation commensurate with each other in theory, it reduces practically to a subject condition all other nationalities that may be within the boundary. It cannot admit them to an equality with the ruling nation which constitutes the State, because the State would then cease to be national, which would be a contradiction of the principle of its existence.

So the "theory of nationality" is condemned as "a retrograde step in history" and, as "nationality does not aim either at liberty or prosperity, both of which it sacrifices to the imperative necessity of making the nation the mould and measure of the State," its cause "will be marked with material as well as moral ruin, in order that a new invention may prevail over the works of God and the interests of mankind." Yet his conclusion is ambivalent. For "criminal and absurd" as the theory is, it has at least served a useful historical purpose in that it "marks the final conflict, and therefore the end, of the forces which are the worst enemies of civil freedom, the absolute monarchy and the revolution."[17]

Where Acton was faced with an apparently insoluble dilemma, another liberal, Ramsay Muir, writing fifty years later, thought the solution might be found in the outcome of the First World War. Muir's book, *National Self-Government,* was published, shortly before the war ended, in 1918. He was more of a traditional liberal and less of a Whig than Acton; in fact, the subtitle to his book, *The Culmination of Modern History,* gives a clue to his commitment. Moreover, one of the main chapters of the book presents a highly lucid, readable and laudatory account of "the era of liberal revolutions" between 1815 and 1855. But, being written when it was, at a time when British liberals were firmly committed to the destruction of Germany's military power, it could hardly fail to distinguish between the German national ideal and that of other states, and between the German and the British in particular. "The nationalist idea," he writes of the aftermath of the revolutions of 1848, "was not destroyed or weakened in Germany by the failure of 1848; but having been disappointed of the dream of securing national unity through democratic machinery,

---

17. Lord Acton, "Nationality" (1862), in *The History of Freedom and Other Essays* (London, 1907), pp. 270–300.

it was ready to use the weapons of blood and iron, force and fraud."
And, as he writes, he sees the "culmination" of the national movements of the nineteenth century in two sharply contrasted types of
representative government: the British type (not merely confined to
Britain) and the German. In the British the organs of government are
subordinate to Parliament, while, in the German, it is the executive
which, free from effective parliamentary restraints and itself control-
ling the army and bureaucracy, directs national policy and effectively
calls the tune. And that, in fact, he suggests, is what the war was really
all about: "The sharp contrasts between these two conceptions may
be said to have come to its issue in the Great War, which will probably
determine which of these two shall survive."[18]

The Second World War and its aftermath raised new "spectres"
and placed the question of nationalism in an altogether wider, international context. New nation-states have emerged in former colonial
dependencies in Asia and Africa, and new vigorous and highly self-
conscious and revolutionary national movements have arisen, in some
cases almost overnight from within formerly feudal or semitribal
societies. All of this must naturally give a new perspective to the
historian's treatment of national movements as a whole, even those
reaching back to the early nineteenth century, or to the so-called age
of nationalism itself. Yet, so far, historians appear to have been slow
to react to these new perspectives and possibilities. Mention should,
however, be made of a work that appeared immediately after the last
war and which reflects at least one aspect of these end-of-war or
postwar preoccupations. This is Hans Kohn's book, *Prophets and
Peoples: Studies in Nineteenth Century Nationalism,* which was published in New York in 1946. As his title suggests, Kohn is concerned
as much with the "prophets" as with the national movements themselves—with men like Mazzini, Michelet, Treitschke and Dostoevsky,
each of whom, he considers, "made a highly significant contribution
to the understanding of nationalism and helped to shape the age of
nationalism." These "national prophets," he argues, helped to give

18. Ramsay Muir, *National Self-Government. Its Growth and Principles* (New York,
1918), pp. 62–82.

their people a sense of national identity and an awareness of history and, therefore, to strengthen their national character. All this was well and good; but nationalism "carries with it a strange and sometimes pernicious fascination" with the past and "nothing is more dangerous than the wish . . . to have nations haunted by its ghosts." Moreover, the differentiation that nationalism brings has the further danger of weakening a country's traditional ties with its neighbors and, specifically among the countries of Europe, of stifling the sense of a "common heritage of Western civilization." These dangers, intensified by "the uncertainties and confusions of the aftermath of the two great wars," call for an effective remedy in the constitution of "an interdependent community of nations." So Kohn's book, though formally set in the context of nineteenth-century nationalism, is clearly a tract for our times: a plea for the closer unity of the nations of Europe.[19]

After this, it may seem a little pedestrian to suggest that some of the more significant of postwar writing on nineteenth-century nationalism has been that which, as in the case of liberalism, attempts to place it in a social or economic context. If (to choose an obvious example) the main social prop of nineteenth-century liberalism lay in the middle class, can the same be said of nationalism? Those historians who have been concerned with the matter have generally agreed that this was so, though few have been as specific as Hobsbawm, who writes that "the great proponents of middle class nationalism at this stage were the lower and middle professional, administrative and intellectual strata, in other words the *educated* classes"; and he notes, in particular, the part played by university professors and students.[20] Yet this is hardly contentious and need not, therefore, detain us further. But other questions arise, such as what other classes became involved, and at what stage? Here again, there does not seem to be any significant disagreement. Valsecchi, for example, having noted that the aristocracy was "far from having played . . . a purely conserv-

19. Hans Kohn, *Prophets and Peoples. Studies in Nineteenth-Century Nationalism* (New York, 1946), pp. 1–9
20. Hobsbawm, p. 135.

ative role," adds that "in some cases it even took a lead in the national and liberal movements as in Italy, Poland and Hungary." Renouvin, too, attributes to the large landed proprietors an active part in the Italian *Risorgimento*. Hobsbawm, however, differentiates in these countries (he is referring particularly to Poland and Hungary) between the landed magnates, generally pillars of the Catholic Church and the political establishment, and the lesser gentry, often with "little but their birth to distinguish them from other impoverished farmers." "Such gentlemen," he continues, "had long been the stronghold of opposition to absolutism, foreigners and magnate rule in their respective countries, sheltering [as in Hungary] behind the dual buttress of Calvinism and county organizations. It was natural that their opposition, discontent, and aspirations for more jobs for local gentlemen should now fuse with nationalism."[21]

What of the mass of urban workers and country-dwellers? Once more divergences between historians have been slight, though admittedly they are not always writing about the same country or the same decade. Boyd Shafer, in his *Nationalism Myth and Reality*, discusses the support given to nationalist movements by various social classes in the wake of the Vienna Congress, and concludes: "The lower economic classes, especially the growing number of city workers, never evinced as much nationalism as the middle classes. Neither among them nor among the peasantry was there much evidence of it in 1815."[22] Pierre Renouvin, in writing of post-Congress Italy, appears to share his view. He notes that in the 1820s and thirties the most active elements were drawn from the urban *bourgeoisie*, supported by a sprinkling of landed proprietors; and he adds: "No doubt, 'the people' played a part as well: the artisans of Romagna, the workers of certain industrial cities or certain ports lent occasional support to the activities of the patriots, particularly to the Mazzinians; but the peasant masses remained inactive." Yet he sees a marked change, with

21. Valsecchi, p. 266; P. Renouvin, *Histoire des relations internationales*, V, p. 162; Hobsbawm, pp. 133–4.
22. Boyd C. Shafer, *Nationalism Myth and Reality* (New York, n.d.), p. 156.

a greater popular involvement in events, after 1846 when Pius IX, the "liberal" Pope, became elevated to the Papal Throne.[23]

In concurring with this general view, Hobsbawm gives it greater precision and attempts an explanation. Conscious nationalism, he argues, was the sole affair of an educated *élite*, while the great mass of Europeans at this time were uneducated—even Britain, France and Belgium had, in the 1840s, an illiteracy rate of between 40 and 50 per cent. Admittedly, illiteracy was in itself no bar to political awareness, but the absence of a common written, or even spoken, language most decidedly was: he instances the Hungarians who only acquired Magyar as their national tongue in 1840 and the Italians "who did not even speak the national literary language but mutually incomprehensible *patois.*" So he discounts the possibility of any widespread popular national feeling against the French among Germans or Spaniards before Waterloo, among Italians before 1848, or among the rebellious anti-Polish peasants of Gallicia in 1846. In fact, before the great turning point of 1848, he sees only one exception to the rule: the Irish, who, in the Repeal movement against the British during the period of 1820–40, formed a genuine national mass movement, solidly based on the peasantry and centered on Daniel O'Connell. Elsewhere, nationalism could only acquire a genuine mass base at this time in developed industrial countries like France, Britain and the United States. For nationalism, he concludes, "like so many other characteristics of the modern world, is the child of the dual revolution."[24]

13. *Romanticism*

Of all the intellectual *leitmotifs* of the early nineteenth century in Europe, romanticism has proved the hardest to define and place in any precise historical context. Its characteristic modes were more often literary and artistic than political or philosphic; yet it undoubtedly deserves a place in history and historiography, and some historians,

23. Renouvin, p. 162.
24. Hobsbawm, pp. 132–45.

as we have seen, have chosen it among all other *idées-force* as expressing most aptly the intellectual currents of the day.[25]

Formally speaking, romanticism began as a literary movement,
with a name and a program of its own, in Germany in the late 1790s.
But, as there was already a similar literary trend in Britain and as both
owed a great deal to eighteenth-century precedents, it may be more
sensible to place the movement in a wider historical and national
context. Romanticism proper may be said (though this is clearly a
personal judgment) to have had three main phases—if we include the
eighteenth-century precedents, four. The first (to start with the
preliminary or "curtain-raising" phase) goes back to the thirty-or-so
years before the French Revolution. The common elements were
"sentiment," "nature" and (on occasion) the cult of the Gothic or
medieval past. This was the time of MacPherson's *Ossian* in Scotland;
of Sterne's *Sentimental Journey,* Horace Walpole's novel *The Castle
of Otranto,* and Wesley's religious revivalism in England. In France,
it was the time of Rousseau's *Confessions,* the *comédie larmoyante,*
Greuze's paintings, Diderot's art criticism, and Queen Marie-
Antoinette's antics as a dairy-maid at Versailles; and, in Germany, of
Sturm und Drang, Goethe's *Werther, Weltschmerz,* and Hölderlin's
Romantic Hellenism. On the whole, this preliminary phase was a-
political, though it often had rebellious undertones, a mood that was
most notably expressed in the *Sturm und Drang* movement in Germany.

The next phase (or the first phase of romanticism proper) was set
almost exclusively—if we except the Frenchman Châteaubriand—in
Germany and Britain and began in both around 1798. This phase
arrived at a time when there was considerable disillusionment among
poets and writers concerning the French Revolution, which many of
the new romantics (Wordsworth, Southey, Coleridge, Herder, Wie-
land, Tieck and Schlegel) had saluted in the past. This mood was
particularly strong in Germany, where the romantic writers (men like
Novalis, Wackenroder, Tieck, Müller, Schelling and the brothers

25. See, for example, R. B. Mowat's *The Romantic Age* (London, 1937); and J. L.
Talmon's *Romanticism and Revolt 1815–1848* (New York, 1967).

Schlegel) accompanied their evocation of the Gothic and Germany's medieval past with a return to Christianity and denunciations of the atheistic French and Napoleonic tyranny. In fact, this "backward-looking" phase in German romanticism has led some writers to see it as the most characteristic feature of romanticism as a whole. "The most significant feature . . . of the romantic age," writes Valsecchi, "is the sense of tradition, the cult of the past. The nineteenth century is the century of history, as the eighteenth has been the century of reason."[26] But it was at this time, too, that, in England, Wordsworth and Coleridge produced their *Lyrical Ballads* (1798) and began to seek nature in the Lakes; that Blake wrote his *Jerusalem,* and Burns was writing his folk-ballads and Scott (the sole "antiquarian" among them) his first historical novels in Scotland.

The third phase started with the importation of romanticism into France from Germany and England, after Madame de Stäehl published her book, *De l'Allemagne,* in 1813. Among its first fruits were Lamartine's *Méditations* (1820) and the early poems of Hugo and de Vigny. Meanwhile, in England, three more illustrious romantic poets had appeared in Byron, Keats and Shelley. In France, during this period (the Restoration), romanticism remained politically conservative or (as with Constant and Madame de Stäehl) mildly liberal. In England on the other hand, only Southey remained conservative; the prevailing mood was radical, as in Byron's epics and in Shelley's *Masque of Anarchy* (1819).

The last and most productive phase of romanticism has generally been dated from the revolutions of 1830; yet it might be reasonable to push the date back to the middle-1820s. With the accession of Charles X in France (1824), poets began to move left, and more decidedly so with Charles's expulsion in 1830. In fact, this phase was, both artistically and politically, the most radical and forward-looking in the whole history of romanticism; and several of the poets, writers, musicians and painters of the day openly allied themselves with liberal and revolutionary movements. In the early 1820s, even Lord Tennyson (a doubtful romantic) gave his sympathies to the foreign liberal

26. Valsecchi, p. 258.

volunteers who went to fight for liberalism against clericalism in Spain; and Byron became the most popular of all romantic heroes by his death at Missolonghi in Greence in 1824. In France, Victor Hugo hailed the revolution of 1830 as a victory for romanticism and wrote, in his preface to *Hernani* the same year, that "Romanticism is liberalism in literature." It was also the time of Delacroix's revolutionary painting, Lamennais's *Paroles d'un croyant,* Michelet's histories of France and Daumier's satirical barbs at Louis-Philippe. It was the age, too, of Chopin and Mickiewicz in Poland; Liszt and Petöfi in Hungary; Manzoni and Mazzini in Italy; Uhland, the brothers Grimm, Freiligrath, Herwegh and Heine (though an exile in Paris) in Germany; and, in Russia of Lermontov's *Ode on the Death of Pushkin,* and of Dostoevsky, who, in 1849, narrowly escaped execution for revolutionary activities. All these were romantics with a distinctly liberal or radical commitment.

The single common denominator in all this, whatever the phase and whatever the country in which it found expression, is that romanticism was a movement of revolt; and this has been generally accepted. But a revolt against whom or what? Was it a revolt against Society *tout court* (see Rousseau, Hölderlin or Musset)? Against the established Church (see Pietism or Evangelical Christianity)? Against Classicism (see August Schlegel, Wordsworth's *Prelude,* or Hugo's Preface to *Cromwell*)? Against French culture (see Germany's *Sturm und Drang*)? Against Isaac Newton (see Goethe)? Against the Age of Reason (see Novalis or Goethe's *Werther*)? Against the French Revolution (see Burke, Bonald, de Maistre)? Against Napoleon (see Fichte, Görres, Müller)? Against Metternich (see Mazzini)? Against aristocracy (see Shelley)? Against absolutism (see Mickiewicz, Freiligrath, Herwegh)? Or against philistinism or the *bourgeoisie* (see Gautier, Shelley, Bryon, Heine and many others)? Moreover, if such were the romantics' villains, who were their heroes? Was it Byron's Corsair or Don Juan, or Byron himself? Stendhal's Julien Sorel? Napoleon (he remained so for many)? The Wandering Jew? William Tell? Rienzi? Garibaldi? Carlyle's Frederick the Great? Or Delacroix's heroes of the barricades? Who, for that matter, was the typical romantic in a movement, which extended over eighty years and comprised such a diversity of talents as, among poets, Wordsworth, Blake, Burns, Lamartine, Herwegh, Manzoni and Lermentov; among novelists, Hugo, Balzac, Mérimée, Stendhal and Scott; among critics and philosophers, Hegel, Schelling, Schlegel and Châteaubriand; among playwrights, Kleist, Grillparzer and Dumas; among painters, Delacroix, Turner, Daumier, Goya and Géricault; among musicians, Chopin, Schubert, Liszt, Verdi, Beethoven and Weber—not to mention such political activists as Mazzini and Garibaldi?

It is, of course, this diversity in romanticism that has made it so difficult to pin it down to any neat definition and that has caused such a wide divergence of opinion among literary critics and historians as to its nature and historical role, and as to whom and what it represented. So much so that one critic, Arthur Lovejoy, long a professor of philosophy at Johns Hopkins, wrote after the last war that "the word 'romantic' has come to mean so many things that, by itself, it means nothing," and that there was no single movement of Romanticism but many.[27] Another writer, the Columbia University historian Jacques Barzun, while not sharing Lovejoy's pessimism, has commented, in his own way, on the bewildering diversity of romanticism by expounding what it is *not:*

Romanticism is not a return to the Middle Ages, a love of the exotic, a revolt from Reason, an exaggeration of individualism, a liberation of the unconscious, a reaction against scientific method, a revival of pantheism, idealism and catholicism, a rejection of artistic conventions, a preference for emotion, a movement back to nature, or a glorification of force. Nor is it any more of a dozen generalities which have been advanced as affording the proper test.[28]

Yet, with all the confusion, others have thought to see a clear unifying thread and a recognizable common pattern running through the movement as a whole. René Wellek, for example, professor of Comparative Literature at Yale, considers the diversity to be purely "relative" and finds in romantic literature, wherever it appears in Europe, "the same conception of poetry and of the workings and nature of poetic imagination, the same conception of nature and its

---

27. See John B. Halsted (ed) *Romanticism,* (Boston, 1968), pp. 32–44.
28. Halsted, *Romanticism,* p. 30.

relation to man, and basically the same poetic style, with a use of imagery, symbolism, and myth which is clearly distinct from that of eighteenth-century neo-classicism." An Italian literary critic, Mario Praz, also sees a unity in romanticism, but with him the common historical context disappears altogether: "The word 'romantic' thus comes to be associated with another group of ideas such as 'magic', 'suggestion', 'nostalgia', and above all with words expressing states of mind which cannot be described, such as the German 'Sehnsucht' and the English 'wistful'." Irving Babbitt, an earlier and more conservative critic (he was writing in Boston in 1919) and one-time professor of literature at Harvard, saw this unity from quite a different angle; for to him romanticism, in whatever guise it appeared, was a kind of disease. "When the romanticist," he writes, "is not posing as the victim of fate he poses as the victim of society. Both ways of dodging moral responsibility enter into the romantic legend of the *poète maudit*. . . . It is hardly necessary to say that great poets of the past have not been at war with their public in this way." Croce also sees an "unhealthy aspect" in romanticism; but he distinguishes between one type and another—between the "theoretic" and the "moral." Theoretic romanticism he considers highly commendable. It is "the revolt, the criticism, and the attack against literary academicism and philosophic intellectualism, which had dominated in the illuminist age. It awakened the feeling for genuine and great poetry . . . and it reintegrated and retouched all the aspects of history, civil and political history no less than religious, speculative, and artistic." It also played a creative political role, for it "grasped life in its active and combative sense, and thus prepared the theoretical premises for liberalism." *Moral* romanticism, on the other hand, or romanticism as a "malady" or *mal de siècle,* represented not strength but weakness, a crisis of faith of those reaching for, but failing to grasp, the new liberal ideal. In Croce's words: it "possessed neither the old nor the new faith, neither the authoritative one of the past nor the clear one of the present, and showed precisely that it was a lack of faith, travailing in eagerness to create one and impotent to do so."[29]

29. Halsted, *Romanticism,* pp. 22, 27, 62, 17; Croce, pp. 42–54.

Other historians, too, have drawn a distinction between one type or one period of romanticism and another. Thus Dr. Kitson Clark sees the year 1830 as a watershed separating the earlier "poetic" and more "excited" period of romanticism (he is writing specifically of England) from the more "stabilzed," politically conscious romanticism of the 1830s and 1840s, when the novel was catering to the tastes of a greatly extended reading public. This fact, he adds, gave a new dimension to romanticism, which "must be considered not only as something which affects some of the leading minds of the day, it must be considered as a popular movement, even as a vulgar movement." For his part, Jacques Barzun, having decided what romanticism is not, concludes that it has two distinctive aspects, one of which is permanent or "intrinsic" and the other temporary and "historic." The permanent aspect is that stressed by Mario Praz and other literary critics, and is represented by "human traits which may be exhibited at any time or place." The historian's definition, on the other hand, presents it as "a European phenomenon, occurring within certain historical dates and possessing certain characteristics." More precisely, he defines this "historic romanticism" as "comprising those Europeans whose birth fell between 1770 and 1815, and who achieved distinction in philosophy, statecraft, and the arts during the first half of the nineteenth century . . ."[30] This simple formula has at least the distinction of neatly begging all the questions.

Historians have, in fact, unlike several of their "literary" colleagues, generally been concerned to see romanticism as a historical phenomenon, fixed within certain boundaries of time and place. Some have gone further and attempted to relate it to a particular social context. Hobsbawm believes that the remarkable flowering of the arts during these sixty years (he is writing of 1789 to 1848) "must be sought first and foremost in the impact of the dual revolution." "If," he writes, "a single misleading sentence is to sum up the relations of artist and society in this era, we might say that the French Revolution inspired him by its example, the Industrial Revolution by its horror, and the bourgeois society, which emerged from both, transformed his

30. Halsted, *Romanticism,* pp. 95, 119–21.

very existence and modes of creation." Yet he denies that romanticism may be properly classified as either a distinctly "bourgeois" or "antibourgeois" movement; for, depending on the period, it was both. On the one hand, the early romantic or preromantic movement of the late eighteenth century had voiced the moods and opinions of the middle class and served to glorify the simple, homely virtues at the expense of an artificial, aristocratic and corrupt society. But, he continues, "once bourgeois society . . . had triumphed in the French and Industrial Revolutions, romanticism unquestionably became its instinctive enemy and can be justly described as such." Moreover, as writer and artist were becoming increasingly alienated from the new society, romanticism (in his view) made a comparatively small impact on the culture of the middle and lower-middle class. "Romanticism," he writes, "entered middle class culture, perhaps mostly through the rise in day-dreaming among the female members of the bourgeois family"; but that culture itself retained its "unromantic" qualities of "soberness and modesty." Popular culture, too—and here he differs from Kitson Clark—retained its old "preindustrial" pattern (its traditional folksongs, festivals and costumes) until industry and urban life, but not romanticism, destroyed it after the 1840s.[31]

Arnold Hauser and Albert George, the first an art historian and the second a professor of Romance Languages at Syracuse, have both treated romanticism in the context of the industrial revolution. Hauser writes of it as being "essentially a middle-class movement; indeed it was the middle-class literary school par excellence, the school which had broken for good with other conventions of classicism, courtly-aristocratic rhetoric and pretence, with elevated style and refined language"; and he adds that "the fact that so many of the representatives of romanticism were of noble descent no more alters the bourgeois character of the movement than does the anti-philistinism of its cultural policy." And, in England in particular, he traces the origins of romanticism to the reaction of "liberal" poets and writers to industrialization and the substitution of a cash-nexus for the old traditional values—a reaction that he sees exemplified in the poetry of Goldsmith, Southey, Coleridge, Blake and Shelley. So Hau-

31. Hobsbawm, pp. 253–76.

ser's thesis ends in a paradox; for his middle-class romantics (and here he comes closer to Hobsbawm) are shown to reject and turn away in despair from the very values that their middle-class society projects. But the outcome, as Hauser sees it, is escape and not struggle; for "everywhere the struggle ends with a turning away from reality and the abandonment of any effort to change the structure of society."[32]

Albert George, who makes a more positive contribution to the debate, traces the interrelation between romanticism and industrialism in France. He divides romanticism into two main periods with a dividing-line around 1830; and, like Kitson Clark in England, he is far more concerned with the second than with the first. For, at about this time, France began her industrial revolution and the new technology, emanating from across the Channel, brought revolutionary changes not only to industry in general, but to the tools and materials at the writers' and artists' disposal. For, he writes, "the arrival of the machine age, changes in the technology of printing, the slow spread of education, and the creation of a huge audience of limited literacy, all combined to influence the direction Romanticism would take after 1830." One of the forms it took (and here again he comes close to Kitson Clark) was to give a new stimulus to prose. For the industrial revolution, in his view, "opened the way for a mass literature, and . . . the very machines which fashioned that age split romanticism in two factions, one of which continued the poetic revolution that the first generation had begun. To the other it presented new possibilities for artistic expression. It helped focus attention on prose, thereby aiding the shift from the romance to the novel . . . In short, it was a major factor in the development of French romanticism."[33]

14. Socialism

Socialism, during this period, is of a somewhat different order from the other *idées-force* we have been discussing. For one thing, it arrived

---

32. Halsted, *Romanticism*, pp. 71–5.
33. Albert J. George, "The Romantic Revolution and the Industrial Revolution in France," *Symposium*, Syracuse, VI, 1952; reproduced (in part) in *The Shaping of Modern France*, Friguglietti and Kennedy (eds.), pp. 242–8; and see Halsted, *Romanticism*, p. 87.

late on the scene and, in consequence, played only a comparatively minor role in the political events of Europe in the early nineteenth century. Secondly, socialism, unlike liberalism and nationalism, is, quite peculiarly and distinctly, a product of what has been called the "dual revolution." The socialist *idea,* it is true, grew, like the concepts of political liberty and "happiness" and of popular sovereignty and nationhood, out of the earlier political revolutions—in particular, the French. But whereas the other political movements acquired merely a new dimension through the second—the industrial—revolution, socialism as a *movement* could not exist at all without industrialization and the new classes it called into being.

The *idea,* then, grew out of the great political debate that accompanied the French Revolution. Its germs have, in fact, been traced back to earlier political thinkers like Mably and Morelly, and to Rousseau's teaching regarding the subordination of the private to the public good. The idea was further fostered, though unconsciously and indirectly, by a number of Jacobins and extreme democrats and was first given formal substance by Babeuf in his "communist" program and "conspiracy" of 1796. But it remained a theory and had no significant following until Buonarotti, Babeuf's old associate and disciple, published his *Conspiracy of the Equals,* based on the *babouvist* experience, in 1828. France was on the eve of an industrial revolution and ideas that had been largely rejected or ignored before now found a remarkable reception among the craftsmen of the small Paris workshops—heirs to the revolutionary *sans-culottes*—and the new industrial working population. In 1831, the term "socialism" was coined by a Frenchman, Pierre Leroux; and other socialist, or near-socialist, projects and ideas came to supplement the "communist" ideas of Babeuf and Buonarotti: the industrial blueprints of the Saint-Simonians, Fourier's self-governing industrial communities, Cabet's plan for a communist *Icarie* or island-utopia, Proudhon's anarchism, Blanqui's theories of class struggle and proletarian dictatorship, and Louis Blanc's scheme for establishing cooperative "social workshops" with government finance. So by 1840, in a variety of guises, French socialism was already a political force to be reckoned with, though it was mainly confined to Paris.

Meanwhile, in England, socialism, like liberalism, had taken root in its own way; indeed, it is probable that Robert Owen used the term, though in a more informal and casual manner, a dozen years before Leroux. English socialism had the advantage of having a more developed industry and working-class movement in which to spread its teachings than the French; but, on the other hand, English socialism was more pragmatic, more piecemeal and untheoretical. Moreover, it lacked the political experience of the French Revolution and it remained more closely attuned to the ideas of the middle-class political economists. In fact, the ideas of the earliest socialist writers, Thomas Hodgskin and William Thompson (both writing in the 1820s) were only a short step ahead of Ricardo's Labor Theory of Value. Hodgskin and Thompson were followed by Robert Owen, the one-time progressive manufacturer of the New Lanark Mill in Scotland. Owen's socialism was strictly moralistic and didactic: he believed that it would grow from the force of example, through education and the development of character. So he discouraged strikes, class war, and even political activity, and launched a wide variety of social-cooperative experiments: self-supporting "Harmony" communities, labor "bazaars," "grand" national trade unions, and (his most durable legacy) consumers' cooperative societies. Thus early English socialism, largely under Owen's influence, remained moralistic, experimental, nonprogrammatic and largely nonpolitical.

In the rest of Europe, socialism made very little impact until the latter half of the nineteenth century. A typical example of this late development can be seen in Russia, whose industrial working class did not exceed 2 or 3 percent by the middle of the century and where socialist ideas (in their post-1850 Marxist form) did not penetrate to any effect before the 1870s: before this, only Populism had any mass followimg among the workers and peasants.[34] Outside England and France, however, the earlier socialism found a limited base in Germany. But German socialism, before Marx, was largely a French importation and made few converts. A crucial year was 1842, when

34. See Isaiah Berlin's Introduction to Franco Venturi, *Roots of Revolution* (New York, 1960), pp. vii-xxx.

Ludwig von Stein wrote his *Socialism and Communism in France Today* and Wilhelm Weitling, a radical Paris-educated tailor of Magdeburg, put forward a medley of Christian, humanitarian and Communist ideas in his *Guarantees of Harmony and Freedom*. It was the year, too, that Marx began to edit the west-German *Rheinische Zeitung;* and Marx's and Engels's new "scientific" socialist writings began to appear, with the *Holy Family*, in 1844; the far more explosively influential *Communist Manifesto* followed in the winter of 1847-8. But the enormous influence that Marxist writing was to exercise on the European socialist and working-class movement lay in the future; and it is generally agreed that, outside the Rhineland (and there only marginally), the *Manifesto* arrived too late to make any significant impression on the German events of 1848.[35]

If, then, we can virtually discount Marxist socialism as playing any part in the ideological battle of the early nineteenth century, what about the earlier scattered threads of "preindustrial" socialism, whose evolution we have briefly outlined above? What, in the first place, were its general and distinguishing features? We have already noted the moralistic qualities in Owen's socialism in England and Weitling's mystical-Christian brand of socialism in Germany. In France, too, as Professor Labrousse points out, early socialism was strongly impregnated with a moral concern for social equality and justice. "The French socialists of the nineteenth century," he writes, "were at once economists and moralists." They were (he goes on) powerfully influenced by the ideas of the eighteenth-century moralists (Mably, Morelly, Rousseau), "whose main concern was with the distribution of property, which they wished to see more equal and more just"— even to the point where they would willingly accept, if this were necessary to assure a just society, a retreat to a more primitive economy.[36] Labrousse adds that French socialism of this period had not yet made a break with the ideas of the more advanced of the bourgeois democrats and that, for some time to come (it was still

35. T. S. Hamerow, *Restoration, Revolution and Reaction. Economics and Politics in Germany, 1815–1871* (Princeton, 1958), pp. 138–40.
36. C.-E. Labrousse, *Le mouvement ouvrier et les théories sociales en France de 1815 à 1848,* Cours de Sorbonne (Paris, 1948, 1954), pp. 6–7.

evident in the Paris Commune of 1871), Jacobinism and socialism would remain closely, and sometimes inextricably, related. So French socialism had not established itself as an independent body of ideas; and English historians have said the same about the British.[37] A third point to note is that this early socialism, unlike the later socialism of Marx and Engels (or, for that matter, the British "reformist" kind of the later nineteenth century), was millennial and cataclysmic, that is, that the ideal society which the socialists wished to bring about might happen overnight like the Second Coming of Christ. There is a great deal of this in Owen's numerous experiments, such as his scheme for a "New Harmony" community in Indiana; the same may be said of Cabet's plan for a communist settlement in Icaria; and even Blanqui's numerous *putsches* and conspiracies were based on the belief that a sudden stroke by a small body of enthusiasts could lead the workers, after a brief interlude, into the Promised Land. So the early socialist vision was largely unhistorical, eclectic (Engels called it a "mish-mash"), often "backward-looking", and divorced from the realities of the emerging industrial society. Their message, therefore, important as it had been in their time, had, by the midcentury, become spent; and Professor J. F. C. Harrison, Robert Owen's most recent biographer, writes that "there is no evidence to suggest that Owen or the Owenites were much read after the 1850s."[38]

So much has, I believe, been generally accepted; and for this reason, there has been a widespread willingness to agree that the early, pre-1850 type of socialism was "utopian," as contrasted with the later Marxist kind which has been called "modern" or "scientific." The terms were first used in this antithetical manner by the early Marxists themselves: their classic formulation was made by Engels in his *Socialism Utopian and Scientific*, which was first published in pamphlet form in 1880.[39] But there have been a number of dissenting voices, with Marxists and near-Marxists among them. Professor Labrousse,

---

37. Labrousse, pp. 7–8; Hobsbawm, pp. 242–5; George Lichtheim, *The Origins of Socialism* (London and New York, 1969).
38. J. F. C. Harrison, *Robert Owen and the Owenites in Britain and America. The Quest for the New Moral World* (London, 1969), p. 260.
39. F. Engels, *Socialism Utopian and Scientific* (London, 1932), p. vii.

for instance, while he accepts the broad distinction, is not altogether happy about Engels's choice of terms. To "utopian" socialism he would prefer a "conceptual," or "theoretic" socialism (though this would hardly apply to Owen) in contrast to the "positive" socialism advanced by Marx and Engels. Professor Harrison, in the case of Owen, considers the appropriate term to be "millennial" and that millennianism, far from being visionary or impractical, was, in the context of the times, both a natural and a necessary means of communication. A further objection—this time in relation to the French —comes from Jacques Droz after reading the work of the Soviet historian V. Volgin on the secret societies under the July Monarchy in France. Volgin published an article, entitled "Egalitarian and socialist tendencies in French secret societies" in the Soviet journal, *Voprosi Istorii,* in 1947. This shows, argues Droz, that there were in circulation, in these societies in the 1830s and 1840s, developed ideas on the class struggle closely related to those of the *babouvists* and bearing little affinity with "idealism" (which he presumably equates with "utopianism"). And he instances, in particular, the egalitarian and socialist ideas of the republican writer and activist, Voyer d'Argenson, and of Vignerte, a member of Blanqui's Society of the Rights of Man.[40]

Of rather greater importance is the question, what influence did socialism and socialist ideas have on the revolutionary and popular movements of the day? Before 1830, even in England, it must without much doubt have been quite negligible; yet, in the next few years, Owenite ideas played an important part in the new trade unions (as witness the affair of the Dorset Labourers of 1834). In France, although Buonarotti's book had appeared in 1828, it had hardly begun to circulate in Paris before the revolution of 1830: and Blanqui and others who adopted Babeuf's conspiratorial methods only began to play an active part in political demonstrations in 1832, after the earlier Lyons outbreak (1831). From this time on, judging by entries in police registers, we may presume that socialists played a leading part in the insurrections of 1832, 1834 and 1839, though it would be hard to

40. Labrousse, p. 7; Harrison, *Robert Owen,* pp. 102, 231; J. Droz, *L'époque contemporaine,* I, pp. 60–61.

prove that they influenced their outcome. With the revolution of 1848, the socialist impact would appear to have been on a far greater scale. As is known from the political literature of the time, Tocqueville and Marx disagreed profoundly about the scope and importance of that impact. Strangely enough, it was Tocqueville, the antisocialist, who played it up and Marx, the revolutionary socialist, who played it down. Where Tocqueville saw socialism as "the essential characteristic" of the February revolution, which, he believed, was "made entirely outside the bourgeoisie and against it," Marx saw its outcome as the creation of a "bourgeois republic," though one "surrounded [as the result of popular intervention] by social institutions."[41] We shall return to this debate, in the context of the revolutions of 1848, in a later chapter.

In England, the equivalent to France's 1848 was Chartism, whose main outbreaks were in 1839, 1842 and 1848. What role did socialism play in the Chartist movement? Evidently, very little, as Feargus O'Connor, by far the most influential of the Chartist leaders, was a radical Tory and antisocialist, who said that his Land Scheme of 1845 was about as "socialist" as the Comet; and Ernest Jones, Marx's friend, arrived on the scene too late to play anything but a minor role, except possibly in the final outbreak of April 1848. The case was clearly put by the late G. D. H. Cole, the greatly respected and most prolific among British labor historians. Cole believes that, at the very tail-end of Chartism, socialism, through Bronterre O'Brien who was one of the principal Chartist leaders, made a distinctive, though somewhat nebulous and short-lived, contribution. This was in the *Propositions of the National Reform League,* which were partly Owenite and partly based on the French socialist ideas of the 1840s. He adds that "they mark a significant stage in the transition from utopian Socialism to the formulation of an evolutionary Socialist program to be worked for by conquest, rather than overthrow of the existing State." But nothing came of them, the National Reform League melted away, and O'Brien's ideas only came back with the appearance of the Independent Labour Party half a century later.

41. J. P. Mayer (ed.), *The Recollections of Alexis de Tocqueville,* (New York, 1959), p. 78 ff.; K. Marx, *Class Struggles in France 1848–1850* (New York, 1934), p. 59.

But why, Cole asks, "was there so little Socialism in the Chartist movement, why did the Socialists in it have so little influence and find what they had slipping away from them even in the 'Hungry Forties?' " Partly, he says, it was due to Britain's more advanced industrial and more stable political situation; partly, too, because Britain's industrial workers and potential recruits for socialism were dispersed over a great number of manufacturing districts and not, like the French, largely concentrated within the metropolitan area. So capitalism in Britain was stronger and the government less vulnerable to civil unrest. Yet these are, of course, generalities that explain rather why Chartism failed or why there was no 1848 in Britain than why socialism—a product of industrialization—should be weaker in the most highly industrialized country in Europe. But he adds two further, highly relevant, points. One is that the Chartist movement "produced no Socialist theory of its own—only echoes of Owen, of Louis Blanc, and of Karl Marx to which the workers, for the most part, failed to listen"; and, in respect to Marx, he adds that "attempts have been made to build up Ernest Jones [a Marxist] into a major Socialist thinker, but he was nothing of the sort." But more important is his observation that in Britain (unlike France) socialism was already a declining force before 1848. He writes that:

the significant thing is that these ideas were losing their appeal in the 1840s, whereas on the Continent Socialism during that decade was a rapidly growing force. European Socialism suffered a very great set-back after 1848, as a consequence of the defeat of the mainly *bourgeois* revolutions of that year. In Great Britain, on the other hand, Socialism declined *before* 1848, not because it shared in a *bourgeois* defeat, but because it was robbed of its appeal by a *bourgeois* advance.[42]

15. Religion and the Churches

Of the bewildering range of issues affecting the Churches in the early nineteenth century, we may perhaps select the following as being of more or less general interest and application: the decline in the close

---

42. G. D. H. Cole, *Socialist Thought. The Forerunners, 1789–1850* (London, 1962), pp. 154–7. Cole's dig at "attempts to build up Ernest Jones" is presumably a reference to John Saville's *Ernest Jones, Chartist* (London, 1953).

partnership of Church and State; the proliferation of sects; the crisis or secularization of belief; and, in some countries but not in others, the attempt made by the Churches to preach a "social gospel" to the new industrial masses.

Of Church-State relations Professor John McManners writes: "The nineteenth century saw the decay of the venerable assumption that Church and State are necessarily and properly in alliance." Other historians have agreed.[43] And yet this decay was not much in evidence in the religious reaction that followed Napoleon's overthrow, when Alexander launched his Holy Alliance, the Inquisition was revived in Spain, the Jesuits returned, and the closest unity of Throne and Altar was almost universally proclaimed. Yet with the exception (in western Europe) of Italy and Spain, the unity was not long-lived: in the first place, in countries whose altars were Catholic and whose thrones were occupied by heretics or foreigners, such as in Ireland, Belgium, the Prussian Rhineland, and Russian Poland.[44] In Ireland, O'Connell's campaign for Catholic Emancipation (realized in 1829) was an early and obvious example. In Belgium, where Catholics and Liberals joined forces to achieve their separation from the Dutch, the alliance was cemented in 1831 by a Constitution which gave the Church a much envied freedom and virtually separated Church from State. In Prussia, the Protestant State had to contend with a predominantly Catholic Rhenish population; yet Protestants were favored for civil and military posts, mixed marriages were settled in the Protestant rather than in the Catholic interest, and a rationalist professor of theology was installed at Bonn. This all led in 1837 to the "Cologne affair," in which, after a head-on collision between the Catholic Archbishop and the government, the Archbishop was imprisoned, which, in turn, provoked noisy Catholic demonstrations, cavalry charges and a pamphlet war.

But opposition in the Rhineland was crushed by 1835 (as it was also

---

43. For what follows, see John McManners, "Church, State and Society," in *Lectures on European History 1789–1914* (Oxford, 1966), pp. 307–24; J. Walsh, "Religion: Church and State in Europe and the Americas," *New Cambridge Modern History,* IX, pp. 146–78; N. Sykes, "Religion and the Relations of Churches and States," *ibid.,* X, pp. 76–103.
44. Walsh, p. 173.

in Westphalia), and Germany remained largely Erastian; as did the obstinately Protestant Scandinavian countries, where it was illegal to agitate for separation from the Lutheran Church. In Italy, too, the State remained firmly wedded to the Church; it was only in the 1850s that Cavour's slogan of "a free church in a free state" had any chances of success. In France, however, the firm alliance of Throne and Altar was only imperfectly upheld even under the Restoration, and as Bourbon legitimism weakened, Liberal Catholicism began to make itself heard. Its chief proponent was Lamennais, who, in 1828, called on the Church to cut loose from political entanglements and to "isolate herself completely from a politically atheist society." Lamennais had been a royalist and remained an ultramontane; but, by 1830, he had become a liberal and a social reformer and, with Montalembert, Lacordaire and others, campaigned for the separation of Church and State. "Men tremble before liberalism; make it Catholic and society will be reborn." In this undertaking he found unexpected, and certainly reluctant, allies in the Catholic hierarchy which otherwise condemned him; for the Bishops, having suffered materially from the 1830 revolution, remained legitimist and hostile to the July Monarchy, and like the Liberal Catholics whose liberalism they detested —they welcomed the revolution of 1848.[45]

In England, too, the role of the Established Church had become eroded: in the first place, by the rapid growth of both Catholic and Protestant Dissent. The repeal of the Test and Corporation Acts in 1828 and Catholic Emancipation in 1829 struck twin blows at the Church's old monopoly; and the religious census of 1851 revealed that, by this time, the combined membership of Protestant and Catholic dissenters fell little short of that of the Church of England. Another cause of erosion was the prolonged campaign for greater "freedom" of the Church waged by the far from liberal Oxford Movement, some of whose leaders (first Newman, then Manning) later went over to the Roman Faith. A similar dissenting agitation in Scotland achieved far more substantial results, when the Free Church was set up in 1843 and, within four years, had raised £1¼ million to build 654 churches.

45. Droz, *L'époque contemporaine*, I, 342.

The analogy between the two movements, though not immediately apparent, was noted by Harold Laski: "Each," he wrote, "was essentially an anti-Erastian movement. It was against an all-absorptive state that each group of men was contending. . . . In each case, as was well enough admitted by contemporaries, the attempt was made . . . to work out a doctrine of the church which, neglecting the State, gave the church the general organization of a perfect society."[46]

Accompanying these divisions and the disruption of Church-State relations went an intellectual ferment and questioning, both within and outside the Churches and often at the Churches' expense. On the one hand, there was the new, mystical Christian "experience" formulated by Hegel's old colleague, the German Protestant theologian, Schleiermacher. There were also the German Liberal Catholics and friends of Lamennais, Görres, Baade and Döllinger (who claimed Lord Acton as a convert). There was Lamennais himself, with his *Paroles d'un croyant* and other social theological tracts. There were the English Evangelicals—like the Clapham "Saints"—the German Pietists, and the Oxford Movement in England, all of whom sought to "purify," or beautify, the existing doctrines or practices and return to older, more conservative principles of faith. On the other hand, there was the new scientific criticism of the Scriptures; Strauss's *Life of Jesus* (1835) and Ernest Renan's renunciation of the Church (1845) with the words: "A single error proves the Church is not infallible; a single weak link proves a book is not a revelation." In addition, there were the many hundreds of European thinkers, writers, poets and painters who had abandoned Christianity on ethical grounds, and the many thousands who, whether they made any formal renunciation or not, stayed away from the churches—as so eloquently attested by the English religious census of 1851.[47]

From all this historians have naturally drawn differing conclusions. Hobsbawm, for example, sees its essence as a turning away from religion by both the middle classes and the people at large. "The

---

46. H. J. Laski, *Studies in the Problem of Sovereignty* (New Haven, 1917), pp. 112–13; Sykes, p. 84.
47. G. Kitson Clark, *The Making of Victorian England* (London, 1962).

general trend of the period from 1789 to 1848," he writes, "was one of emphatic secularization." He instances the new trends in historical-Biblical scholarship and the anti-Christian writings of Strauss and Lachmann, and adds that "by 1848 educated Europe was almost ripe for the shock of Charles Darwin." As for the workers, he considers that the great mass of the unskilled and the poor of the great cities (with the possible exception of London and Paris) remained "profoundly pious and superstitious"; but the ideology of the new working-class and socialist movements was secular from the start, with a strong leaning towards eighteenth-century rationalism. And he concludes that "the working class as a group was undoubtedly less touched by organized religion than any previous body of the poor in world history."[48] McManners disagrees. "There was a crisis of belief," he writes, "but the nineteenth century was not an irreligious or sceptical age: it was an age of tremendous religious vitality. . . . The intellectual attack on the foundations of Christian belief was serious, but it did not run through the moods of materialism, nihilism and indifference characteristic of the generations that followed the first World War." He believes that the "ethical rebels" helped to purify the Churches and, in consequence, whether they were themselves believers or not, they did religion a useful service. In short, the nineteenth-century "crisis of belief," far from marking a "drift from religion," marked, rather, "a passionate dissatisfaction and disappointment with dogma amd institutional churches in the interests of religion itself."[49]

Some of the other themes discussed and debated by historians—generally within the context of their own particular country—have been: in France, the role of the French hierarchy under the Restoration and July Monarchy, and (a favorite theme) Lamennais's position as liberal Catholic and social critic; in Germany, the part played by ultramontism in Mainz and Cologne, the German Catholic "renaissance," and the social role of Pietists and Lutherans; and, in England, the contribution of the Oxford Movement to the Catholic revival, and the social policies of the Protestant sects. These are briefly, but admi-

48. Hobsbawm, pp. 220–23.
49. McManners, pp. 308–10.

rably, set out by Jacques Droz in his "état des questions" at the end of the relevant chapter in his *Epoque contemporaine.*[50] I do not propose, however, to repeat them all here but will confine myself to one single problem. It is that of the "social" role of the churches and sects in France, Germany and England, and the extent to which they offered the people a "social gospel" (to borrow McManners's phrase), or attempted to deal with the new explosive situation caused by the growth of cities and population and the impact of the industrial revolution.

Lamennais, as we have seen, was both a liberal and a social reformer. In 1839, for example, he wrote a small book, *De l'esclavage moderne,* which G. D. H. Cole has described as "one of the great documents in the history of the class struggle."[51] But there were other socially-conscious Catholics as well, such as the Abbé Gerbet who in 1830 denounced "the new feudalism, the feudalism of riches"; and Ozunam, a liberal and the founder of the charitable Society of St. Vincent de Paul. There was also Buchez, moderate socialist, journalist and historian of the French Revolution, whose views were strongly reflected in the *Atelier,* one of the earliest working-class newspapers, which was both socialist and anticlerical. In writing of these matters, a French historian, J.-B. Duroselle, argues that the social ideas of men like these began to circulate at the same time as the ideas of socialism and that both had their origins, through a number of mutually independent channels, in the poverty and social disorientation of the near-industrial society of the 1820s. French historians have also argued that through all the varying facets of Lamennais's thought—whether ultramontane, liberal or socialist—there runs a single unifying thread: a concern for the material ills of society and the conviction that only faith in a Divine Will can bring a remedy. In short, he was as much a sociologist as a believer.[52]

According to Droz, German historians are agreed that there was no similar movement of social concern within either the Protestant or

50. Droz, pp. 341–5.
51. McManners, p. 311.
52. Droz, p. 343.

Catholic Churches in Germany. The sole exception lay in the South-west, where liberalism and Protestantism joined forces. Elsewhere, German Lutheranism (like Calvinism in France), true to the traditions established by the founder, was conformist, legitimist, conservative and submissive to the dictates of the State. Even the Pietists, noted for their charitable works, were conservative, paternalistic and antiliberal; and H. Wichern, one of the most respected of their preachers, described the poverty of the masses as a "punishment for impiety."[53]

In England, the role of the dissenting or nonconformist sects was vastly different. The political radicalism of Unitarians, Quakers, Baptists and Congregationalists of various kinds went back to the seventeenth century; and although many of them (notably Independents, Baptists and Quakers) had become socially and politically respectable since, there was still a politically dissenting minority which had, after Wesley's death, found new allies among the break-away Methodist sects, such as the Bible Christians and the Primitive Methodists. Unitarians, in particular, had close relations with the Benthamite Radicals: so much appears from F. E. Mikeka's study, *The Dissidence of Dissent: The Monthly Repository 1806–1838* (1944);[54] and it has long been accepted that dissent played an important part in securing the liberal reforms (such as the abolition of the Test and Corporation Acts and of Negro slavery) of the 1820s and 1830s.

The relations between dissent and liberal reform in nineteenth-century Britain are, then, reasonably well established. But here a somewhat different, and perhaps a more interesting, question arises. What part did religion and religious ideas play in stimulating or discouraging radical movements or revolutions? We may perhaps assume that, on the Continent of Europe, the Liberal Catholics in France and Protestants in southwest Germany, and the French Catholic hierarchy (though for quite different reasons), behaved in such a way as to encourage people to take part in the revolutions of 1848; and, conversely, that French and German Protestantism in general

53. Droz, p. 348.
54. Droz, p. 143.

acted as a conservative brake. But what about Britain where, as is well known, no revolution took place either in 1848 or in 1830 or 1789? This is the way the French historian, Elie Halévy, put the question in the first volume of his *History of the English People* in 1912: "Why was it that of all the countries of Europe England has been the most free from revolutions, violent crises, and sudden changes?" A present-day historian, if he posed such a question, could hardly fail to relate his answer, in large part at least, to the social and political situation of Britain at the time. To Halévy, however, the heart of the matter lay in religion: Britain's immunity was essentially due to the large number of Englishmen, particularly from the artisan and working class, who had been exposed to the socially conservative contact of Methodism and other revivalist and evangelical sects. Admittedly, other factors come into the picture, but they are lightly brushed aside. He maintains, for instance, that Britain's political institutions and economy were such that society might easily have lapsed into anarchy if workers and *bourgeois* had a mind to unite in order to enforce their will on the rulers of the day. But, he insists, "the élite of the working class, the hard-working and capable bourgeois, had been imbued by the evangelical movement with a spirit from which the established order had nothing to fear".[55]

This was written of England in 1815; but in the fourth volume of the *History*, completed with the aid of Paul Vaucher after the author's death in 1948, Halévy carried the story forward to the middle of the century and repeats his answer, though in a somewhat modified form. The same year, Paul Vaucher, at an international history conference in Paris, held to commemorate the centenary of the revolutions of 1848, answered the question why Britain was not involved in broadly similar terms. It was not due to the absence of an economic crisis (the European crisis, in fact, started in Britain) but to the "solidity" of the middle classes (like Halévy, he includes the skilled workers in the term), "who were imbued with a body of ideas which prevented them from desiring the advance of democracy"; in consequence, it was

55. Elie Halévy, *History of the English People in the Nineteenth Century.* Vol. I, *England in 1815* (New York, 1949), pp. 423–8.

nonconformity which, more than any other factor, contributed to the defeat and isolation of the revolutionary movement.[56]

The view has been challenged by a number of labor historians in recent years and, somewhat earlier, by two historians of Methodism. The first of these two, E. R. Taylor, wrote a prize essay on *Methodism and Politics,* which was published at Cambridge, England in 1935. Taylor argues that Halévy, in writing of Methodism as a single conservative *bloc,* has overstated his case; and he points to the various break-aways from the old Methodist Connexion between the date of Wesley's death (1791) and the middle of the nineteenth century; several of these, he insists, were, unlike the founder, liberally inclined and contributed both to the working-class movement and to liberal reform. And, even within the Old Connexion itself, where the redoubtable Jabez Bunting ruled for many years as a "methodist Pope," the authority of the leader was often challenged, and occasionally overruled, by an active minority of liberals; and this was even before the general turn to liberalism among Methodists after 1849.[57]

But Taylor is, of course, only touching the fringe of the problem: he is merely concerned to defend Methodism from the charge of having been a wholly conservative force. Robert Wearmouth, in his *Methodism and the Working-Class Movements of England* (first published in 1937), goes nearer to the heart of the matter, which relates not so much to the politics of the Methodists as to the political influence they had on others. For, whether Methodists were self-styled Liberals or Tories, did they, in fact, exercise a radical or a conservative influence on the mass, or a vital part of the people of England? Wearmouth agrees with Halévy that Methodism saw a phenomenal advance during the first half of the nineteenth century: according to his figures, the number of registered members increased six-fold and, by 1850, at least two million people came under their influence, of which the great proportion were drawn from the working

56. Droz, p. 142.
57. E. R. Taylor, *Methodism and Politics 1791–1851* (Cambridge, England, 1935), p. 138 ff.

class. But in which direction was this influence exercised—was it radical or Tory? It was, he insists, the first far more than the second. For, he argues, the admittedly authoritarian, conservative and reactionary Wesleyan Conference must not be confused with the Methodists at large; for Conference did not represent "the democratic elements" within Wesleyanism, and still less within the other Methodist sects. These sects, he continues, were formed on democratic principles, and as their number increased "a religious democracy developed." But this democracy could not be confined to the four walls of the Methodist meeting; it inevitably "filtered into the industrial and political activities of its members," and thus became "a pattern and parent for their democratic exercises and idealism." So he concludes that, whatever the inclinations of the Wesleyan leaders, Methodism became the ally of radicalism and working-class movements rather than the reverse.[58]

K. S. Inglis, an Australian, in a more recent book, *Churches and Working Classes in Victorian England* (1963), points to the weaknesses in Wearmouth's case. Yet he in no way lines up with Halévy; in fact, implicitly or explicitly, he rejects them both. In the first place, he questions Wearmouth's assertion that the rapid expansion of Methodism (which he does not deny) was bringing in an ever larger proportion of working-class recruits. In fact, he argues from the Methodists' own evidence that the contrary was the case; so much so that "socially the Church of England and Methodism were moving in opposite directions; the Church was turning slowly and clumsily to face classes which it had long ignored, and the Methodists, sprung from these same classes, were in many places shedding their humble associations." So, in relation to the working classes, Methodism (even Wesleyanism, which had by far the largest number of members) was a declining rather than an expanding force; and this was particularly true of the large towns and cities, where Methodism shared with the other Protestant churches in the extraordinary decline in church

---

58. Robert W. Wearmouth, *Methodism and the Working-Class Movements of England 1800–1850* (New York, 1969), pp. 16, 223–5.

attendance revealed by the religious census of 1851.[59]

Inglis's argument can, of course, be used as much against Halévy as against Wearmouth; for if the census showed a general falling-off in church-going, and notably in the large towns, how can this be made to accord with the picture of an increasing evangelization of the masses as an antidote to riot or revolution? Inglis, more specifically, makes the point that the Wesleyans, at this stage, "worried far less about the heathen at home than about the heathen abroad."[60] Yet, as I say, his criticism of Halévy is implicit rather than explicit. The frontal assault on the Halévy thesis was left to two British historians, whose names have already figured more than once (and will figure again) in this volume: Eric Hobsbawm and Edward Thompson. Hobsbawm opened the attack with an article, which first appeared in the London journal *History Today* in 1957 and was subsequently reprinted in his *Labouring Men.* He agreed that Britain was almost unique among European countries in not having had a revolution at this time; also that the Wesleyan Connexion was politically conservative and opposed to violent change. "There was thus no revolution and Wesleyan Methodism was hostile to one; but it does not follow that the second fact was the cause of the first." In fact, he disputes the connection all along the line and uses four main arguments to support his view. First, he does not believe that the Wesleyans, though the strongest of the Methodist groups, were strong enough to carry the influence that Halévy suggests. Even if the Old Connexion remained largely Tory and antireformist, the seceding Methodist sects (and here he agrees with Wearmouth) were decidedly not; and, like others before him, he cites such radically-oriented groups as the Kilhamites, the Bible Christians, and the Primitive Methodists, the largest and the most "proletarian" group of all. Secondly, he argues from the religious census of 1851 that the Methodists were not evenly spread all over the country and that large parts of England were virtually untouched by Methodist teaching. "Speaking broadly, they

59. K. S. Inglis, *Churches and the Working Classes in Victorian England* (Toronto, 1963), pp. 9–13.
60. Inglis, p. 11.

were not a serious force south of a line drawn from the Wash to Dudley in the Black Country and thence west to the Welsh coast, except for certain parts of Norfolk. They were also extremely strong in Cornwall . . . Methodism, as a whole, therefore, could be expected to have a major political influence or popular agitation only in the North, Midlands, East Anglia, and the extreme South-west; Wesleyanism as such only in the West Riding." Given this distribution, he goes on to ask, can one detect in these areas "any major moderating influence" on the part of the Wesleyans? He decides that political (though not social) radicalism was weak among the Cornish miners, but that the West Riding, the main Wesleyan stronghold, became successively a centre of Luddism and Chartism as well. So Methodism (even Wesleyan Methodism) and radicalism often existed side by side and were by no means, as so often assumed, directly exclusive the one of the other. In fact, religious revivalism might, on occasion, be a stimulus rather than a barrier to revolution; and he cites the influence of the Primitive Methodists in the Durham pits a century ago and the activities of "masses of deeply pious men and women, adhering to religious bodies—whether Hindu, Christian or Buddhist," in the revolutions of today.[61]

Edward Thompson is almost equally sceptical of Halévy's thesis, but his reasons are different. In the first place, he casts considerable doubt on the *permanence* of the Methodist conversion, which he sees, rather, as "a revivalist pulsation, or an oscillation between periods of hope and periods of despair and spiritual anguish"; indeed "the great Methodist recruitment between 1790 and 1830 may be seen as the chiliasm of despair." He also compares the years most notable for "revivalist" recruitment with those of the maximum political activity, and he concludes that they are sufficiently close to justify Hobsbawm in drawing attention to the "parallelism" between the two. But while the relationship is "obviously intimate," its nature remains obscure; and he criticizes Hobsbawm's over-confident assumption that "Methodism advanced when Radicalism advanced and not when it grew

61. E. J. Hobsbawm, *Labouring Men. Studies in the History of Labour* (New York, 1965), pp. 23–33.

weaker." On the contrary, he continues, "it is possible that religious revivalism took over just at the point where 'political' or temporal aspirations met with defeat." The suggestion, he adds, is only a "tentative" one; but, to lend it substance, he points to the Primitive Methodist revivals in the frame-work knitting areas of the Midlands after the defeat of Luddism and, again, in the wake of the abortive Pentridge rising of 1817.[62] He makes an impressive case and Hobsbawm, in the later edition of his *History Today* article, added a postscript which modified his own and accepted Thompson's point of view. More recently, he has put theory into practice by testing the validity of Thompson's "tentative suggestion" in relation to the aftermath of the "Last Labourers' Revolt" of 1830. He found that, in the immediately following years, there was a considerable increase in recruits to the Primitive Methodists in Norfolk and the southwest, to the Wesleyans in Bedfordshire and Lincoln, and to the Baptists in East Anglia, Berkshire and Kent—all of them counties notably touched by the disturbance; and he sees this revival as "an escape from, rather than a mobilisation for social agitation."[63]

Admittedly, the case against Halévy is not finally proven. "To take it further," writes Thompson, "we should know more about, not the years of revivalism, but the months; not the counties, but the towns and villages." So there has been no knock-out blow and the argument goes on, even if the Halévy thesis has become badly mauled in the course of the dispute. It is to be hoped, though, that the debate will broaden as well as narrow and that historians from other countries will join in with similar problems of their own. For the issues raised (as those raised by the debate on the industrial revolution and society and on Chevalier's theory of the city) are such as deserve examination in a far wider context than that of a single European country.

62. E. P. Thompson, *The Making of the English Working Class*, (New York, 1964), pp. 427–9.
63. E. J. Hobsbawm and George Rudé, *Captain Swing* (London and New York, 1969), pp. 288–91.

IV

The Political Challenge

Historians are generally agreed that the years 1815 and 1850 in Europe witnessed a continuous, and often successful, struggle of the new political forces against the old—of liberalism and absolutism, of middle classes and aristocracy, of reformers and reactionaries, of nationalists and foreign occupants—at the end of which the system established by the victor powers at Vienna had largely disintegrated and fallen apart. In 1817, hard on the heels of the launching of the Holy and Quadruple Alliances, Serbia declared and won her independence from the Turks. There were revolts and revolutions in Cadiz, Naples and Portugal in 1820, and the Greek war of independence began in 1821 and was successfully concluded in 1829. 1825 saw the revolt of the Decembrists in Russia. In 1830, the Belgians revolted against the Dutch and the Poles against the Russians; and there were revolutions in France and parts of Germany. In 1832, after a two-year nationwide campaign, the Reform Bill was passed in Britain; and Mazzini founded his "Young Italy" movement, to be followed by "Young Europe" two years later. The same year, there were further revolts in Naples and Piedmont. A twelve-year lull followed, during which reaction strengthened its hold in Italy, Germany, Russia, Poland and France and took up arms (the Carlist war) in Spain; it was broken by working-class revolts in France and by further liberal-nationalist insurrections in Italy: at Aquila (Naples) in 1841, in Calabria in 1843, and in the Papal States in 1846. Finally, after a brief prelude in the food riots and Swiss *Sonderbund* war of 1847, the year 1848 saw the most extensive series of revolutions since the last dozen years of the previous century.

16. A "Middle-Class" Challenge?

Traditionally, historians have presented the struggle in terms of a middle-class challenge to the old aristocratic or absolutist rulers of Europe, and it has been portrayed as a significant stage in "the rise of the bourgeoisie." Among those who witnessed these events, it is perhaps not surprising that a socialist like Louis Blanc should have seen it in this light. Looking back from the 1840s, Blanc saw the history of France during the preceding half-century—through the Revolution, the Napoleonic Empire, the Restoration and the Revolution of 1830—as a protracted struggle for the assertion of the rights and interests of the middle class. Napoleon, he believed, continued the work of the Constituent Assembly by strengthening "the basis of bourgeois domination"; even the Restoration "was essentially a bourgeois transaction"; while the July Monarchy, following on the revolution of 1830, was nothing "but the reign of the bourgeoisie."[1] Marx and Engels saw the political struggle, whether in France or elsewhere, in similar (though by no means identical) terms. Marx, as we have seen, believed the Paris revolution of February 1848 to be the necessary prelude to the creation of a "bourgeois republic"; and Engels, in his articles on Germany, Austria and Italy, continually presents the *bourgeoisie* as the principal contender, and often the victor, in the contest for political power.[2]

But such a presentation has by no means been peculiar to socialists or Marxists. In Marx's own day, as we noted, Tocqueville, although not sharing Marx's view of the outcome of the February revolution, saw the nature of the struggle that followed it in similar terms, that is as one between "the people" (or "proletariat") on the one hand and the *possédants* (or *bourgeoisie*) on the other. In fact, Marx and Engels's use of the term "bourgeoisie" appeared no more unusual or misguided to Tocqueville than it did to others of their nonsocialist contemporaries. And this is a tradition that, in France and other European Continental countries, has persisted to the present day and

---

1. Louis Blanc, *The History of Ten Years, 1830–1840*, I, pp. 3, 19; II, p. 648.
2. See F. Engels, *Revolution and Counter-Revolution, or Germany in 1848* (Chicago, 1914), *passim;* and his article on the outcome of the *Risorgimento, cit.* S. J. Wolf, (ed.), *The Italian Risorgimento* (London, 1969), pp. 81–2.

is shared by historians of all political persuasions. Recently, for example, we find Charles Morazé, a leader of the French *Annales* school, entitling a work covering the period 1780 to 1890 *Les bourgeois conquérants*—a title that might well have appealed to Louis Blanc. Jean Lhomme, another French historian, has, similarly, given a book devoted to the half-century of French history after 1830 the title *La grande bourgeoisie au pouvoir*. Jacques Droz, too, sees "the new feature of the 1830s" as "the establishment of the supremacy of the *haute bourgeoisie*"; and he believes the whole period 1815–1848, not only in France but in Europe generally, to be "characterized by the steady rise of the bourgeoisie." Jean Lhomme and Droz may be classed as historians of the Left; but this is hardly the case with Bertier de Sauvigny, whose apologia for the Restoration we have already noted. In a recent paper on "French Politics, 1814–47," contributed to the *New Cambridge Modern History*, Sauvigny writes of the aftermath of the revolutionary events of 1830:

Thus the French bourgeoisie, having a monopoly of wealth and, to a large extent, of intellectual culture also, arrogated to itself the monopoly of political power as well. In the administration it occupied every road of advancement, for the nobility had been driven out, or had voluntarily retired out of fidelity to Charles X.[3]

In Italy, a similar tradition has persisted, though it has been somewhat obscured by the idealist historio-philosophy of Croce. Croce preferred, as we have seen, to present the political struggle in the more abstract terms of a contest between liberty and absolutism and it is but rarely that he descends to the "grass-roots" level of a conflict between two opposing social classes. Yet he has such moments; in writing, for example, of the Restoration in France, he points to the succession of "aristocratic chambers and liberal chambers," the former "full of nobles" and the latter "full of bourgeois"; and, in the course of their contest, he contrasts "the aristocrats of the old

3. Charles Morazé, *Les bourgeois conquérants* (Paris, 1957); Jean Lhomme, *La grande bourgeoisie au pouvoir (1830–1880): essai sur l'histoire sociale de la France* (Paris, 1960); J. Droz, *Europe between Revolutions 1815–1848*, pp. 37–43; G. de Bertier de Sauvigny, "French Politics, 1814–1847," in *New Camb. Mod. Hist.*, X (1965), p. 357.

régime," who "were emptied of their not very copious contents," with "the men of the middle class" who "issued from the struggle with renewed vigour." Valsecchi, no longer tied to the Crocean formula, is less inhibited and, like his French counterparts, writes of the "domination of the bourgeoisie"; while, more specifically, he notes:

If the economic revolution opened to the bourgeoisie the road to wealth, the political revolution [he is writing of the European events of the 1820s and 1830s] opened the road to power.[4]

It is in fact mainly in Britain and North America that such formulations have come to be considered somewhat suspect; yet this has happend only in the last twenty years. Indeed, before the war, English and American historians—at least the liberals among them—were almost as inclined to resort to them as their European colleagues. So R. B. Mowat, in his *The Romantic Age* (1937), writes of "the great European revolution which took place between 1789 and 1848" as marking "the overthrow of the aristocracy"; while the post-Napoleonic era was a time "when the *bourgeoisie* all over Central and Western Europe was beginning to assume the leadership of public life." Again, Frederick Artz, in his *Reaction and Revolution* (1934), sums up the achievements of the radical and revolutionary movements up to 1834 as follows:

In England, France, and Belgium—the European states most advanced economically and socially—the middle class had, since 1815, made substantial gains and succeeded in establishing the political machinery to ensure them.

Moreover, this old liberal tradition is by no means dead. Asa Briggs, for example, in his Introduction to *The Age of Improvement* (1959), looking back from the Reform Bill of 1867, writes that "the previous seventy years of English history had been dominated by the rise of the middle classes."[5]

---

4. Croce, *History of Europe in the Nineteenth Century*, pp. 60–70; Valsecchi, "L'évolution politique," in *L'Europe du XIXe et du XXe siècle*, p. 256.
5. R. B. Mowat, *The Romantic Age*, pp. 109, 249; Frederick B. Artz, *Reaction and Revolution 1814–1832*, pp. 290–91; Asa Briggs, *The Age of Improvement 1783–1867* (London and New York, 1959), p. 3.

But such terms as "the rise of the middle classes" and "the overthrow of the aristocracy," while still common form on the Continent and among British labor and Marxist historians, had already come under fire from certain of the more conservative among their colleagues. In the United States, Professor J. H. Hexter set the pace with his appeal for a greater precision in the use of such terms as "the rising middle class." Hexter was more particularly concerned with the seventeenth century, as was H. Trevor Roper when (in 1954) he took R. H. Tawney to task for including aristocrats among his "rising gentry." The discussion, however, has moved to the eighteenth and nineteenth centuries in the work of Alfred Cobban. In *The Myth of the French Revolution* (1955), Cobban first argued that the members of the Revolutionary Assemblies were more typically landowners and officeholders than bourgeoisie. Extending his attack, he went on to cast doubt on the "bourgeois" nature of the governments of Louis-Philippe. The facts, he believes, do not support the prevailing view: "Louis-Philippe had in all 60 ministers in the course of his reign. Of these 8 were aristocrats, 36 civil or military officials, 9 lawyers and professors, and 7 representatives of trade, industry and finance." "Such facts," he continues, "suggest that the 'bourgeois monarchy' deserves a little more investigation before we can take it for granted."[6]

Dr. Kitson Clark, the Cambridge historian, believes that a similar misuse of the term "middle class" has bedevilled and stultified thought on Victorian England, and that phrases like "the rising middle class," "the predominant middle class," "middle-class taste" and "middle-class morality" are not only wearisome but misleading and confusing. "Who precisely," he asks, "were the middle class?" He decides, having toted up the score, that the bracket was a very wide one; in fact, that the term could be used so widely, and has been used so indiscriminately, as to be virtually meaningless. Moreover, however widely used, it cannot reasonably be applied to all those aristocrats and gentry who played so conspicuous a part in passing the Reform Bill and repealing the Corn Laws. Nor, he concludes, "did

6. Alfred Cobban, "The Vocabulary of Social History," *Political Science Quarterly,* LXXI, (March 1956), pp. 1–17.

the middle class, however defined, dominate the country after 1832";
for "after the Bill the final control in politics still lay without question
in the hands of the old governing classes, the nobility and gentry."[7]
This last is a point we shall return to later.

So who is right: is it the "traditionalists," such as Asa Briggs,
Morazé, Valsecchi and Bertier de Sauvigny? Or is it the "revisionists,"
like Cobban and Kitson Clark? Yet the differences are perhaps not
quite so great as they at first appear: both Cobban and Clark, for
instance, for all their tilting at the malpractices of their fellow-historians, concede that such terms as "middle classes" and "bourgeoisie"
have their uses and should not be too vigorously thrown out, like the
proverbial baby, with the bathwater. Moreover, as we have noted
before, historians, in the course of their polemics, are not necessarily
arguing about the same things. Nobody, for example, among the
traditionalists is suggesting that the term "middle class" or "bourgeoisie" is as readily applicable to Russian Decembrists or Polish and
Hungarian rebels as it is to the nationalists and liberal protesters in
the more economically developed countries such as Britain, France or
Belgium. (We noted that Frederick Artz makes this very point in a
passage quoted above; and Hobsbawm, though decidedly a "traditionalist" in this respect, frequently makes the distinction in *The Age of
Revolution.*) Moreover, the traditionalists tend to use the term "bourgeois" in a political as well as a purely social or occupational sense,
so that, by extension, it acquires the same sort of socio-political attributes as Marx's "proletariat" or the *sans-culottes* of the French Revolution. The revisionists, on the other hand, are applying a more
strictly sociological test, as is evident in Kitson Clark's question,
"Who precisely were the middle class?", and in Cobban's analysis of
Louis-Philippe's ministers. They have every right to do this if they
wish, but at least we should recognize that they are talking a different
language from those whose terminology they criticize. But, of course,
there is more to it than that, and it is not simply a question of
semantics and of an appeal for greater precision in the use of social
terms. There is an underlying political element as well. Cobban, a

7. G. Kitson Clark, *The Making of Victorian England,* pp. 5–7.

liberal-conservative, is quite right when he argues that the traditional presentation of political conflict in class terms owes a great deal to Marx and that many historians, who readily use such terms as "bourgeoisie," while not professing to be Marxists, have been influenced by Marx's view of history. Perhaps we may add that it is a revolutionary tradition as well; and it may therefore perhaps be more natural for historians (even conservatives like Sauvigny) whose countries have had a recent revolutionary past to resort to such terms than others. This may help to explain why Englishmen, or Anglo-Saxons, have, in this respect, shown a greater tendency to be the odd men out.

17. The Revolutions of 1830

The political challenge, then—whether we term it a "middle-class" challenge or not—took the form of a prolonged series of battles and engagements with the established rulers of the day. It is not proposed to enumerate them here at greater length than we have done already; but, rather, as in previous chapters, to pick out certain issues, arising from these disputes, that have divided and exercised historians. The themes selected here are the French Revolution of 1830 and the July Monarchy that followed; the Italian *Risorgimento;* the so-called *Vormärz* in Germany; the revolution and counterrevolution in Spain; and the Reform Bill, Corn Law Repeal and the powers of government in England.

The revolutions of 1830 have been, almost exclusively, related in political terms; and this is almost as true of recent historians as it is of contemporary observers. The Belgian revolt against the Dutch in August took place because the Belgians' sense of nationhood, which had long lain dormant, had been aroused to the point of explosion by a series of recent vexations at the hands of the Dutch. Charles Poplimont, a Belgian historian, writing of these events in 1852, describes this sense of nationhood as going back to the days of Julius Caesar and writes that its realization "was only a matter of time, accessory to and dependent on events."[8] Unlike the Belgian revolution, the

8. Charles Poplimont, *Révolution belge 1830–1848. La Belgique depuis mil huit cent trente* (Brussels, 1852), p. 52.

French, which had obviously far less time to germinate, has been pin-pointed to a single, sudden, explosive cause: Charles's revocation of the Charter. To cite a recent book of edited texts:

When the country refused to return a Chamber which would support royal policy, Charles and his minister [Polignac] decided to invoke Article XIV of the Charter against the Chamber: "The King is the supreme head of state . . . and makes the ordinance necessary for the execution of the laws and the security of the State." The use of this provision to dissolve the newly elected Chamber precipitated the Revolution.[9]

This sums up in a nutshell the gist of these events as told by most historians. Of course, this is not to say that they have not differed, and differed profoundly, as to the propriety or impropriety of what took place. Among those who lived through the July events in France, there were Liberals like Guizot (and this could probably be said of the great majority of the Liberal opposition in the Chamber), who, while strongly opposed to Charles's policies, had no intention whatsoever of overthrowing the dynasty by force, and therefore, though Liberals, deplored the revolution. Lamartine's view was somewhat different. In his own words, he had "a tenderness" or "weakness of mind" towards the Restoration, and there seems little doubt that his later aversion for the July Monarchy made him look back on the July revolution, which he termed a mere "subversion," with less than enthusiasm. Blanc, on the other hand, took a far more detached view. He had no reason to detest (like Lamartine) or to deplore (like Guizot) what he took to be just another manifestation of the bourgeois struggle for power. "The struggle," to quote his own words, "which began in 1815 and which was to terminate in the revolution of 1830, was but the continuation, for the benefit of the bourgeoisie, of the struggle which the états généraux had maintained previous to 1789 against the monarchial principle."[10] But to Blanc, as to the others, the battle was essentially seen "from above" and fought out in political terms.

9. *The Shaping of Modern France*, Friguglietti and Kennedy, (eds.), p. 197.
10. Guizot, *Memoirs to Illustrate the History of my Time*, I, pp. 356–7, II, pp. 16–31; Lamartine, *The History of the Restoration of Monarch in France*, I, p. xiv; Blanc, *The History of Ten Years*, I, p. 32.

Similarly, historians, writing in the century that followed, have bestowed their approval or condemnation on the contending parties according to their political sympathies or affiliations. It is only natural that monarchists like Bainville, Gazotte and Lucien Romier (the last two writing as recently as the 1950s) should have viewed the Restoration with some affection and therefore, even if they had some reservations about Charles X, lamented his violent overthrow, while an old-style republican like Charléty, in his volume in Lavisse's *Histoire de la France contemporaine* (1921), should have justified the same event. There have also been more subtle differences dividing monarchists, republicans, conservatives or liberals among themselves. Such a case is that of two conservative historians, separated by a quarter-century of time and of quite unequal merit: Lucas-Dubreton and Bertier de Sauvigny. Dubreton, as we noted earlier, admired the Restoration; but he had the poorest opinion of the wretched Charles, who had "nothing great about him, not even his pride" and allowed himself to be drawn into adventurist policy by Polignac, and thus deserved his fate. Sauvigny's view, as we saw, was altogether different: as an admirer of Charles, he thought the revolution which overthrew him a great disaster.[11] Finally, English historians, being less directly touched by these events, have generally displayed a greater Olympian detachment than the French. They have tended to distribute their praise or blame with some aloofness and with what some may consider a commendable degree of impartiality or non-involvement: we may cite the histories of Leonard Woolf (1939), J. P. F. Bury (1949), D. W. Brogan (1961), Alfred Cobban (1961) and Gordon Wright (1962).

One American historian, however, has broken fresh ground by bringing the popular element into closer focus in relating the July events in Paris. In so doing, he has given this phase of France's history a new dimension, similar to that given by a number of historians in recent years, under the inspiration of the late Georges Lefebvre, to the

---

11. J. Lucas-Dubreton, *The Restoration and the July Monarchy*, p. 173; Bertier de Sauvigny, *The Bourbon Restoration*, pp. 454–60.

political events of the French Revolution of 1789. The rudiments for such a treatment, of course, were always close at hand. Poplimont, for example, as far back as 1852, presents the Brussels uprising of 25–26 August in two successive stages: the "armement du peuple" and the "intervention des bourgeois"—in short, in a succession remarkably similar to that of the Paris events of July 1789. Again, Lucas-Dubreton, looking back from Louis-Philippe's monarchy, sums up the problem in a nutshell: "Those who had profited by the revolution of 1830 were not those who had made it; the men of July, the bourgeoisie, were not the combatants of July, the proletariat."[12] It is to David Pinkney's merit that he has made the first significant effort to bring this "proletariat" into the picture as an active historical force. The conventional history of the July revolution, he notes, "written in the single dimension of politics, leaves much unexplained, many questions unanswered." And these are the questions that Mr. Pinkney pertinently asks:

Why did the workers of Paris risk their lives in July 1830? To defend the Charter of 1814, as many fatuously pretended to believe?
To defend the abstract principles of 1789? To re-establish the Republic, which was to some a distant memory, to most only a hazy ideal? . . .

He concludes that the workers had compelling reasons of their own for their intervention. These, he believes, are not so much political as economic. After a ten-year period of prosperity, a turn for the worse began in 1826. Industrial prices fell, and with them wages. Thousands of looms became idle, and building workers were thrown out of work. A succession of bad harvests began in 1828 and, a year later, the price of bread—the most vital element in the poor man's diet—was double what it had been in 1825. The middle classes, in turn, blamed the government for the crisis and, in the summer of 1830, further provoked by the threat to the Charter, joined the workers in resorting to arms. So, in many respects, it was a remarkable repetition of what happened in Paris in July 1789.[13]

12. Poplimont, p. 33; Lucas-Dubreton, p. 366.
13. David Pinkney, "A New Look at the French Revolution of 1830," *Review of Politics*, XXIII, 1961, pp. 490–501; in *The Shaping of Modern France*, pp. 217–22.

18. The July Monarchy in France

Many régimes have been more repressive and more detested than the French July Monarchy of 1830 to 1848; but few have left so ignominious a mark on the historical record. The Restoration, as we have seen, has found eloquent supporters; and whereas Louis XVIII (and, more rarely, Charles X) might command the loyalty of conservatives, neither conservatives, liberals nor socialists have been overwilling to shed a tear for Louis-Philippe. To conservatives he stands condemned as the son of Philippe-Egalité, a Jacobin of 1793, and as the usurper of the Bourbon throne, to liberals as the betrayer of the hopes raised by the "trois glorieuses," and to socialists as the butcher of the Cloître Saint-Merri and the patron of the *haute bourgeoisie*. There are other factors besides to blacken the indictment. The "backstairs" manner of his rise to power; Daumier's cartoons; the bloody suppression of working-class revolt; the ambivalence of foreign policies, reactionary and cravenly submissive in turn; his old man's obstinacy in resisting reform; his dismissal of Guizot to save the throne, followed hot-foot by his own humiliating flight and abdication: all have built up an impression of indecision, cowardice, philistinism, stupid reaction, or bumbling ineptitude. Above all, it is a picture that inspires contempt. "It was a government," writes Lamartine in a passage with which we are already familiar, "with two faces, neither of which spoke the truth." The King himself, conscious of his tarnished image, expressed late in life the belief that posterity, at least, might do him justice.[14] It was a forlorn hope. Historians (with certain notable exceptions) have continued to treat him and his régime with a similar disdain. Even Alfred Cobban, who has not been ungenerous to lost causes, dismisses the régime as one "that had been so lacking in principles that it could only be known by the name of the month of its founding, the July Monarchy."[15]

14. T. E. B. Howarth, *Citizen-King. The Life of Louis-Philippe King of the French* (London, 1961), p. 11.
15. A. Cobban, *A History of Modern France*, II, p. 129. For historians who have said a kind word for the July Monarchy, see Lucas-Dubreton, *op. cit.*, p. 367; and J. P. T. Bury, *France 1814–1940*, pp. 68–71.

It is natural that the King and his régime should have become tarred with the same brush. Yet some of his ministers have escaped the taint. Casimir Périer, for instance, has emerged as something of a hero—first to the Right for his strong measures against the rioting workmen of 1832 and, more generally, as a victim of the cholera epidemic of the same year. Thiers has retained a separate identity, both because he went into opposition in 1840 and appeared as a critic in 1848; and, above all, because he survived long enough to present a new image—even more detestable to some, though not wholly contemptible—as a pillar of the successive *bourgeois* republics of 1848 and 1871. Guizot has been less fortunate. He was the King's closest adviser and confident in the crucial years 1840 to 1848 and, having fallen from power the day before the King, retired from office without any hope of reinstatement or redemption.

Guizot has found more defenders than the King; but, until recently, in spite of his many obvious talents (as journalist, historian and orator, and as a skillful diplomat and politician), the odor of his final failure has persisted. And this is the odor that Douglas Johnson, an English historian, now professor of history at University College, London, has attempted to dispel. In an article in *History* in October 1962 (and in a later book), Johnson concedes that Guizot failed in his main political task of holding Louis-Philippe's régime together. (How could he do other, with the catastrophe of 1848 as an all-too visible reminder?) He concedes, too, that his intellectualism was a hindrance to the practical conduct of affairs. (Here Guizot differed from Thiers who attuned his day-to-day policies to the situation at hand.) Moreover, he sees Guizot as an eclectic, who attempted to reconcile the past with the present, the Revolution with the *ancien régime*, autocracy with representative institutions, the privileged classes with *bourgeoisie* and people. As a believer in such diversity, he sapped all sense of reform and creation, appeared as a man of no ideals and, professing to be the friend of all, he ended with the loyalty of none. Johnson thinks, nonetheless, that Guizot's critics have dealt too harshly with him and, mesmerized by his ultimate failure, have refused to give him credit where it was due. He writes:

In fairness to Guizot there are certain things that must be added . . . The difficulties of governing France, like the difficulties of economic development in France, are to be largely explained by a varied social structure and by a historical development which had created new divisions and intensified old ones. In this situation, as Guizot believed, there was no single or self-evident way in which representative government could be organized . . .

It was during the July Monarchy that France began to resemble a modern state and that the government began to provide the equipment necessary for economic development. In this, the period from 1840 to 1848 is of vital importance, and if one considers the very heavy expenditure incurred by the government in those years, it is ironical to think how they were accused of doing nothing . . . When one remembers the law of 1833 on primary education, the freedom of the press, the importance and vitality of the parliamentary debates, and the way in which the whole period was alive with intellectual speculation, it seems inappropriate to dismiss the "liberalism" of Guizot as a sham.

Moreover, he commends Guizot for the sanity and realism of his foreign policy, which was aimed to restore better relations with England, and he insists that, over such explosive incidents as the Tahiti affair and the tangle of the Spanish marriages, it was he rather than Palmerston who kept a sense of proportion; and he was astonished that the English, over this affair, should have reacted with such indignation. "The historian," comments Johnson, "shares his astonishment, and history confirms his conviction." And he rounds off his portrait with a tribute from Sainte-Beuve to "a considerable man of whom there is much to say."[16]

It is a noble attempt to give Guizot his due, though perhaps the historian protests too much. Even with these additions to his credit, Guizot still emerges as a doctrinaire, wedded to eighteenth-century concepts in a nineteenth-century situation, failing to appreciate what was new in the industrial and social changes going on before his eyes, stubbornly espousing the cause of the *haute bourgeoisie,* whom he saw as rightly filling an important role in the state, and yet (they are the author's own words) "without reference to its economic interests."

16. Douglas Johnson, "A Reconsideration of Guizot," *History,* XLVII, No. 161, October (1962), pp. 239–53.

19. The Risorgimento

If the 1830 revolution and the July Monarchy in France have failed to inspire a rich and varied literature, the same cannot be said of the Italian *Risorgimento*, which is perhaps the most important and has certainly been the most heatedly debated episode in Italy's whole history.

The *Risorgimento* is generally said to have been completed with Italy's national unification in 1870 (though some would say 1861). But when did it begin? On this point there is no such unanimity. The word (meaning national "rebirth" or "resurrection") was first used by S. Bettinelli in a cultural history, entitled *Del Risorgimento d'Italia dopo il Mille,* published in 1775. Some have traced its intellectual origins, if not its vocabulary, further back. Croce, for example, among the liberals, placed its starting-point at the end of the Italian Renaissance of the sixteenth century. Other liberals, such as Franco Valsecchi and Luigi Salvatorelli, have seen it rather in the reforms and intellectual climate promoted by the enlightened depots of the eighteenth century —by men like Charles III of Naples, Leopold of Tuscany, and his brother Joseph II in Lombardy; for, they have argued, their ideals of better government laid the basis for the later and more specific movements for national unity and political rights. After 1922, Fascist historians also chose the eighteenth century, but for them the *Risorgimento* was a purely native movement stripped of its European context and of all connection with the Enlightenment and Revolution. Socialists, on the other hand, have tended to begin with the French Revolution, in particular with Filippo Buonarotti and the Italian Jacobins of the 1790s; more precisely still, they have pointed to the abortive republican attempts, native and not French-inspired, to overthrow the governments of Turin and Naples in 1794 and Palermo in 1795. Others, still, have seen the point of departure rather in Napoleon's invasion of Italy in 1796, his various constitutional reforms and the secret societies—*Carbonari* and *Federati*—that the French occupation and dominion progressively provoked. To others, again, these are mere curtain-raisers or antecedents, and the real struggle for Italian "rebirth" or unification—the political *Risorgimento*—only began after Napoleon's defeat and the return of the old rulers in 1815.[17]

This question of origins is important, as it tells us something of what different groups of historians mean by a national "rebirth," and also how far their sense of national pride will allow them to admit the intrusion of influences from outside. But of equal or greater importance perhaps are such further questions as, did the *Risorgimento* take the right turn? who actually took part? and, above all, what has been its significance for Italy's national history? Let us consider some of these questions, with particular reference (where this is possible) to the period up to the revolutions of 1848.

In the confusion following Napoleon's defeat, Italian reformers and patriots were faced with a number of alternatives, which only gradually found political expression. All were agreed on the desirability of national independence and on some degree of unity; but what form should they take? Should the aim be a unified or a federal state, a monarchy or a republic? Should it be achieved by calling in the masses, or should it be left to the educated or propertied classes? By the 1830s, the practical choices had narrowed to three. First, there was Mazzini's "democratic" solution of a single unified republic to be achieved by continuous popular insurrection. Next, there was Gioberti's (and Balbo's) "aristocratic" solution of a confederation of states under the aegis of the Pope, and with only a minimum of popular participation; and, lastly, a "monarchical" solution emerged around the person of Charles Albert, the ruler of Piedmont. All three alternatives were championed, with varying fortunes, in the revolutions of 1848; but, with their outcome, the Papal solution (with Pius IX) was eliminated altogether and, when the next round opened in 1859, it was the Piedmontese solution, with Cavour as its new champion, that firmly took the lead. In consequence, Italian patriots closed their ranks and, whether monarchist or republican, liberal or radical, saw Cavour's solution as the *only* solution and adopted him as the spokesman for the nation as a whole. And it was only after the new Kingdom had been formed and after the first deceptions of the 1870s that

17. Agatha Ramm, *The Risorgimento* (London, 1962), pp. 4–7; J. Droz, *L'époque contemporaine,* I, p. 215.

radicals looked back with nostalgia to Mazzini's republicanism and
the single-minded patriotism of Garibaldi.

Yet, by and large, after the dust had settled down, a pattern of
loyalties emerged that was not altogether unexpected. For radicals
and some socialists, Mazzini's revolutionary republicanism has continued to exercise its spell. Garibaldi has retained an enthusiastic
following among radicals and nationalists (both of the Right and Left)
alike; while more conservative elements, whether among traditional
liberals or Fascists, have tended to see Cavour as the man of order and
good sense and the true architect of unity, while relegating his rivals
for popular favor, Mazzini and Garibaldi, to a sometimes venerated,
but less significant role.[18]

Outside Italy, no leader, or would-be leader, of the *Risorgimento*
has aroused such conflicting opinions as Pius IX, the "liberal" Pope.
Was his liberalism genuine, or was it a fake? Or was the whole idea
of a "liberal" Pope, as Metternich suspected, a misconception or a
contradiction in terms? Let us contrast the views of three historians.
To G. F. H. (with the occasional support of J.H.) Berkeley, who wrote
a three-volume history of *Italy in the Making,* his liberalism was
genuine enough. To him he is the embodiment of intelligent Moderation, at a time when the Moderate party (he claims) was more responsible than any other for popularizing the national cause, which
Mazzini's excesses were dragging into disrepute. In short, Pius is
"Gioberti's Pope come into being. He inaugurates the regime of
progressive ideas in Italy, and does not abandon the great effort to be
a Liberal Pope until, some two years later, he is driven from his home
by the Revolution."[19]

Two more recent accounts—the first by an Englishman, the second
by an American—take a contrary view. E. L. Woodward, in his *Three
Studies in European Conservatism,* presents Pius as a man of mediocre
intelligence, vain and remote from realities, who paraded a shallow
liberalism to court popularity and applause. He writes:

18. D. Mack Smith, *Italy. A Modern History* (London, 1959), pp. 13–16.
19. G. F. H. and J. Berkeley, *Italy in the Making,* 3 vols. (Cambridge, England,
1932–40), I, p. xix; II, p. xxiii.

His liberalism was never much more than the vague goodness of heart of a weak man; nor was it free from that vanity and sense of his own superior knowledge and importance which became almost tragic at the time of the Vatican Council . . . He loved adulation and popularity. His emotional nature needed excitement and the continuous stimulus of a crowd, because it was without independence, consistency or fire of its own. Pius thought of the political consequences of his actions as little as he foresaw the effects of his dogmatic extravagance. He was never cynical, because he never lived in a world of real things.[20]

Bolton King, in his *History of Italian Unity* (1899), is equally sparing of praise. He concedes that Pius was "too intelligent to be altogether weak"; however, he continues:

But he was a coward morally and intellectually; he pined for applause, he shrank from responsibilities; there was always in him something of the supple, cringing ecclesiastic . . . He never fronted the situation, so long as he could drift and threw the responsibility on Providence. Feebly optimistic, with no master grasp or foresight or caution, he refused to look below the surface, and provided for the moment.

Such was the man who was called to decide the future destinies of the Papacy.[21]

And who were the activists who manned the barricades and took part in the numerous insurrections and commotions? Modern historians have generally rejected the claims of the early liberal enthusiasts that the *Risorgimento* was a spontaneous patriotic uprising of the whole Italian nation; indeed, perhaps the reaction against this kind of extravagance has swung the pendulum back too far. We noted in our last chapter that Hobsbawm and Renouvin both ascribed a relatively modest role to "the people" in the national movements of the time. And Mr. Denis Mack Smith adds that the insurgents formed a small minority, "for the wars and risings of the *risorgimento* had little effect on ordinary people." The peasants, he continues, formed 90 percent of the Italian population, but "few of them knew what the word 'Italy' meant," and where (as in the south) they lent their support to the rebellion it was to obtain land and security and not to exchange one

20. E. L. Woodward, *Three Studies in European Conservatism*, p. 282.
21. Bolton King, *A History of Italian Unity, being a Political History of Italy from 1814 to 1871*, 2 vols. (1967), I, pp. 171–2.

set of landlords or rulers for another. Miss Ramm writes that, in Sicily, the peasants invaded the demesne lands and demanded their division; but elsewhere they did not rise. Both writers agree that, even in the towns, it was the professional classes—lawyers, doctors and students—rather than the workers, that manned the barricades (as at Palermo in January 1848). Garibaldi's volunteers, who defended the Roman Republic against the French, included men of all social classes —except peasants and laborers. Milan and Venice were something of an exception: in fact, it was the workers of the arsenal that began the Venice rising; but even here their enthusiasm was kept in check by the restraining hand of others. "In short, everywhere in 1848–49," concludes Miss Ramm, "the people gave a mandate to the bourgeoisie, or even to the nobility, and did not themselves claim power."[22]

Yet this is a comparatively minor aspect of the *Risorgimento* which has, as yet, received only casual attention by historians. A far wider debate has been conducted—particularly among Italian writers—on what the *Risorgimento* was really all about and what it contributed to Italy's national history. It is hardly surprising, in view of the issues involved, that the debate has been largely conducted on political, or party-political, lines. First in the field were the liberals of the 1860s and seventies, who, as victors in the struggle so recently concluded, wrote with unrestrained enthusiasm of the national achievement. "Hear what posterity will say of us," the Neapolitan patriot Luigi Settembrini wrote in 1879. "It will say that this was a generation of giants . . . We suffered much in that night of servitude, but we gained equal pleasure to see that dawn, to greet that sun, to become Italians."[23] This liberal myth of national amity and concord was the particular creation of moderate or conservative liberals, like Stefano Jacini and Nicomede Bianchi, who believed that the monarchical solution achieved by Cavour was that best calculated to assure "the liberty and unity of the national patria." "With what justice," asked Bianchi in an early biography of Cavour, "would you forbid us paying

---

22. Ramm, pp. 14–15; D. Mack Smith, *Italy. A Modern History,* pp. 12–13; and "Italy," in *New Camb. Mod. Hist.,* X, pp. 560–574.
23. S. J. Woolf (ed.), *The Italian Risorgimento* (London, 1969), p. 69.

that posthumous and solemn reparation demanded by historical truth and exacted by the most vital interests of our national *Risorgimento* to that glorious man, who should be respected because he raised us all out of the mire of servitude?" And, outside Italy, the refrain was repeated, almost half-a-century later, by the British liberal historian, G. M. Trevelyan, whose admiration for Garibaldi did not prevent him from expressing an even greater enthusiasm for the memory of Cavour. In a review submitted to the *Atlantic Monthly* in 1911, he wrote:

Italy produced the most wise and beneficent of all the European statesmen of the nineteenth century, if not of all time . . . Germany is a greater country than Italy, but Cavour was greater than Bismarck, almost in proportion to the inferiority of the material with which he had to work.

And he added (ironically enough, in view of Italy's pending conquest of Tripoli): "Bismarck used a maximum and Cavour a minimum of force, Cavour thought force bad in itself, and Bismarck thought it good in itself."[24]

But, within Italy, dissenting voices had already long been raised—both among those to whom the *Risorgimento* had been a defeat or a betrayal, like the Catholic Church and the South; and those, like the republicans and socialists, who believed that it had not gone far enough or had taken a wrong turn. Already in the 1860s, Giacinto de Sivo, a Neapolitan conservative historian, was denouncing the conquest of the South by Piedmont: "Piedmont cries Italy, and makes war on Italians; because she does not want to make Italy—she wants to eat Italy . . . Naples wants truly to unite Italy, so that she can advance in civilization, not regress in barbarity." And Alfredo Niceforo, a Sicilian, echoed the theme with his picture of *"two Italies, quite distinct"*: the North on the one hand, the South on the other. Cesare Cantù, a Catholic, voiced the protest of the defeated Catholic Church: "The pope, after eighteen centuries of Christianity, saw a universal and radical negation burst forth, religion corroded not so much from hatred as from ignorance of those eternal truths which have been made even clearer by a century of revolution." Among

24. *Ibid.*, pp. 70–72.

republicans, the poet Giosuè Carducci contrasted the heroic vision of Garibaldi and Mazzini with the squalid intrigues of Italy's late nine-teenth-century rulers.

Oh, those days of sun, liberty and glory of 1860! Oh, that struggle of titans between Garibaldi and Cavour in 1861! What have we become! The epic of the infinitely great has been followed by the farce of the infinitely small, the busy little farce of ponderous clowns. For how much longer must this go on?

The socialists were more realistic. Instead of crying over the spilt milk of broken promises or shattered hopes, they accompanied their indictment of Italy's new rulers with an attempt to explain the weakness and immaturity of "the people" in the national revolution. So they presented a picture of an uncompleted revolution, which therefore had a future as well as a past. Engels's writings in the early 1890s set the stage. In Italy, he wrote, modern industry was still in its infancy; and "the working class was still far from being completely expropriated and proletarianized . . . [and] the energy of the bourgeoisie had not yet been broken by the antagonism of a modern, class-conscious proletariat." So the *bourgeoisie* was the natural leader in the struggle for national independence. But having won power, it was neither able nor willing to complete its victory: "it has not destroyed the relics of feudalism, nor reorganized national production along the lines of a modern bourgeois model." Hence the survival of antiquated methods of production in industry and agriculture, the financial swindles, and "the most voracious taxes that a bourgeois system has ever invented." Following Engels, the Italian Marxist Antonio Labriola pointed to the ingenuous idealism of the early socialist and radical youth, who had expected that "a social revolution would inevitably and immediately come after a political one," whereas, "in reality, Italian affairs have taken a wholly different course," with "a highly oppressive army," a conservative monarchy and a greatly strengthened upper *bourgeoisie*. The implication was, of course, that it was only by learning such lessons that a more genuine national revolution might be brought about.[25]

25. *Ibid.*, pp. 75-83.

With the turn of the century, this picture of an inadequate or uncompleted *Risorgimento* assumed other forms as well. As industry developed, nationalists began to write of Italy's "civilizing mission," and there was much talk, in imitation of the European great powers, of building a "greater Italy" across the seas. One such nationalist, Alfredo Oriani, wrote from Bologna in 1908: "Thus there was a need to affirm ourselves in an enterprise beyond the national boundaries; we had now been preparing for this for thirty years, and as the major effort of Europe was in Africa, Italy had to be present." With Italy's entry into the Great War on the Allied side, the talk of "completion" assumed the form of a demand for the return of the "unredeemed lands" (Trentino, Istria, Trieste) from the Austrian Empire. Among those who voiced it was Gaetano Salvemini, a democrat, liberal historian and later anti-Fascist, who was certainly no colonialist or national extremist. "Today," he wrote, "either we make good the error of 1866 and complete the work of unification and national consolidation, miserably blocked at that time, or we shall never be able to resolve this problem."[26]

As is known, the problem was not fully solved by the Peace Treaties of 1919, and the milder "irredentist" claims of liberal democrats gave way to the far more strident demands for a place in the sun by conservative nationalists, and Mussolini and the Fascists. But Fascist historiography went much further than merely using the *Risorgimento* as a springboard for voicing additional nationalist aims. True to the doctrine, "Everything for the State, nothing outside the State, nothing against the State," Italy's national history, and the history of the *Risorgimento* in particular, was rewritten to accord with the new national image. Giovanni Gentile, a former Crocean philosopher and historian, became Mussolini's minister of education; and C. M. de Vechhi di Val Cismon, one of the leaders of the March on Rome, was in 1932 appointed president of the Societa Nazionale per la Storia del Risorgimento and made editor of its journal, the *Rassegna*. By statutory declaration the *Risorgimento* became, almost overnight, "the creation of Italian unity and . . . the presupposition of the Fascist

26. *Ibid.*, pp. 84–6.

Revolution." But how could the *Risorgimento,* as the precursor, continue to be associated with liberalism or such alien instrusions as the Enlightenment or the French Revolution? Already in 1923, E. C. Bollea had written:

It is no mystery that the Italian national movement . . . was born of the spiritual and economic needs of our people, and would of itself have followed —perhaps in a slower but certainly in a fairer form—its natural parabola, like every other human phenomenon.[27]

Similarly, in the work of Gentile, Giacchino Volte and others, liberalism, nationalism's traditional twin, became abandoned as well. In 1931, Gentile wrote: "One speaks of 'liberalism' . . . The individual Italian wanted liberty to become a citizen; and hence he wanted the state, in which there was room for the citizen. This is the reality . . . So one must state that the *Risorgimento* was liberal, but more or less in the same way that Fascism today means to be liberal: that is, not aiming at the liberty of the individual, but that of the state, without which there is no liberty for anyone."[28]

The Fascist revision called forth a spate of new interpretations from their opponents, both during Mussolini's heyday and after his fall. Piero Gobetti, a young radical journalist who died in 1926, argued that Fascism itself was an outcome of the *Risorgimento*'s failure to win and unite the people: "The men of our Risorgimento did not succeed in viewing their historical position clearly; they did not overcome feudalism, they did not fecundate the needs which arose from the French Revolution in Italy. This is the significance of the failure of our revolution . . . Fascism . . . has been the autobiography of the nation." Croce, as an old-style liberal, disagreed. While rejecting the Fascist concept of Italy's "special mission," he vindicated the achievements of the *Risorgimento* and of the statesmen who brought Italy into the First World War. Ten years later, Antonio Gramsci, the imprisoned communist leader, wrote a book that was only published after the last war. He revived the old socialist and radical theme of

27. K. Robert Greenfield, "The Historiography of the *Risorgimento* Since 1920," *Journal of Modern History,* VII, 1935, pp. 49–67.
28. Woolf, pp. 91–2.

the failure of the *Risorgimento*, and added a new and significant element: the failure of the liberal revolutionaries to win the support of the peasants. Moreover, the Italian revolution, unlike the French, had had no "Jacobin" phase. In consequence, the Italians of 1848 and 1859 had lacked the dynamism and purpose of the French and been compelled to "piece together a unified nation by any possible means." So "the great programmes of Gioberti and Mazzini had to give way to the political realism and empiricism of Cavour."[29]

Since then the discussion has become more muted and few books on the *Risorgimento*, apart from Mr. Mack Smith's *Italy: A Modern History* (published in 1959), have caused much of a stir. Mack Smith briefly revived the political debate by attributing Italy's collapse, her turn from liberalism and her defeat in the twentieth century to constitutional weaknesses in the nineteenth. But he added, "perhaps one can push the story back one stage further still and explain constitutional by social and economic weaknesses." And since Gramsci, in fact, it is the economic aspect that has taken over and economists, like the Italian Rosaro Romeo and the American Alexander Gerschenkron that have mainly held the stage. These writers have been less concerned with the rights and wrongs of the founding fathers, or even with the social aspirations of peasants, craftsmen and intellectuals, than with the size of farms and factories and banks and with the stages reached in Italy's industrial and agrarian development. So much of the heat has gone out of the debate. Yet, in this new direction it has taken, it is perhaps predictable that it may continue fruitfully for some time to come.[30]

20. The Vormärz in Germany

Unlike the *Risorgimento* in Italy, which enveloped the whole period of national unification, the *Vormärz* in Germany was limited to the thirty-three years between the Vienna Congress and the "spring" revolution of March 1848. The first phase was marked by the students'

29. *Ibid.*, pp. 95–6, 98–9, 101–2.
30. *Ibid.*, pp. 104, 105–9.

national movement known as the *Burschenschaft,* which, after the Wartburg Festival of 1817 and the assassination of the poet Kotzebue, believed to be a Tsarist spy, was ended by Metternich's Carlsbad Decrees (September 1819), ushering in a ten-year period of reaction. The second phase was the liberal-national phase of the 1830s, when, following the Paris revolution of July 1830 and the Polish revolt of 1831, liberal constitutions were won in Brunswick, Hesse-Cassel, Hanover and Saxony, and a new Festival—this time a "liberal" rather than a "national" one—was held at Hambach in the Bavarian Palatinate in May 1832. Once more, reaction followed: the new constitutions were suspended and Metternich's System appeared to be as firmly entrenched as ever. Meanwhile, however, liberal-national hopes were raised by a new creation—the *Zollverein,* or German Customs Union, which Prussia promoted in 1834. Similar hopes were raised by the accession of Frederick William IV to the throne of Prussia in 1840. Liberalism revived in the Rhineland and, under its impact, the King agreed, as a mild measure of reform, to convene a United Diet, with representatives from the provincial diets, in Berlin in August 1847.

So the *Vormärz* is essentially a liberal phase and, as its name implies, it is (again unlike the *Risorgimento*) a curtain-raiser to the liberal revolution of 1848. In fact, the concept of *Vormärz* is hardly one that could commend itself to German nationalist historians, to whom the "year of revolutions" marked a break with a foolish past rather than a stepping-stone to a glorious national future. For German nationalist historiography has been intimately bound up with national unification on the Bismarckian-Prussian model and has, in consequence, been contemptuous of the discarded liberal models of the period up to 1848; and this, broadly, has been true of most historians of the nineteenth and a great many historians of the twentieth century. In general, this history has been highly "political" (history, wrote Dahlmann, Treitschke's Liberal teacher, should be a school for political action). It has seen itself as the servant of the Prussian State and the German Reich and has shown a marked tendency to be hostile to foreigners and Jews.[31]

31. John A. Moses, "The Crisis in West German Historiography: Origins and Trends,"

A moderate exponent of this nationalist trend was Heinrich von Sybel, whose seven-volume history, *The Founding of the German Empire by William I,* with an opening section on the *Vormärz,* began to appear in 1890. The work is dedicated "to the Memory of Emperor William I with Reverence and Gratitude"; and, in his preface, the author makes clear that, in no part of it, has he tried "to conceal [his] Prussian and National Liberal convictions." A hostile French critic wrote of him that, as a Rhineland Protestant, his brand of liberalism naturally meant that he was "Prussian in spirit, anti-clerical, and anti-French."[32] The charge is overdrawn. Although a Protestant, Sybel shows no particular antipathy to Catholics and, in his treatment of the *Vormärz,* his hostility to Metternich and the petty German princes is certainly more pronounced than his hostility to France. Moreover, he shows considerable sympathy for the fumbling efforts of the liberal moderates, particularly those of the Rhineland who (after 1840) pinned their hopes on Prussia and its King. In contrast, as a Prussian with conservative-liberal views, he condemns the radicalism of the Baden democrats at Offenburg—the "hot-headed and vain" Hecker and the "cold-blooded fanatic" von Struve—while Frederick William IV, the romantic conservative King of Prussia, receives almost unqualified praise.[33]

If Sybel may be termed a moderate, it is the last word that springs to mind when one writes of his fellow-Prussian (though a Prussian by adoption), Heinrich von Treitschke. Treitschke began political life as a Liberal, and he wrote in 1860 that it was "only as a constitutional State that Prussia can become a true centre for all the Germans." But his views changed as the new Germany developed; and he had already gone a long way towards becoming a thorough-going Prussian conservative nationalist by the time he finished the first volume of his *History of Germany in the Nineteenth Century* in 1879. The book stops

Historical Studies. Australia and New Zealand, XIII, April, 1969, pp. 445–59.
32. Antoine Guilland, *Modern Germany and Her Historians* (Westport, Connecticut, 1915), p. 175. This work is admittedly tendencious: note the author's nationality and the date at which he is writing.
33. Heinrich von Sybel, *The Founding of the German Empire by William I,* 7 vols. (Westport, Connecticut, 1890–98), I, pp. 28–141.

short (for our purposes conveniently) at 1848. It is, for all its perversity, a work of immense power and imaginative sweep and far more readable than Sybels's. Moreover, it is a work of considerable scholarship in the best Rankean tradition. Yet it is from start to finish a political polemic, an undisguised *apologia* for Prussia by a man who glories in his chosen task of "awaken[ing] in the hearts of his readers [they are his own words] a delight in his fatherland." "In the history of Prussia," he writes in his preface, "there is nothing to cloak, nothing to conceal." So the hero of the book is Prussia, her Kings, her army and administration. And the villains of the *Vormärz* (but, of course, he never uses the term) are the forces that stood in the way, or appeared to stand in the way, of the Prussian, or *kleindeutsch*, solution of Germany's national problems: such "alien" forces as Metternich, the petty German states and princes, the Roman Catholic Church, the Jews, the Liberals, the French and the English. Metternich, as we noted earlier, is said to be "the greatest liar and rascal on the Continent." The Jesuits and the Roman Church become almost synonymous terms. "The Jesuitical faith," he writes, "always remained foreign to the spirit of our people. The rich spiritual forces of the New Roman Church developed proudly in their Roman fatherlands; but on this hostile German soil, among this people of inveterate heretics, they could never take root." Palmerston is presented, in his pro-Liberal intervention in Spain, as "lightheartedly trampling international law underfoot." The small German states are objects of pity and contempt, a continuous stumbling block in the way of national unity. "Small states," he says, "are to appear ludicrous, for the State is power, and weakness stultifies itself immediately should it attempt to masquerade as power." As for France, "she will always be the country of police, of soldiers lowered to the rank of policemen, of partial tribunals, of phrases in Parliament, of the besottedness of the people and of Catholic fanaticism."[34]

Among those against whom some of Treitschke's most vindictive and ill-tempered shafts are directed are the Liberals and Jews. Liberal-

34. H. von Treitschke, *History of Germany in the Nineteenth Century,* I, pp. xv, 25; IV, pp. 265, 423; V, p. vii; VI, p. 12.

ism, he thought, was an alien importation from the French; and he sneers at "the arid and ready-made formulas of the fashionable doctrines of liberty." The Jews, for their part, are charged with a long list of offenses: for their "dangerous spirit of aloofness and arrogance," their cosmopolitanism, their hatred of Christianity, "the evil Jewish custom" of self-mockery, their affinity with the French, and their natural inclination to espouse the radical cause. "In so far," writes Treitschke, "as the Jewish cosmopolitan was competent to understand western nations, he was chiefly attracted towards the French, not merely from reasonable gratitude, but also from a sense of inner kinship." And the Jews, having derived their radicalism from the same source, now turned it to undermine the solid virtues of the German *Volk*. And so, Treitschke laments, "it came to be regarded as a mark of genius to speak dispassionately, with shameless disrespect, of the fatherland, as if the speaker had neither part nor lot therein, as if the mockery of Germany need not inevitably cut every individual German to the heart."[35]

Treitschke's views and his store of invective were to become a rich treasure-house for later German nationalist historians, and particularly (though by no means exclusively) for the National-Socialist historians of the 1930s and 1940s. But, of course, there have been exceptions and liberals have been found to write the history of Germany's past in entirely different terms. Among them has been the moderate liberal historian, Veit Valentin, whose book, *The German People*, was published abroad in 1941. Only a small part of the book deals with the *Vormärz*, but it is enough to show how profoundly Valentin's view of these events differs from Treitschke's, and to a lesser degree from Sybel's. Like Sybel, he believed that the French Revolution failed in its aim to create a better world: "It ended in world tyranny, destruction and bloodshed without precedent." But happily, out of the turmoil, he writes, there emerged two new concepts, "liberty" and "nationality"; and the author, being a moderate liberal, has a friendly word for both. But German nationalists, he argues, took a wrong turn. Whereas liberalism, estranged by the

35. *Ibid.*, IV, pp. 501, 555–7.

egoism and reactionary obstruction of the two German great powers and by the parochialism of the princely states, inevitably became more radical, nationalism, though faced with the same opponents, from a hatred of Jews, foreigners, revolutionaries and cosmopolitans tended to turn towards counterrevolution and to become the enemy of liberal reform. So, unlike Treitschke and Sybel and the other Imperial historians, Valentin is no apologist for Prussia, no advocate of Prussian claims. In fact, as he looks back, he sees a greater promise for Germany's future—for the new German Empire that was being looked for—not in Prussia with its reactionary Junkers and its semifeudal institutions, but among the patriots of the southern states—Württemberg, Baden and Bavaria—the states that at first opposed the Prussian-sponsored *Zollverein* and later resisted Bismarck's *kleindeutsch* solution till after the war of 1866. He sees it, too, in the patriots of the smaller German states; for "no other German longed with such bitter intensity as the one who lived within this system of small states for a Germany of the future that should be really great, free and strong." But how could it be achieved against the obstruction of Austria and the counterrevolution, which "had strangled any possibility of reform"? "The future," he concludes, "could only be realized through a German revolution."[36]

So to Valentin, unlike the German nationalist historians, the *Vormärz* was a preparation for and a justification of the "year of revolutions." Yet they had at least in common that they discussed the preparation and the outcome in almost exclusively political terms, and it was the activities of liberals and nationalists, of Metternich, the German Confederation, the petty princelings and the Prussian State that determined the outbreak of 1848 and its aftermath, and not so much the peasants, workers and industrialists, or even the growth of industry and the German Customs Union. These economic and social forces, in fact, play a comparatively insignificant part in their presentation. An American historian, Theodore Hamerow, has reversed the process and looked at the problem the other way round. He opens his

36. Veit Valentin, *The German People. Their History and Civilization from the Holy Roman Empire to the Third Reich* (New York, 1946), pp. 363–87.

book, *Restoration, Revolution, Reaction* (1958), by considering the calamitous consequences, for both Germany and Europe, of the failure of German liberalism in 1848: "the penalty for the mistakes of 1848 was paid not in 1849, but in 1918, in 1933 and in 1945." So important an event, therefore, required to be closely examined; but, in considering the causes of 1848, he soon realized that to grasp the significance of the political events "involved an investigation of the economic and social forces which drove the masses of Germany to insurrection." For

it became apparent that the Revolution was the expression not only of ideological forces like nationalism and liberalism, but also of deep-seated popular dissatisfactions engendered by the transition from agrarian manorialism to industrial capitalism. Indeed, throughout the first half of the nineteenth century, politics in Central Europe were profoundly affected by a painful social adjustment to new economic conditions. While parliamentarians and businessmen fought the policies of princes and landowners, the lower classes were engaged in a life-and-death struggle against the consequences of industrialization. And their influence on the direction of national growth was of paramount importance. My purpose is to study that influence.

In Hamerow's presentation, the central theme of the *Vormärz* becomes the social and political upheaval caused by the growth of a capitalist economy and an industrial revolution in a formerly "sleepy land of noblemen and peasants." It was a lop-sided development, which brought profits and new opportunities to some, but hardship and dislocation to the majority. In industry, handicraftsmen, who formed the bulk of the producers, faced ruin and became bewildered and resentful. On the land, also subject to capitalist pressures, manorialism and serfdom progressively disappeared from large parts of the country; but the peasant, like the handicraftsman, traded his old servitude for an illusory freedom, lost his former security, and, "after centuries of bondage, he was left to shift for himself in a world of bankers, industrialists and landlords." Even landowners, unable to hold their own in a world of new competitive values, sank into debt and insolvency; and, in a few years, one-third of the Junker estates in Prussia passed into middle-class hands. Meanwhile, government remained rooted in the past and tied to the old concepts of legitimacy and benevolent despotism of the previous century; so "in the age of the factory and the railway it became a parasitic relic of a bygone age commanding neither loyalty nor respect." From these new conflicts and tensions different classes sought different means of escape. Manufacturers, journalists and professional men looked to nationalism and liberalism and demanded political rights, a share in goverment by men of property, an end of national subservience, and the removal of tariff barriers between the states. The aristocracy, like the old rulers, tended, in resisting these claims, to cling more firmly to the past and to entrench themselves in the old system of legitimism, privilege and prerogative. Some workers and peasants (as in the Rhineland, Baden and Silesia) began to look for salvation through the new political ideas: through liberalism, radicalism, democracy, and even socialism or revolution. But the great majority, Hamerow insists, remained indifferent to politics or ideologies: "For the uprooted guildsman, the unemployed journeyman, the lackland peasant, and the agricultural labourer, the conflict betwen liberal and conservative, between nationalist and particularist was of little interest . . . they looked only for relief from want."

It was the events of the 1840s, Hamerow argues, that brought matters to a head by both sharpening antagonisms and imposing a degree of unity on the scattered forces of opposition. On the one hand, there were the constitutional promises which Frederick William dangled before the Liberals, thus whetting their appetite for more. But far more cataclysmic, in his view, was the great depression of the forties whose consequences he outlines as follows:

For the masses it came as a climax of a long series of disasters extending over thirty years, intensifying the disruptive effects of capitalism in industry and agriculture, accelerating the decline of the master handicraftsman and the independent peasant, and driving the proletariat of Germany from Europe to America in a great wave of emigration. To the middle class it brought new courage and new resourcefulness, providing constitutionalism with a mass following ready to use violence for the overthrow of the old order. Some of the liberals even came to feel that a civilized revolution, a revolution of maximum enthusiasm and minimum bloodshed, might compel the government to share its power with the bourgeoisie without inviting the danger of mob rule. The economic crisis thus prepared the way for the spring rising of 1848 by endowing the political opposition with popular support and forcing it to adopt more radical tactics.[37]

21. Spanish Revolution and Counterrevolution

In no country in Europe had the Restoration turned the clock back so quickly and so thoroughly as in Spain. When Ferdinand VII returned to his subjects in 1814, the liberal Constitution of 1812 was revoked, liberals were exiled or imprisoned, the Inquisition was reimposed and the Jesuits recalled, the convents were reopened and their properties restored, and all the paraphernalia of government and administration reverted to the ministerial despotism of the past.

Counterrevolution, in turn, bred revolution; and, in 1820, a mutiny by troops under Major Riego touched off a successful liberal revolt which, following the political convention of the times, "pronounced" for the Constitution and compelled Ferdinand to establish a moderate liberal administration. But a near-state of civil war persisted, fostered on the one hand by the radical liberals (the *exaltados*) at Madrid and a clerical-legitimist *Apostolic Junta,* which formed at Seo de Urgel, on the other. When the radicals won the elections of 1822, Ferdinand called in the French and, with their help, reasserted his old authority. Riego was executed and the liberal reforms were annulled; but, attempting to steer a more moderate course, the King resisted the more conservative aims of his brother Don Carlos, crushed an ultra-Royalist rebellion (1827) and, to block Don Carlos's succession to the throne, annulled the Salic Law by proclamation, and thus assured the succession to his infant daughter Isabella on his death in 1833.

Ferdinand's death was followed by the Carlist War. The Regency at Madrid, set up to govern in the name of Isabella, was challenged by Carlos, who was proclaimed King in the north, mainly with the support of the Catalans and Basques. The war ended with the defeat

37. T. S. Hamerow, *Restoration, Revolution, Reaction. Economics and Politics in Germany, 1815–1871* (Princeton, 1958), pp. vii-ix, 3–93.

of the Carlists in 1840. But, meanwhile, the Regency party had been split between Moderates and Progressives, and the reign of Isabella (1843–68), depending mainly on Moderate support, was punctuated by a series of popular or radical rebellions (Madrid riots in 1848, another revoltuion in 1854) and a further Carlist challenge in 1849. In short, as Droz has written, "the political history of nineteenth-century Spain is dominated by *pronunciamentos* and civil wars."[38]

Political historians, in presenting these events, have been guided by their aversion or sympathy for Ferdinand, Don Carlos, or the liberals whether radical or moderate. The British have, perhaps not surprisingly, tended to be critical of Ferdinand and more so of Don Carlos, and (like Canning and Palmerston in their day) bestowed their favors on Isabella and the more moderate of the liberal groups. But there has been at least one notable exception: a certain W. Walton Esq., who, in 1837, published a plea on behalf of the Carlist pretender, entitled *The Revolutions of Spain from 1808 to the End of 1836*. As a Carlist and a Tory, Walton criticizes Ferdinand not for any lack of charity to liberals but, on the contrary, for having allowed himself to become the tool of liberal intrigue; so much so that, on his death (the writer avers), "not a single royalist held a military command or filled a civil station." And the "lawful successor," in his view, was not Ferdinand's daughter, Isabella, but Carlos, the ultra-Royalist claimant, whom he calls Charles V throughout. For the liberals, he writes, "have failed in all their endeavours" and have resorted to "expedients which would have disgraced the worst days of the French Revolution"; while "the name of the young queen is a mere cloak under which the revolutionary party seek to conceal their ulterior designs." "Who then," he asks, "can restore order to such chaos?" And, of course, the answer is not in doubt: "The prince alone, who unites sufficient wisdom, temper, and influence to devise and establish a system of government that may be acceptable to the great majority of Spaniards." So British governments, from Canning's on, are roundly condemned for

38. Droz, *L'époque contemporaine*, I, p. 308.

intervening on the liberals' and Isabella's side; and, he concludes, "it is the duty of Europe to raise her voice against an interference in itself unprincipled and unjust, ruinous to the Peninsula, and dangerous to the tranquillity of the civilised world."[39]

More typical of British attitudes are two works that appeared at the turn of the century: Martin Hume's *Modern Spain 1788–1898* (1899) and Butler Clarke's *Modern Spain 1815–1898* (1906). Butler Clarke's book is a typical narrative history of the day, broadly liberal in its sympathies, factual and devoid of all analytical discussion. The style is dispassionate and the author hardly ever stops to comment on the events he is relating. Yet his views, although not overtly paraded, appear to be those of Canning, who became (the author tells us) "the peaceful friend of the moderate Spanish liberals." Hume's views are not dissimilar, but his manner is altogether different. Like an old-style Whig, he hammers remorselessly, and with fine moral fervor, at all who fail to conform to the British liberal-constitutional ideal. The *exaltados* are given short shrift for their excesses; and "the servile crowd," which, in 1820, had acclaimed Riego for his revolution and, three years later, "abased [itself] before the lying despot," ends up with "the government it deserves." As for Ferdinand, he is doubly condemned as a despot and a perjurer. "He had learnt nothing from his suffering and experience. His father had been absolute, and he wished to be absolute too. So all the old abuses were re-enacted; the friars, the tithes, and the entails came back; the Spaniards became 'dear vassals' again and gloried in the name . . ."[40]

In sharp contrast to the Whig historian, Marx and Engels, in the articles they wrote for the *New York Herald Tribune* in the 1850s, were less concerned with personalities than with what the revolution and counterrevolution were all about. It had been suggested in Britain that the 1820 revolt was no revolution at all, but a military conspiracy or the mere outcome of a Russian intrigue. Both views are rejected.

39. W. Walton, *The Revolutions of Spain from 1808 to the End of 1836*, 2 vols. (London, 1837), I, pp. iv–ix, 350–55; II, pp. 1–20, 34–8, 66–74, 532–5.
40. Butler Clarke, *Modern Spain 1815–1898* (London, 1906), p. 57; Martin A. S. Hume, *Modern Spain 1788–1898* (New York, 1900), pp. 242–7.

Riego's rebellion, they argue, was a limited operation and it involved only 5,000 men; but an army of 35,000, which was sent to suppress it, adopted its demand for the Constitution and made it their own. Moreover, the belief that Riego's revolt had succeeded touched off popular-liberal movements all over the country, and "those most remote from the spot were the first to declare themselves for the Constitution of 1812." In fact, they add, "so far was Spain matured for a revolution that even false news sufficed to produce it." As for the Russian intrigue, it was real enough but of a most ambivalent kind. Russia had been the first European power to acknowledge the Constitution of 1812 and, again in 1820, she "first kindled the revolution." But, having done so (they continue), she "first denounced it to Ferdinand VII, first lighted the torch of counter-revolution on several points of the Peninsula, first solemnly protested against it before Europe, and finally forced France into an armed intervention against it." So Russia most decidedly played a part in these events; but what does this prove? "That Russia produced the revolution of 1820? By no means, but only that she prevented the Spanish Government from resisting it." That the revolution would have occurred in the Spaniards' own time, with or without the Russian intervention, they argue in their clinical and thoroughly un-"Whiggish" way, is proved by the following facts:

1. By the series of conspiracies which since 1814 had followed each other; 2. By the testimony of M. de Martignac, the French Commissary, who accompanied the Duke of Angouleme at the time of the Legitimist invasion of Spain; 3. By a testimony not to be rejected—that of Ferdinand himself.

In short, "no Tatischeff [Russian Ambassador to Spain] was needed to bring about a Spanish revolution."[41]

Finally, let us note the observations of a modern British historian, Raymond Carr, whose *Spain 1808–1939* was published in 1966. Mr. Carr, though probably no socialist, is as clinical, analytical and un-"Whiggish" as Marx and Engels; moreover, he has had the advantage of writing over a century later. He is no more concerned than they

41. K. Marx and F. Engels, *Revolution in Spain* (New York, 1939), pp. 75–84.

are with the vices or virtues or the personalities of Ferdinand, Don Carlos or Riego. Like theirs, his concern is with the nature of the revolution of 1820: what sort of revolution was it, and why was it so successful when a more "respectable" liberal attempt to make one a few months earlier had been a dismal failure? According to Carr, the revolution developed in four stages: first, Riego's *coup* or "military sedition"; secondly, a larger military rebellion at Corunna; thirdly, mixed military and civilian risings at Barcelona, Saragossa and Pamplona; and, lastly, the adoption of the military and provincial-sponsored revolution by the capital, where "civilian liberalism had waited on events." In short, it was a process directly at variance with what had happened in France in 1789 and with what would happen there again in 1830 and 1848. Why was this? Because, writes Carr, the officer corps in Spain had, by established tradition, become "the ultimate repository of a general will"; in consequence, "the *pronunciamento* (voiced by an officers' revolt) was the instrument of liberal revolution in the nineteenth century." So there was a kind of rough division of labor between the army and the civilians: the liberals and Masonic Lodges provided the ideas, the army supplied the activist cadres, while the civilian crowds stamped the whole operation with the seal of popular approval. But why should this particular *pronunciamento* in this particular revolt have succeeded where numerous others in the previous half-dozen years had failed or gone off at half-cock? Because, argues Carr, the army, already soaked in liberal and Masonic ideas, were incensed by orders to embark to crush rebellion in America; and, as the troops, lying in cantonments round Cadiz and awaiting the order to sail, became increasingly disaffected, the government became progressively weakened and powerless to crush revolt. So it became possible for Riego's "military sedition," which no one expected to succeed, to escalate into a full-scale national revolution, whose consequences (both in America and Spain) neither Riego nor the Moderates, neither Ferdinand nor the *exaltados,* neither the French, the English, nor the Russians could possibly have conceived.[42]

42. Raymond Carr, *Spain 1808–1939* (Oxford, 1966), pp. 124–43.

22. Reform, Party and Government in Britain

The political history of early-nineteenth century Britain has been largely rewritten in the past fifty years. What is sometimes termed the "older history" is that presented, in its classical form, by G. M. Trevelyan who, a half a century ago, published his *British History in the Nineteenth Century*, which carried on the Whig tradition established by Macaulay's *History of England*, written sixty to seventy years before.[43] According to the classical "Whiggish" view, there was a Tory "reaction" after the Napoleonic Wars, followed by the reforming "new" Toryism of Canning and Peel, succeeded in turn by the era of Whig reforms of 1830 to 1841, in the course of which the twin pillars of middle-class ascendency were laid in Free Trade and Parliamentary Reform. The emphasis is all on ordered progress and continuity; and not only did the Reform Bill, and its attendant legislation, spring from the initiative of the reforming Radicals or Whigs, but it was also a stage in an inevitable chain of events, reaching back to the early Reform movement of the 1760s and leading by an equally inevitable progression to future stages in the Reform Acts of 1867, 1884 and 1918. So, writes Trevelyan, "there has been no solemn revision of the principles of our Constitution, only a constant amendment and extension of its details, and an entire though gradual change of view".[44]

There are other points to note about the Whig view of the nineteenth century as well. It is essentially a political view: progress and reform are presented as the outcome of a struggle between opposing Whigs and Tories in the successive Parliaments of the day. It is, moreover, a political view as seen "from the top": the heroes in this line of development are Earl Grey, Lord Durham, Cobden and Bright, Peel (a Tory defector) and Gladstone (only temporarily a Tory), while working-class movements, Luddism, Chartism, Robert Owen, or the rebellious laborers of 1830, are mere casual intruders on the stage of events. Above all, it is the battle of Whigs and Tories, in

---

43. G. M. Trevelyan, *British History in the Nineteenth Century and After (1782–1919)* (New York, 1966).
44. *Ibid.*, p. xv.

which it is generally the Whigs that are the "goodies" and the Tories the "baddies," that dominates the scene.

All recent British historical revision of the period has tended to be directed, often quite deliberately, at this old-style Whig interpretation. Conservative historians, in particular, with their distrust of patterns, broad historical sweeps and generalizations, or of any ferment of ideas, have been conspicuous in this act of revision; but others, whether liberals, socialists or Marxists, have also played a hand. In fact, "knocking Trevelyan" (or at least the Whigs) has, like "knocking the Hammonds," become a fashionable pastime among British nineteenth-century historians.

Let us briefly consider some of the issues involved, beginning with the two great land-marks of 1832 and 1846. No measure during the century has figured so prominently in the whole Whig armory as the Great Reform Bill of 1832. After its eventual hard-won passage through the Lords, Trevelyan sums up its significance as follows:

It had asserted the power of the whole nation, enfranchised and unenfranchised, because it had been carried by the popular will against the strenuous resistance of the old order entrenched in the House of Lords.[45]

Historians have objected to this type of simplification. How had the Bill in fact been won? By the Whigs and Radicals alone? By the combined "good sense" of all parties? By mass popular action—or by the threat of revolution? While the "older history" tended to see the Whigs (with popular support) as the sole heroes of the piece, conservatives have, somewhat naturally perhaps, been inclined to give the Tories a greater measure of credit; or, alternatively, the more old-fashioned among them might even praise the Tories for refusing to take so hazardous a "leap in the dark." Among such old-style conservatives was Sir John Marriott, who, in his *England since Waterloo* (1913), argued that the Lords behaved very sensibly in resisting a measure which was likely, by opening the floodgates to reform, to have far more dangerous and far-reaching consequences than its promoters had foreseen or intended. "Nor can it be denied," he contin-

45. *Ibid.*, p. 241.

ues, "that their estimate of the results to be apprehended from reform was far nearer the mark than that of their opponents." For the reform of 1832 led inevitably to those of 1867 and 1884; and though Grey and his colleagues denied any such intention, "they opened the gates; the capture of the citadel was merely a question of time."[46]

It is unlikely, however, that such views as Marriott's would find much support even among conservative historians today. The issue now is not so much whether reform was good or bad (it is generally assumed to have been good, or at least something that could not have been avoided), but how far the honors can be shared between the parties. Among recent historians, D. C. Moore is one of those who believe that too much credit has been given to the Whigs and that there were Tories, too, without whose energetic contribution the Reform Bill might have been stillborn. To prove his point, he argues that a large number of "country," or "ultra," Tories, incensed by their leaders' concessions to Roman Catholics and free-traders, had, even before 1830, turned to reform as a means of keeping ministers in check. "Their adoption of reform", he writes, "was their way of demanding that the Government remain true to the principles of which they were the major custodians." Nor does he believe that they thereby "cut off their noses to spite their faces" by increasing the influence of the middle class; for "in practical terms, the first Reform Bill was far less a blow against the powers in the State of the aristocracy and gentry than it was against the powers of the Ministers."[47]

It is a part of Moore's case that there are no solid grounds for accepting the views of those historians who have argued that the Reform Act was a concession made to stave off revolution. The "fear-of-revolution" theory may be expressed in one of two forms. On the one hand, there are those, like Cole and Postgate, authors of *The British Common People*, who have held that, after the city riots of 1831, the Whigs were persuaded by their Radical and working-class allies that "nothing less than the Bill" would suffice to avert a revolu-

46. *Cit.* in *The Reform Bill of 1832. Why not Revolution?*, W. H. Maehl, Jr., (ed.) (New York, 1967), p. 20.
47. D. C. Moore, "The Other Face of Reform," *Victorian Studies,* V, 1961–2, pp. 7–34; *cit.* Maehl, pp. 63–70.

tion. The other view is that it was not so much the Whigs as the Tories who surrendered to the threat of revolution and that this was why the Lords, in the "May crisis" of 1832, so hastily withdrew their opposition to the Bill. This threat of revolution was certainly used by Francis Place and the Philosophical Radicals, with all their talk of barricades and a run on gold, to force the measure through; but was there substance behind the threat or was it largely bluff? Some historians, both Whigs and others, have been inclined to take Place and his allies at their word. Trevelyan, for one, appears to have done so, for he claimed that it was only the passage of the Reform Bill that saved "the cultivated upper classes" from "violent revolution" on the Continental model. J. R. M. Butler, the author of *The Passing of the Great Reform Bill* (1913), is more specific as he pinpoints the date of the Lords' "ultimate surrender"; for, he writes, "in the eyes of the people of the Three Kingdoms it was May 18 on which the battle was won and which brought the country nearest to a revolution." The view is shared by an American scholar, J. Salwyn Schapiro, who observes in his *Liberalism and the Challenge of Fascism* (1949): "The fear of a revolutionary upheaval from below was the prime reason why the Lords yielded to the Commons in the great crisis of 1832." Elie Halévy, the French historian, however, was not convinced: writing at about the same time as Butler, he merely describes Place's threat of a run on gold as a "successful manoeuvre." Others have gone much further and have dismissed the threat of revolution as a sham. James Hamburger, for example, in *James Mill and the Art of Revolution* (published at New Haven in 1963), has argued that the whole thing was a gigantic piece of bluff stagemanaged by Place and his Radicals to bring both hesitant Whigs and obstructive Tories to heel. Edward Thompson, more cautiously, considers that "a revolution was improbable." For myself, after searching through the Home Office papers relating to these events, I have found that the evidence for any revolutionary situation in England is considerably slimmer for 1832 than it is for 1830 or 1831. I have added the comment:

The view that it was Wellington's surrender to the Political Unions that averted a revolution is based on the assumption that there was in England at this time a revolutionary situation and that it needed but a spark to set it off. . . . [T]hese historians appear to believe that a revolution can be switched on, or can spontaneously erupt, almost regardless of the social and political realities of the day . . . Is it conceivable that the various movements that have been described could, either singly or in unison, have provoked a revolutionary explosion? If so, what sort of revolution, and on whose behalf would it have been carried through? . . . [48]

So doubts continue to linger as to how or why the Bill was passed; but there have also been arguments about the consequences of Reform. To Trevelyan it appeared that "the 'sovereignty of the people' had been established in fact, if not in law"; he continued: "In England, 'the nation' was defined afresh by each of the Franchise Acts of 1867, 1884, and 1918, but the fact that the nation was master in its own house had been settled once for all in the days of May." And although he gave no support to the view that "the Bill gave all power to the middle class," he claimed that "after the experience of 1832 the landlords shrank from saying 'no' to the great majority of the nation." Later historians have been more guarded, and revision (and not Tory revision alone) has taken the form of questioning the degree to which, or the speed with which, the Reform Bill effected a transfer of power from the aristocracy or the landlord interest to the manufacturing or middle class. Some of the earlier revisions of this kind were those carried out, in the 1930s and 1940s, by S. F. Woolley and J. A. Thomas on the composition of the House of Commons, by Harold Laski on the Cabinet, and A. S. Turberville on the House of Lords. They are generally agreed that the changes that took place between the First and Second Reform Bills were comparatively slight. More recently, the point has been emphasized by Asa Briggs: "In many ways . . . the political world after 1832 resembled that which preceded it"; and Kitson Clark has, less cautiously, asserted that "after the Bill the final control in politics still lay without question in the hands of the old governing classes, the nobility and gentry." It is a point that has been explored more fully and more subtly than by any other

48. Maehl, pp. 2, 56, 77–84, 105–6. See also Halévy, *The Triumph of Reform 1830– 1841*, p. 7; G. Rudé, "Why was there no Revolution in England in 1830 or 1848?," in *Studien über die Revolution,* M. Kossok (ed.) (Berlin (G.D.R.), 1969), pp. 239–40.

historian by Norman Gash, now professor of history at St. Andrews' University in Scotland. Gash has devoted two books to the task: his *Politics in the Age of Peel* appeared in 1953, and his *Reaction and Reconstruction in English Politics 1832–1852*, first presented as Ford Lectures at Oxford, in 1965. In the first of these he draws up a sort of balance-sheet of change and continuity, from which it appears that "there was scarcely a feature of the old unreformed system that could not be found still in existence after 1832"; and he instances the survival of "pocket" and nomination boroughs, electoral corruption, borough-mongering, landlord-control, and organized violence at the hustings. In the second book, however, he shows how the Reform Act substantially contributed to the weakening of the Hanoverian Monarchy in its declining years; for "if the Act enhanced the power of the Commons, it inevitably diminished that of the other two branches of the legislature: the Crown and the House of Lords." Moreover, it brought a whole number of further reforms in its train; for

In a sense, it was only after the Reform Act had passed that the real crisis began: the post-Reform crisis of adjustment between what had been done and what men thought should be the consequences of what had been done. Many of the subsequent reforms are important; but equally significant is the phenomenon of reforms attempted and defeated, and those defeated or transformed.[49]

There has been a similar debate on that other great victory for the middle class, the repeal of the Corn Laws in 1846. To whom (or to what), primarily, should the credit be due? To Peel? to Cobden and Bright and the Anti-Corn Law League? to the "good sense" of the ruling classes? or to the potato famine in Ireland? In the traditional Whig presentation, pride of place went to the League and its leaders, Cobden and Bright; and it is hardly surprising to find Kitson Clark complaining that "in most of the older histories the account of the behaviour and the case of each side to this controversy came directly

49. Trevelyan, pp. 240–41; Droz, *L'époque contemporaine*, I, pp. 143–4; Briggs, *The Age of Improvement*, p. 5; Kitson Clark, *The Making of Victorian England*, p. 7; Norman Gash, *Politics in the Age of Peel. A Study in the Technique of Parliamentary Representation 1830–1850* (New York, 1964), pp. ix–xi; and *Reaction and Reconstruction in English Politics 1832–1852* (Oxford, 1965), pp. 1–3.

from the political statements of the leaders of the Anti-Corn Law league, unmodified and unquestioned"; and there is considerable justice in the complaint. Later research and historical writing, whether conservative or not, has tended to redress the balance. An early attempt was that made, before the last war, by D. Walter-Smith, who, in *The Protectionist Case 1840–1846* (Oxford, 1933), argued that Peel's free-trade measures of 1842 and 1845 were prompted less by free-trade arguments and theories than by the compelling necessities of the day; and that this was even more true of Repeal itself which was forced on Peel more by the Irish famine than by any other factor. Thus the role of the League and its leaders was reduced to less than life-size! Others, while exploring the matter further, have refrained from going quite as far. Norman McCord, for example, the League's most recent historian, strikes a balance between the activities of the League and "the decisive part played by Peel and his followers"; and he argues that the League, for all its noisy propaganda, "had not yet [in 1846] succeeded in its aim of building up its own independent strength to a point at which repeal could be carried in the face of the influence of the united landed interest." Briggs, too, disputes the League's claim to have been the disinterested champion of the small consumer. "[It] was not a democratic body," he writes. "The League was never the pure hearted and utterly unselfish crusade which Bright claimed it to be. Whatever may have been its objective, its arguments were often inconsistent and contradictory." Donald Read, in a recent biography of Cobden and Bright, emphasizes this division of councils by asserting that, contrary to "the received version" of their relationship, "it was Cobden, and not Bright, who was the more progressive of the two." While Kitson Clark, for his part, has even questioned the League's claim, so often repeated by historians, that the opponents of Repeal were the aristocracy and gentry. On the contrary, he writes, "many of the country gentry seem to have been divided in mind, or at least in allegiance, on the matter of the Corn Laws, for they were pushed in one direction by their leader Sir Robert Peel but pulled in the other by their farming constituents, and it seems that the attitude of members of the House of Lords was even more equivocal." "None of this," he concludes, "required very much research to uncover, but the older historians did not feel the need to do research, since they accepted the League's account of the crisis as obvious truth."[50]

Another of the League's familiar claims has been disputed by historians. This was that the repeal of the Corn Laws would (and, in fact, did) reduce the price of bread and usher in a general period of prosperity for farmers and townsmen alike. As McCord has shown, it is not altogether surprising that the view should have found favor with the next generation of Englishmen, who contrasted the evident improvements of the 1850s and sixties with "the bad old days and the hungry 'forties" and were readily persuaded to give some credit to the League for the change. Historians, after a century has passed, have naturally not proved so easy to convince. Among the critics of the old view, once more, have been Briggs, Clark and McCord; also a number of economic historians who have argued that such prosperity as followed was not as immediate as the League had prophesied, nor was it necessarily the result of Repeal. Briggs sums up the case as follows:

The claim of the League that the abolition of the corn laws would open up an enormous range of foreign markets was exaggerated and only sketchily supported by statistical enquiry: the chances of British manufacturers being successful in overseas markets depended on other factors besides the corn laws. The prosperity of mid-Victorian England did not rest entirely or even mainly on the decisions arrived at in 1846, but on a variety of economic circumstances many of which had little to do with either the positive or the negative actions of government. [51]

And it is on this wider question of government action and inaction, on *laissez-faire* and "collectivism," that a further, and perhaps a more significant, debate has taken place. Broadly speaking, the "older" (or Whig) historians had argued that the century was divided into two distinctive periods: the first, running up to 1870 or 1880, when Benthamism and *laissez-faire* prevailed; the second, covering the final twenty or thirty years of the century and beyond, when "collectivism"

50. Kitson Clark, pp. 7–8; Droz, I, p. 144; Norman McCord, *The Anti-Corn Law League 1838–1846* (London, 1958), pp. 208–9; Briggs, p. 315; Donald Read, *Cobden and Bright. A Victorian Political Partnership* (New York, 1968), p. vii. See also G. Kitson Clark, "The Repeal of the Corn Laws and the Politics of the Forties," *Econ. Hist. Rev.*, 2nd series, IV (1), 1951, pp. 1–13.
51. McCord, pp. 209–10; Briggs, pp. 322–3.

or State intervention was the order of the day. Some modern historians have rejected this view. Kitson Clark, for instance, believes that " 'the period of *laissez-faire*' and 'the period of collectivism' run concurrently like prison sentences, and cover most of the nineteenth century." He believes, moreover, that the legislation of the earlier period was guided more by empirical considerations than by Benthamite or other preconceptions, and determined as much by the needs or whims of individuals as by the programs of political groups. "What they thought about these circumstances," he writes, "was no doubt conditioned by their principles, Tory or Radical, Economist or Benthamite, Christian or Medical, and by their professional training or experience, and by their temperaments, sensitive, missionary or negative. What they thought affected what they did, but a preponderant factor in any decision they had to make was always the need to find a practical solution to the immediate problem."[52]

The same type of conservative empiricism pervades an article that Oliver MacDonagh, now professor of history at the University of Cork, in Ireland, contributed to the English *Historical Journal* in 1958. Like Clark, he denies that there was any sharp break, or "revolution in Government," dividing a *laissez-faire* from a "collectivist" phase after the third quarter of the nineteenth century. He denies, too, that there was any distinctive political doctrine, whether Benthamite or other, that inspired the parliamentary legislation of the half-century between 1825 and 1875. The "legislative-cum-administrative process" was, rather, set in motion by a "concatenation of circumstances"; and he constructs a five-stage model of its operation. The first, the "humanitarian," stage begins with the exposure of a "social evil," considered "intolerable" by some but insignificant or irremediable by others; so it ends in compromise. There follow three intermediate stages of more effective legislation; and the whole process ends with a fifth, or "Fabian," stage from which emerges a bevy of executive officers empowered to exact penalties and to frame further regulations. Moreover, MacDonagh insists, administration itself has an

---

52. G. Kitson Clark, *An Expanding Society: Britain 1830–1900* (Melbourne, 1967), pp. 162–3.

inner momentum that carries the whole process forward, and "reforms never correspond too closely to the wishes of their promoters, or even to social needs." In short, "the correlation between a social problem," he writes, "and its administrative remedy is seldom exact."[53]

It need hardly surprise us that such views, empirical and contemptuous of ideology, as those expressed by MacDonagh and Kitson Clark should have aroused controversy. The most methodical and outspoken of their critics, up to now, has been Jennifer Hart, who, in an article published in *Past and Present* in 1965, described their views, and those of three other historians, as "a Tory interpretation of history."[54] In the first place, she takes them to task for their cavalier treatment of Benthamite ideas: both because they appear to confuse Benthamism with *laissez-faire* (the two, she insists, are quite separate phenomena) and because they play them down as a factor of little importance. They also, she complains, belittle the ideological factor in general and substitute for it, as a stimulus to reform, vague "humanitarian" notions and a generalized response to the "intolerability" of social evils. Thus, she maintains, an undue emphasis is placed on "blind forces" and "the historical process" *in vacuo,* while the conscious thought and activity of human beings are reduced to a minor role. The evidence, she insists, points rather the other way; and it "seems to suggest that most social evils were not removed without fierce battles against absurd arguments, vested interests, obscurantism and timidity, and that their removal required considerable effort and determination on the part of men (even if only of obscure men) who realized that it was worth while making a conscious effort to control events." And in this, she concludes, Benthamism, with its emphasis on social action to diminish misery, played, for all its shortcomings, an effective and positive role.

Hart's strictures on conservative revisionism imply, of course, a partial return to the views of the "older historians." The same may

---

53. Oliver MacDonagh, "The Nineteenth-century Revolution in Government: a Reappraisal," *The Historical Journal,* I (1), 1958, pp. 52–67.
54. Jennifer Hart, "Nineteenth-century Social Reform: a Tory Interpretation of History," *Past and Present,* No. 31, July, 1965, pp. 39–61.

be said of Dr. Hobsbawm's discussion of the role of government in economic affairs in his recent work on *Industry and Empire*. Unlike Hart, he does not name the "new" historians from whose opinions he dissents; but his whole argument, in that chapter of his book, is at variance with the views expressed by Kitson Clark and others regarding the concurrence of *laissez-faire* and the "collectivist" State. He agrees that "total government *laissez-faire* is a contradiction in terms"; for "no modern government can *not* influence economic life"; but he insists nevertheless that, far from *laissez-faire* being already a diminishing factor or of little importance, "by the middle of the nineteenth century government policy in Britain came as near *laissez-faire* as has ever been practicable in a modern state"; and he cites the stability of public expenditure per head of population to support his case. But while thus appearing to return to the old Whig tradition, Hobsbawm makes clear that he is not really talking about the same thing as Kitson Clark or Trevelyan. For, he writes,

What is at stake is not the fact of government intervention or even (within certain limits) its weight, but its character. In the classical liberal economy its object is to create and maintain the best conditions for capitalism, which is regarded as an essentially self-regulating and self-expanding system which tends to maximize the 'wealth of the nation'. At the outset of the British Industrial Revolution the major problem was to create these conditions; from about 1846 (the abolition of the Corn Laws) it was to maintain them. From the last quarter of the century it became increasingly clear that they could not be maintained without growing government interference, . . . but until 1931 (the abolition of Free Trade) the attempt to maintain the liberal economy was not abandoned. After 1931 it was. This, in a nutshell, . . . is the history of government policy in the age of British industrial glory.[55]

So here there is clearly a division of opinion between the new conservative historians on the one hand and their socialist and liberal critics on the other. In fact, it might be argued, until the whole matter has been thrashed out more fully, that this is a case of the "new" history (to borrow a phrase from Asa Briggs) replacing the old Whig

55. E. J. Hobsbawm, *Industry and Empire* (Baltimore, 1970), pp. 191–7 (*my Italics*).

"myths" with Tory ones.[56] Yet the same cannot be said of recent historical writing about the events of 1832 and 1846; for on such matters, as we saw, a labor historian like Briggs has been as willing to rewrite the old Whig-type of history as Gash or Kitson Clark. So here, at least, revision has cut across ideologies or party lines; and there is a sufficiently broad consensus of opinion to say that the "older history" of Trevelyan and his associates has been superseded as the result of modern scholarship, the posing of new questions and the opening up of new fields of research.

56. A. Briggs, "Angleterre," in *L'Europe du XIXe et du XXe siécle,* I, p. 489.

V

The Challenge "from Below"

So far, we have been largely concerned with historians' views on what may be termed the "middle-class" challenge to the constituted authorities of the day. A challenge that, as we have seen, assumed a variety of forms, both economic, political and ideological. Meanwhile, "the people"—the peasants, the craftsmen and wage earners of town and countryside—have not been omitted entirely from the account; but they have appeared somewhat as intruders, or as standing on the periphery of events, except when they have been engaged as shock-troops in rebellions or demonstrations inspired by the liberal aristocracy or middle class, as in the insurrections of the Italian *Risorgimento,* the Reform agitation in Britain, and in the Belgian and French revolutions of 1830. (The debate on the events of 1848 will be considered in a later chapter.)

But "the people," even at this time, were not always mere auxiliaries or outsiders. They also, on occasion, played a part in their own right. This could happen in a variety of ways: in riots, labor disputes, working-class rebellions, or, from about the 1830s, through membership of trade unions, socialist clubs or, more simply, of a "labor movement." Not surprisingly, such developments were more frequent at this time in Britain than in the other countries of Europe. So, in England, beginning in the Napoleonic Wars, we have successive outbreaks of Luddism, or machine-breaking, in 1811–12, 1816 and 1822. Meanwhile, there were the march of the unemployed "Blanketeers" and the East Anglian food and machine riots of 1816, the Pentridge rebellion (or Derbyshire Rising) of 1817, and the great Manchester Reform meeting and "Peterloo Massacre" of 1819. After a lull there followed the trade-union agitation and labor disputes of 1829–31, the farm laborers' revolt of 1830, the city riots and Reform Bill agitation of 1831–2; and, most spectacularly, the three great outbreaks of Chartism in 1838, 1842 and 1848.

In France, there were food riots and machine-breaking in the 1820s; but these were of little consequence compared with the insurrections of the Lyons silk-weavers in 1831 and 1834, which, in turn, were followed (or accompanied) by similar outbreaks in Paris in 1832, 1834 and 1839, succeeded by a lull in the 1840s which, in turn, was broken by widespread food riots in 1847. In Germany, such manifestations were rarer still; yet there were riots in Leipzig in 1845, a railway strike in Brandenburg and East-Prussian disturbances in 1846, and food riots in Berlin and weavers' riots in Silesia in 1847. But in France and Germany—as in Italy, Poland and the Austrian Dominions—all such disturbances were eclipsed by the far greater crop of popular outbreaks, both social and political, that occurred in the revolutionary year of 1848.

23. Whigs and Tories Again

It is natural that these protests and manifestations "from below" should not have altogether escaped the notice of historians and particularly those events relating to the birth and development of a trade-union and labor movement. Here, too, there has been a wide diversity of opinion both as to the events themselves and as to the importance that should be accorded to them. To the older school of Whig historians in England, though they were by no means lacking in benevolence towards the working classes, "labor" history was of little importance, or simply no history at all. Justin McCarthy, for example, writing of Chartism in the 1890s, considered that it "did not die of its excesses; it became an anachronism . . . its active or aggressive influence ceased with 1848. The history of the reign of Queen Victoria has not any further to concern itself with Chartism."[1] But such complacency could not, of course, long survive the crises and turmoils of the First World War; and the Whigs of the 1920s (including Trevelyan himself), while still treating such episodes with a degree

1. J. McCarthy, *A History of Our Times* (London, 1895), I, p. 327; *cit.* F. C. Mather, *Chartism* (London, Hist. Assoc., 1965), p. 5.

of condescension, no longer denied them a place in the nation's history. More recently, Trevelyan's disciples, though still loyal to the old Whig tradition, have developed this "assimilative" process further by according the popular element a more honored role. Such is the case with R. J. White, who dedicates his *Waterloo to Peterloo,* an account of the upheavals following the Napoleonic Wars, to the Old Master himself. It is what the author terms "a study in social transition, an essay in what may be called 'suspended revolution' "; and it deals, in particular, with the Luddites, the Derbyshire Rising, the Cato Street conspiracy, and the Peterloo "massacre." It is a warm and compassionate account in which the author shows clearly that his sympathies lie with "the people" and not with the government of Liverpool and Sidmouth and their motley crew of paid informers. Moreover, Peterloo is shown, in true Whig-fashion, to lie along the straight line of progress from Magna Carta to Reform. For "it marked the point of final conversion of provincial England to the doctrine of 'first things first' . . . Henceforth, the people were to stand with ever greater fortitude behind that great movement, which, stage by stage throughout the nineteenth century, was to impose a new political order upon a new society . . . With Peterloo, and the departure of Regency England, parliamentary reform had come of age." Yet he distributes his praises with discrimination. Jeremiah Brandreth and his Pentridge rebels are treated more with contempt than sympathy, as are the "pitiful protagonists" of the Cato Street Plot. "With its frustration," he writes of the latter in roundly denunciatory terms, "the unclean birds who had nested within the Society of Spencean Philanthropists, and who had bedevilled the cause of Radical reform politics for so long, disappeared for ever."[2]

Conservative historians have usually been less generous and compassionate in their appraisal of popular and workers' movements. There are, of course, exceptions and, among them, there is Dr. Kitson Clark. In his article, "Hunger and Politics in 1842,"[3] he shows a considerable sympathy for the plight and an understanding of the

2. R. J. White, *Waterloo to Peterloo* (London, 1957; 1968 edn.), pp. 199–200.
3. In *Journal of Modern History,* XXV, March-December, 1953, pp. 355–74.

motives of the "turn-outs" who marched into Manchester to close down the mills and foundries in August of that year. (It might be suspected, of course, that his strictures on the Anti-Corn Law League, who were suspected of fomenting the disturbance, are as much a blow struck at the Whigs as one struck in the popular cause!) But, generally, conservatives have been more inclined to dismiss such movements as manifestations of the "mob," to side with law and order, and to hold "the people's" leaders up to ridicule. Examples may be found, in an earlier period of British history, in Paul de Castro's *The Gordon Riots* (1926) and Max Beloff's *Public Order and Popular Disturbance 1660-1714* (1938). Nor are they lacking for the first half of the nineteenth century either. One such case is that of Donald Read, whose study on *Peterloo* followed hard on the heels of R. J. White's *Waterloo to Peterloo* which we cited above. But where Mr. White's account is "Whiggish," Dr. Read's is Tory. He largely exonerates Lord Sidmouth and the Manchester Yeomanry of having displayed any excessive harshness in the event, and he takes Mr. White to task for his belief in the political-reforming influence of Peterloo. Moreover, he insists that its designation as a "massacre" "represents another piece of political propaganda"; for "perhaps only in peace-loving England could a death-role of only eleven persons have been so described."[4]

There is also Mr. Gavin Thurston, author of an excellent "whodunnit?" on a little-known episode in London history, *The Clerkenwell Riot*, published in 1967. It is the story of the drama that ensued when a political meeting called by the National Union of the Working Classes off the Gray's Inn Road was set upon by the newly formed Metropolitan Police and a certain Constable Culley was stabbed to death by an unknown assailant. The year was 1833, the year after the First Reform Bill but still one of considerable political commotion. Yet the author's sympathies are so heavily, and uncritically, engaged on the side of the police that he makes little effort to explore the deeper causes and dismisses the rioters as "ready dupes for the agitator" and

4. Donald Read, *Peterloo. The "Massacre" and its Background* (Manchester, 1957), pp. vii–viii.

their organizers as "obscure and maladroit."[5] Perhaps, too (to take a somewhat different example), a similar conservative bias underlies the estimation made of Engels by two Manchester historians, W. O. Henderson and W. H. Chaloner, in the introduction to their edition of *The Condition of the Working Class in England,* published by Blackwell's of Oxford in 1958. "This brash young man," they tell us, "can hardly be taken seriously as a historian." And why was he so angry and intemperate in his attacks on the factory-owners of Manchester? Having returned to Germany to write his book (we learn), he wrote to Marx in March 1845 that he was "living a veritable dog's life" in Barmen. "All this helps," the editors write,

to explain the fury with which Engels attacked the English middle classes in general and the factory owners in particular. At loggerheads with his family and watched by the police, he was a young man with a bad temper who vented his spleen in a passionate denunciation of the factory system as he had recently seen it in England. The unrestrained violence of his language and his complete failure to understand any point of view different from his own may —at any rate to some extent—be explained by the fact that in the winter of 1844–5 Engels was suffering from an overwhelming sense of frustration.[6]

24. The Older Labor Historians

But, more frequently, "labor" history or the history of the common people has been written by "labor" historians or historians with a commitment to the labor or socialist cause. This has been as true of Germany as it has of France and England, though it is natural that it should have been in Britain that such history began to be written first and has assumed the largest proportions. It began with the Fabians, or moderate socialists, of the 1880s; and, under their influence, the Webbs wrote their *History of Trade Unionism* (1911), the Ham-

---

5. Gavin Thurston, *The Clerkenwell Riot: The Killing of Constable Culley* (London, 1962). For a similar approach, see John Stanhope, *The Cato Street Conspiracy* (London, 1962).

6. W. O. Henderson and W. H. Chaloner (eds.), *Engels, The Condition of the Working Class in England* (Stanford, California, 1968), pp. xv, xxix–xxx.

monds their "laborer" trilogy and *The Age of the Chartists,* G. D. H. Cole his trade-union and working-class histories, Cole and Postgate their classic account of *The Common People 1746–1938,* and Mark Hovell and Edouard Dolléans their studies of Chartism. Meanwhile, in France, there there had appeared Emile Levasseur's *Histoire des classes ouvrières* in 1899 and E. Martin Saint-Léon's *Le compagnnonage,* a history of early trade unions, in 1901. These had been followed by O. Festy's work on working-class movements during the July Monarchy in 1908, Pierre Louis's on the working class and trade unions in 1924 and 1927, Fernand Rude's on the silk-weavers of Lyons in 1944, Labrousse's Sorbonne lectures on "le mouvement ouvrier" in 1948, and Jean Bruhat's four-volume study of French working-class movements in 1952. Georges Duveau's study of working-class life under the Second Empire (1946), though mainly concerned with the 1850s and 1860s, has a certain relevance for the earlier period as well. In the case of Germary, where the industrial revolution and working-class movements made a later appearance, there is little to note other than Jürgen Kuczinski's *Die Geschichte der Lage der Arbeiter in Deutchland* (Berlin, 1947). Other books have treated the history of Western European labor as a whole: such are C. R. Fay's *Life and Labour in the Nineteenth Century* (Cambridge, Eng., 1920); Dolléans' *Histoire du mouvement ouvrier* (Paris, 1930); and Kuczinski's *Labour Conditions in Western Europe 1820–1935* (London, 1935).[7]

All these histories have a certain "official" labor stamp about them; they are all, as we have said, whether Marxist or social-democratic, dedicated to labor's cause and, as such, generally quite distinctive in their sympathies from the works we mentioned earlier. But, being "official," or quasi-official, history, they bear certain other hallmarks in addition. One is that they tend to deal with institutions rather than with people. So the focal point is not so much the worker in the street or factory or workshop as the organization, the committee, lodge or

7. For details, see Droz's bibliography in *L'époque contemporaine,* I, pp. 74–8; see also, H. M. Pelling's *History of Trade Unionism* (London, 1963), and E. J. Hobsbawm, "Trade Union Historiography," in *Bulletin of the Society for the Study of Labour History,* London, Spring, 1964.

"movement" (in a purely static sense) to which he may belong. This institutional type of labor history has established a new orthodoxy and respectability of its own, and is common form among this older generation of historians; we find it as much in Cole and Postgate and the Webbs in England as in Levasseur, Dolléans or Labrousse (though here with subtle variations) in France. There are, however, some notable exceptions. Georges Duveau, for example, has made a point of attempting to enter into the "mentality" of the workers he is portraying in the "days" of 1848 and in the Paris of the 1860s; and we shall see in a later chapter how he personalizes the events of 1848 through the eyes of three symbolic Paris tradesmen: a hosier, a cabinet-maker and a mechanic. In England, the Hammonds are a similar exception to the rule. They, too, are concerned with persons rather than with institutions; and in their vindication of the town and country laborers and their savage indictment of early-nineteenth century society, they have brought right to the center of the stage what Mr. Thompson has called "the poor bloody infantry of the Industrial Revolution." It is for this reason perhaps that the Hammonds, for all the criticisms to which they have been recently subjected, have, in many respects, stood the test of time better than any of their contemporaries.

A second feature of this older school of labor history has been a lack of analysis or study-in-depth, an aversion to borrow from the other social sciences, and a tendency to tell a plain and unvarnished tale. This, admittedly, often makes for excellent reading: as witness the great classic on the Chartist Movement left by Mark Hovell when he was killed in action in the First World War. This narrative tradition of labor history has survived and will no doubt continue. A recent (though modest) example is Frederick Harper's *Joseph Capper* (1962), the story of a country blacksmith who became a local Chartist leader and was involved in the riots in the Potteries that followed the "Plug-Plot" strikes of 1842.[8]

Another tendency of the traditional labor historians that has been

8. Mark Hovell, *The Chartist Movement* (New York, 1918); Frederick Harper, *Joseph Capper* (London, 1962).

noted by their critics has been to create a Whig-type of history, or mythology, of their own. Writing of British historiographical trends in the 1950s, Asa Briggs observes that where the newer histories (both conservative and others) have begun to abandon the Whig-style broad historical sweep for the closer examination of problems in depth, the "socialist interpretation" of British history has tended to become fixed in the older "Whiggish" mold. "It tends," he writes, "to trace an uninterrupted line from the radicalism of the eighteenth century to the 'labourism' of the twentieth, with Chartism as a turning-point. Socialist myths, like Whig myths, have their political uses and, like them, they are not entirely false: they contain an important element —but an element only—of truth." And he selects for particular mention Cole and Postgate's book, *The Common People 1746–1938.*[9]

Another aspect of the labor historian's "Whiggery" is picked out by Edward Thompson in commenting on the Hammonds' *The Skilled Labourer.* He is concerned, in particular, with the authors' handling of the nefarious activities of Oliver the Spy and with their discounting of the political element in Lancashire Luddism and in the Pentridge rebellion of 1817. (A similar charge of narrow "economism" has been made by Fernand Rude, in France, against his predecessor, L. Lévy-Schneider's treatment of the Lyons silk-weavers' risings of the 1830s.[10])

The Skilled Labourer [writes Thompson] is a fine book; but its chapters on Luddism read like a brief prepared by the Whig opposition, and intended to discredit the exaggerated claims made by the authorities as to the conspiratorial and revolutionary aspects of the movement. The role of spies and *agents provocateurs* is emphasized to the point where it is suggested that there was no authentic insurrectionary underground and no evidence of delegates passing between the counties . . . Authentic Luddism (it is implied) was without ulterior aims, and was either a matter of spontaneous riot (Lancashire) or an action with strictly limited industrial objectives (Nottingham and Yorkshire).

And why this particular bias, which the Hammonds are said to share with other labor historians, like the Webbs and Cole and Postgate? It

---

9. Briggs, "Angleterre," in *L' Europe du XIXe et du XXe siècle,* I, p. 482.
10. Droz, *op. cit.,* I, p. 76.

is, answers Thompson, because of their "Fabian persuasion," which colors their judgment and prompts them, in looking back on the nineteenth century, to discount such lost causes as food riots, Luddism, and Pentridge and Grange Moor risings, which made no ostensible contribution to the growth of a Labor Movement.[11]

25. The New "Labor" History

A more recent school of labor, or "popular," history has developed since the war; its tendency is Marxist, but even when it professes to be so it is a point that might escape the notice of its readers. Its most distinctive characteristic, perhaps, has been to abandon the old institutional, Labor-Movement oriented, narrative history of the past and to turn towards a more rounded *social* history of both labor and "the people" at large. This new emphasis on people as opposed to institutions is implicit in the title of E. J. Hobsbawm's *Labouring Men* (1964), and it is spelled out more explicitly by the author in his preface:

Most of these [essays] have one negative thing in common. They lie outside the borders of the straightforward chronological or narrative history of labour movements. This was ably pioneered by the Webbs and G. D. H. Cole and in the golden age of British labour history which began about fifteen years ago, a number of excellent scholars have continued, added to, or revised their work. However, *there has been comparatively little work about the working classes as such (as distinct from labour organizations and movements)*, and about the economic and technical conditions which allowed labour movements to be effective, or which prevented them from being effective . . . Most of the essays in this volume belong to the latter category.

And of these eighteen essays, a half-dozen relate to our period, including one on machine-breaking, one on Methodism and revolution, one on the early factory system (the "Dark Satanic Mills"), and a couple on the standard of living debate.[12]

11. E. P. Thompson, *The Making of the English Working Class* (London, 1968 edn.), pp. 629, 647–8.
12. E. J. Hobsbawm, *Labouring Men. Studies in the History of Labour* (New York, 1965), p. vii (*my italics*).

In an issue of *The Times Literary Supplement* of April 1966, devoted to the "New Ways in History," E. P. Thompson welcomed Hobsbawm's book as "the most important" to appear to date in the new historiography of the British trade union movement.[13] In the wider field of labor history, if not of British social history in general, Thompson's own book, *The Making of the English Working Class* (first published in 1963), has probably been the most original and the most influential of all works published since the war. Thompson's concern for "people" as against "movements" or "institutions" is, once more, implicit in his choice of title, and also in the definition of "class" that he gives in his preface: "a historical relationship" which is neither "structure" nor "category," and which "must always be embodied in real people in a real context." Moreover, he sees it as "a social and cultural formation," which can only be studied over a considerable span of time: in this instance over the half-century between 1780 and 1832, which is the span of the book and the time during which "most English working people came to feel an identity against their rulers and employers." The author's presentation, as is usual in this newer labor history, is thematic, not narrative; and, in selecting his themes, he is conscious of challenging the received wisdom of a number of established orthodoxies. He lists these as, first, the "Fabian orthodoxy," in which "the great majority of working people are seen as passive victims of *laissez-faire*"; secondly, the orthodoxy of the empirical economic hsitorians,' with their tendency to reduce workers to "a labour force" or the raw material for statistical tables; and, finally, what he terms the "Pilgrim's Progress" orthodoxy, "in which the period is ransacked for forerunners—pioneers of the Welfare State, progenitors of a Socialist Commonwealth, or (more recently) early exemplars of rational industrial relations." His main quarrel with these orthodoxies is that they smother the working man's own contribution to the "making" of his history and that, by putting a premium on success, they subject the "losers" in the race—the poor stockinger, the Luddite cropper, the "obsolete" handloom weaver, the "utopian" artisan—to "the enormous condescension of posterity"; and to rescue

13. Thompson, "History from Below," *Times Literary Supplement,* 7 April 1966, pp. 279–80.

them from this is one of the major objects of the book.[14]

An essential ingredient in Thompson's "making" of the working class is the use he makes of ideology. The older labor history either ignored this altogether or set its evolution in a conventional trade-union or "labor" mold (though we have seen that writers like Duveau and the Hammonds proved exceptions to this rule). Significant departures from the tradition are found in the work of Hobsbawm and Christopher Hill, such as in the former's *Primitive Rebels* (1959) and the latter's essay on "The Norman Yoke" in the volume on *Democracy and the Labour Movement* (1954), dedicated to the late Marxist scholar, Dona Torr. Hill traces the survival of the legend of "The Norman Yoke," imposed by "the French Bastard and his banditti" on the freedom-loving Anglo-Saxons, through to Chartist times; and he argues that such myths, if "infused with an imaginative spirit," have a valuable part to play in the ideology of a developing working-class movement. Moreover, in his own chosen field of the English seventeenth century, Dr. Hill has long been a foremost exponent of the role of religious dissent as a stimulus to political action; and this is also one of the problems that Thompson sets out to examine in his book. More particularly, he has been concerned with the formative influence of Methodism, which (in contrast to Halévy) he sees equally as an agent of subversion and as an agent of the *status quo*. Moreover, in discussing the extraordinarily pervasive spell exerted by Methodist preaching over men's minds, he picks out for special mention the "obsessional Methodist concern with sexuality" revealed in "the perverted eroticism of Methodist imagery." Elsewhere, in a more conventional mood, he turns, somewhat in the spirit of the Hammonds, to that other great formative influence, the industrial revolution, and to the qualitative changes that it brought to men's way of life. In an earlier chapter, we saw that he characterized the "slight improvement" in living standards experienced in the half-century up to 1840 as "a catastrophic experience"; for, "over the same period there was intensified exploitation, greater insecurity, and increasing human misery." And it is out of this dual experience—of the "slight improve-

14. Thompson, *The Making of the English Working Class*, pp. 9–13.

ment" on the one hand and "the intensified exploitation" on the other
—that "the political and cultural expression of working-class consciousness arose."[15]

One of the established orthodoxies that Thompson objected to was,
as we saw, that of the "Pilgrim's Progress" kind, which puts its money
on the winners and "pioneers" and shovels the losers and lost causes
under the mat. He and other historians have now begun to cast their
nets far wider, to scoop up losers as well as winners, and to depict
labor and laboring men with all their imperfections and weaknesses,
"warts and all." Hobsbawm's "primitive rebels," with their "backward-looking" and irrational manifestations, are an obvious case in
point. In another sense, too, the image of "labor" has become broad-
ened or diluted: a recent paper, for example, argues that the London
Working Men's Association, the author of the famous "People's
Charter," owed a great deal of its impetus and organization to the
radical middle class, thus considerably modifying the traditional picture painted by Mark Hovell and others. Similarly, the "lost cause"
has begun to come into its own. It was, of course, never quite so
systematically cold-shouldered as Thompson would have us believe:
the Hammonds, for instance, painted a searing and compassionate
picture of the greatest "losers" in British labor history, the country
laborers who staged their last desperate revolt in 1830. Some years
ago, too, David Williams wrote his fine study of *The Rebecca Riots*
that convulsed West Wales in the late 1830s and early 1840s. (This,
however, was not entirely a lost cause, as most of the turnpikes and
toll gates destroyed by Rebecca and her "daughters" were never
rebuilt.) And, since Thompson wrote his book, he and others have
turned their attention to the "moral economy" of the "just price" and
to the late-eighteenth and early-nineteenth century food riots that
even the Hammonds eyed with a certain contempt. The first full-
length study to appear in this field has been A. J. Peacock's *Bread or
Blood: A Study of the Agrarian Riots in East Anglia in 1816,* which

15. Hobsbawm, *Primitive Rebels: Studies of Archaic Forms of Social Movement in the
Nineteenth and Twentieth Centuries* (New York, 1963); C. Hill, "The Norman Yoke,"
in *Democracy and the Labour Movement,* John Saville, ed., (London, 1954), pp. 11–66;
Thompson, *op. cit.,* pp. 231, 385–412.

was published, with a commendatory Foreword by Thompson, in 1965. More recently, E. J. Hobsbawm and I have returned to the Hammonds' old theme and rewritten from more extensive records the story of the "last laborers' revolt."[16]

Another development has been to place British labor history in a wider, European and less parochial context. In the case of Chartism, this has resulted, almost fortuitously, from the publication of two new biographies: John Saville's *Ernest Jones: Chartist* (1952) and A. R. Schoyen's *The Chartist Challenge: A Portrait of George Julian Harney* (1958). These both deal with Chartist "physical-force" men, who were generally played down or neglected by the earlier historians. They were also men who developed links with democrats and socialists on the Continent of Europe whose ideas (including socialist ideas) they passed on to their colleagues of the National Charter Association, mainly after the rejection of the third and final Chartist petition of 1848. In consequence, Chartism has become projected, in point of time, beyond its traditionally accepted demise in 1848, and it has also begun to assume a new socialist and international image ignored by the earlier writers. Yet it was an aspect that had not escaped the notice of contemporaries. "Chartism in 1850," wrote a contributor to the first issue of Harney's *Red Republican*, "is a different thing from Chartism in 1840. The leaders of the English Proletarians have proved that they are true Democrats, and no shams, by going ahead so rapidly within the last four years. They have progressed from the idea of a simple *political reform* to the idea of a Social Revolution."[17]

This turn to internationalism has been accompanied by its apparent antithesis, a greater attention to regional studies, to local history; but to a new type of local history which, far from guiding the reader into a cosy parochial niche, gives greater depth, diversity and precision to the picture as a whole. Notable examples of this new type of regional

---

16. D. J. Rose, "The 'People's Charter'," *Past and Present*, no. 36, April, 1967, pp. 73–86; J. L. and B. Hammond, *The Village Labourer* (New York, 1970); David Williams, *The Rebecca Riots. A Study in Agrarian Discontent* (Cardiff, 1953); E. J. Hobsbawm and G. Rudé, *Captain Swing*.
17. Mather, *Chartism*, pp. 5–7; A. Briggs (ed.), *Chartist Studies* (New York, 1959), p. 290.

history are Sydney Pollard's *History of Labour in Sheffield* (1959), C. Wright's *Scottish Chartism* (1952), and the volume of *Chartist Studies* (1959) edited by Asa Briggs. "A study of Chartism," writes Briggs in his opening chapter, "must begin with a proper appreciation of regional and local diversity." For Chartism, as he and his fellow-contributors amply demonstrate, was a many-sided movement, meaning different things to different men, and one whose diversity owed more to local tradition and regional variation in industry, skills and occupations than it did to the particular views and idiosyncracies of its national leaders. So Chartism, writes Briggs, "was a snowball movement which gathered together local grievances and sought to give them common expression in a nation-wide agitation." And it is only by turning the search-light onto what the Chartists called "the localities"—onto London, Manchester, Scotland, Wales, the Potteries, the mining areas and agricultural counties—that a new composite picture may emerge, both fuller and more realistic than the near-monolith presented by the earlier historians. "A new narrative history of Chartism [adds Briggs], long overdue, cannot be written until these and other local histories have been adequately treated."[18]

The turn from institutional to "popular" history has naturally been accompanied by another trend as well: the attempt that has been made by some modern social historians to view their history "from below," by asking new questions and turning for the answers to new grass-roots type records in addition to the old. We have already noted that Dr. David Pinkney, following the precepts of Georges Lefebvre and others, has begun to do this in his studies of the Paris revolutionaries of 1830.* Similar attempts have been made by British historians in their work on "preindustrial" labor movements of the early nineteenth century. There has certainly been no uniformity of method; and, broadly, we may distinguish between two approaches which may, for convenience, be termed the "impressionistic" and the "statistical" or "analytical." The outstanding example of the first is that used by Edward Thompson to construct his great work on *The Making of*

18. *Chartist Studies,* pp. 2–3.
* See pp. 81–82 above

the English Working Class. Not that there is any lack here of analysis based on careful documentary investigation; for Thompson has made fuller use of the Home Office papers in the Public Record Office, the Minutes of the London Corresponding Society in the British Museum and of local collections, both public and private, in Harrogate, Sheffield, Nottingham and the Yorkshire West Riding—not to mention the local press—than any other historian who has worked in this field. Yet his particular concern was to evoke the mood, the mentality and degree of class consciousness of a developing working class, and to do this he could not rely on statistical evidence, which (in his view) would in many cases have proved a positive hindrance and given what he wished to present in a dynamic manner an immobile or static appearance. (Hence, no doubt, his aversion to the practices of "empirical economic historians.") In consequence, he turned to the literary evidence afforded by a wide range of pamphlets and periodicals, mainly from the British Museum and the John Rylands Library in Manchester, which included folk songs, ballads, oral tradition and hymns. And it was largely with the aid of "impressionistic" sources of this kind that he was able to construct his picture of the developing ideology of class.[19]

In writing our book on the agricultural laborers of 1830, Eric Hobsbawm and I were faced with different problems and had different aims in mind; and where Thompson's grass-roots history leaned towards literature, ours leaned more perceptibly towards the social sciences. Apart from the "when?" and "where?" questions relating to the sequence of events, we were concerned with such questions as: what was the society out of which the riots grew? how did they begin and how did they spread? why did they begin and why did they stop? who took part in them? what forms did the rioting take? why was the threshing machine viewed with such particular aversion? how were the riots distributed? why was one region, or one village, affected and not another? who were the rioters' victims and who were their allies? what was the cost both in material damage and in human suffering?

19. Thompson, *The Making of the English Working Class,* pp. 941–4. See also Arthur Marwick, *The Nature of History* (London, 1970), pp. 133–4.

and what was the riots' place in British labor history? (And some of our critics would have had us ask a great many more.) So our enquiry was both descriptive and analytical, but mainly it was analytical: we wanted to know, as precisely as possible, who the rioters were, why they rioted, how they behaved and why their behavior was different in one place from what it was in another. We were admittedly, like Thompson, concerned with motives and mentality, but even more with economic factors (such as prices, wages, Poor Law allowances, tithes, rents and profits), topography and patterns of behavior. In consequence, the records we consulted were often analytical and statistical, less often literary and impressionistic. So we were on common ground in consulting Home Office papers, the London and provincial press, and a variety of memoirs and the descriptive accounts of eyewitnesses and public bodies; in fact, we had this in common with earlier historians as well. But where Thompson's innovation was to lay such store on literary sources, ours was rather to make a fuller use of statistical tables and Parliamentary reports, the records of insurance companies and county treasurers' account books, and a large variety of prison and judicial records—the records of quarter sessions in a score of English counties, assizes records, gaol registers, and the convict records (relating to some 500 transported persons) in the archives of Tasmania and New South Wales.[20]

Sometimes, then, the turn taken by the more recent "popular" or labor history has brought the historian into closer association with the social sciences: in an earlier chapter, we saw how this relationship developed in the case of urban and population studies and studies of the industrial revolution. Historians of popular movements have been slower to respond: except perhaps in France, but their work has been largely concerned with earlier periods of history. In Britain, Hobsbawm was gently impelled in this direction when he became engaged in his study of the archaic and millennial movements that he records in his *Primitive Rebels*. I, too, have felt a similar urge in the course of studying the "crowd"; and I have attempted to construct a model, on broadly social-scientific lines, of popular movements arising in

20. *Captain Swing*, pp. 367–71.

France and England in the century leading up to 1848. This "preindustrial crowd", as I have termed it, has (in my view) certain features that distinguish it from those arising in earlier and postindustrial times. I have classified these distinguishing features as follows: first, the prevalence of the rural food riot as the typical form of disturbance; second, the resort to direct action and violence to property; third, "spontaneity" and lack of organization; fourth, leadership drawn from outside the "crowd"; fifth, the "crowd's" mixed composition, with the emphasis on small shopkeepers and craftsmen in towns and weavers, miners and laborers (or peasants) in villages; and, sixth, as a prime motive of rebellion, a "backward-looking" concern for the restoration of "lost" rights. All these features, I have argued, are the reflection of society itself and, as society changes—as it moves into its next, industrial, phase—they tend to disappear and to give way to others, with a period of transition (in the case of France and England) somewhere about the 1840s.[21]

But these are only broad and tentative conclusions, arrived at by somewhat unsophisticated means; and, like all norms and patterns in history, those I have attempted to establish are riddled with exceptions. Much more work will obviously have to be done to give them more solid substance, particularly around the "twilight" period of transition leading from the old society to the new, somewhere around the 1840s or 1850s. And this is where, in the case of France, Mr. Charles Tilly, with his far more sophisticated training in the social sciences, comes to the historian's aid. For Mr. Tilly, as was mentioned in an earlier chapter,* is engaged on a long-term investigation of all the social and political disturbances occurring in France from 1830 to 1960, with particular and more immediate emphasis on the thirty years between 1830 and 1860. During this shorter period, he has already, with the aid of computer and punched cards and his own considerable skill as a social analyst, compiled a list of 674 disturbances that he has begun to classify. In the course of assembling his

---

21. G. Rudé, "The 'Pre-industrial' Crowd," *Flinders Journal of History and Politics,* I, 1969, pp. 4–18. See also my *The Crowd in History, 1730–1848* (New York, 1964).
* See p. 83 above

data, he has been concerned with one particular set of questions that have a bearing on my own: how and why and at what precise point did the forms of popular protest change somewhere between 1845 and 1855? His findings are not completed (nor can they be until he has pushed his enquiry up to at least the 1860s); but he has already (he is writing in mid-1969) made a number of observations that have some relevance not only for France, but for "preindustrial" disturbances as a whole. They are roughly as follows:

(1) The composition of participants remained remarkably constant up to about February 1848, being mainly based on the craftsmen and shop-keepers of the typical Paris trades. After that (in June 1848) there was a dramatic shift: fewer shopkeepers and craftsmen in the luxury trades (e.g. goldsmiths and printers), and more factory-based mechanics and semiskilled construction workers. But, in view of the different nature of the next great outbreak—in 1851—it is not possible to say that this was a permanent trend.

(b) The character of political conflicts in France changed significantly be-tween April and December 1848. Demands become more "forward-looking," disturbances more carefully timed and better organized; and this set the pattern for all subsequent political activity and protest.

(c) The general pattern of protest changed significantly somewhere about 1850. Specifically, Mr. Tilly writes: "The 1850s saw a decline of property damage, of struggles for control of particular commodities or persons, of protests against particular actions of others, of demands for specific local changes; struggles for control of places, protests against contrasts like prices, and demands for general social changes assumed larger places than before. Concretely, the attack on machines, the tax rebellion, the invasion of land and the food riot virtually disappeared."

(d) It appears likely that the new ("industrial") pattern of disturbance was well established by the time of the great strikes that took place at Saint-Etienne, Anzin and other industrial centers in the late 1860s.

Yet (Mr. Tilly tells us) there is a strong element of doubt: partly because the investigation has not yet reached the 1860s; partly because of the paucity of disturbances during the 1850s (a period of severe repression); partly, too, because such disturbances as there were (but were they typical?) appear to revert to a "preindustrial" pattern. So he concludes: "We leave our painting on the easel, unfinished . . . It will take more chipping and rubbing, greater subtlety, more powerful tools." Yet he adds that his findings, incomplete as they are, have perhaps the merit of underlying a simple, but neglected truth: that "collective violence depends intimately on the political process, and its very nature changes as political men change their ways of organizing political action."[22]

But, of course, such studies as these, with their highly sophisticated analysis of data, provide no more certain guarantees that we shall arrive at a perfect understanding of the "submerged" classes and movements of the period than does Thompson's *Making of the English Working Class.* They are two entirely different methods of looking at a similar problem in depth; neither can claim a monopoly of wisdom, and the one is no adequate substitute for the other. We shall need both types to unravel—on a far wider front than has been attempted up to now—the numerous and mainly unsolved problems attending the study of history "from below."

22. Charles Tilly, "How Protest Modernized in France, 1845 to 1855," paper read to the Conference on Applications of Quantitative Methods to Political, Social and Economic History, Univ. of Chicago, June, 1969 (in typescript), esp. pp. 36, 38–9, 55–7, 61–5. My thanks are due to Mr. Tilly for allowing me to cite this paper.

VI

The Revolutions of 1848

The year 1848, "the year of revolutions," forms a fitting climax to the movements and events we have been considering in our last three chapters. In that year, revolutions broke out in France, Germany, parts of Poland, Italy and the Austrian Empire and may be said, broadly speaking, to have tapped the resources of all those ideological, political and social movements that we have seen developing since the close of the Napoleonic Wars. Even in England, which had no revolution, it was in that year that Chartism, the most developed expression of the "preindustrial" working-class movement, had its third, and virtually its final, phase. The first of the revolutions broke out in Sicily in January, but the crucial spark was provided by the February events in Paris which toppled the monarchy of Louis Philippe. Within a few days there followed revolutionary outbreaks in Naples and Tuscany; in March, there were revolutions in Turin, Prague, Vienna, Budapest, Milan, Venice, Berlin and Baden; in April, there were insurrections in Poland and throughout the Austrian provinces; and there was a short-lived Irish rebellion in July.[1] In November, a popular uprising drove the Pope from Rome; a Roman Republic was proclaimed in the following February and an independent Hungarian Republic in April. But long before this, the revolutionary tide, having reached its peak in April 1848, had begun to recede. Revolution was crushed in Naples in May; in June, Prague was bombarded into submission and a workers' insurrection in Paris was stamped out in blood; in July, the Irish rising was crushed almost as soon as it had begun, and the Habsburgs, after defeating the Piedmontese and their allies at Custozza, reestablished their authority in Lombardy; and Vienna was recaptured by the Imperial army in October. In March of the next year,

1. For Ireland, see Denis Gwynn, *Young Ireland in 1848* (Cork, 1949).

the Austrian Parliament was dissolved. In April, the German revolution collapsed after Frederick William IV had refused the crown offered him by the Parliament at Frankfurt. In July, the Roman Republic fell to the French and the Venetian Republic to the Austrians, and the Hungarian revolution was crushed by a combined Austro-Russian force in August. In November 1850, the Prussians capitulated to the Austrians at Olmütz and solemnly renounced all further attempts to unify Germany. Finally, in December 1851, the era of revolutions was rounded off by Louis Napoleon's *coup d'état* in France and the suppression of the liberal Constitution and the return to absolutist government in Vienna.

26. *Causes and Origins*

Historians have naturally differed and argued about the nature and significance of these events, both in their European and their purely national context. Let us first consider certain views concerning the origins and causes of the outbreaks of that year.

The older historians—those of the nineteenth and earlier twentieth century—though often deeply divided by their sympathies and antipathies towards these revolutions, were generally agreed that their origins must be sought in political conflicts and the fermentation of ideas; anything like an *economic* or a *social* explanation was far from their thoughts. Moreover, they were inclined to treat their own national revolutions in isolation and, in so far as they sought a wider context for the events of 1848, they sought it rather in their own national history than in any common European experience. Thus to Italians, the outbreaks of 1848 naturally appeared to lie within the context of the *Risorgimento* as a whole, to Germans as a curtain-raiser to the more "realistic" unification of 1871, and to Frenchmen as another step in the long series of political convulsions that had rent their country since the abdication of Napoleon. Such is the case with that unusual, and sometimes perceptive, chronicler of the events of 1848 in France, the Comte Imbert de Saint-Amand. His book, *The Revolution of 1848*, appeared in English translation in 1895. It is not particularly distinguished and it is conventional enough in its treatment of the outbreak of February 1848 as a largely political event arising in a setting that is exclusively French. Yet it is unusual for the points of resemblance and divergence that it draws between the two successive revolutions of 1830 and 1848; in fact, in the author's words: "February was the imitation—I had almost said the parody—of July." Some of the points of resemblance are trivial enough: he notes, for example, that the February "days," like those of July, were three in number; and that, on both occasions, the ladies of the Court "showed more energy than the men." Other judgments, however, are more significant, as when he notes the remarkable indifference of Parisian opinion, already exercised by other affairs, to French military victories in Algiers in both July 1830 and January 1848. He observes:

People were as ungrateful to the older branch of the Bourbons as to the younger. Under the Restoration, as under the government of King Louis Philippe, there were Frenchmen ungrateful enough not to rejoice at the successes of France, because those successes might consolidate a dynasty which they detested.

More curious is the difference that he notes in religious attitudes in the two revolutions; for "the second had not the same character of impiety as the first," and "the Revolution of July remained as Christian as that of 1830 was Voltairian." He records in particular the chorus of approval that greeted Lacordaire when he ascended the pulpit of Notre Dame in his Dominican habit three days after the revolution began. And he concludes the volume by observing that these same revolutionaries had sacked the Tuileries and Palais Royal and burned down the *château* of Neuilly; "but they had not profaned the churches. They had burned the throne, but had respected the altar. France has not ceased to be the great Catholic nation. The crowns are broken. The Cross remains."[2]

Where Saint-Amand is a traditionalist, whose relatively favorable picture of the revolutionaries of 1848 is influenced by evident hostility to the monarchy of Louis Philippe, the first English historian to comment on the European events of 1848, Edward Stillingfleet Cayley, a barrister of the Inner Temple in London, is a typical middle-to-

2. Imbert de Saint-Amand, *The Revolution of 1848* (London, 1895), pp. 4, 329–35.

late century Whig. He is, therefore, in general sympathy with the revolutionists' aims, though he naturally deplores the "savagery" and violence of the "mob." But the main interest of his book lies in the fact that it is probably the first attempt made (it appeared in 1856) to present a detailed and comprehensive account of all the revolutions occuring in that year. Not only does the revolution in France (the one most familiar to English readers and to which he devotes six chapters of his first volume) come into his picture, but those in Italy, Germany and the Austrian Empire as well; and, for good measure, he has a chapter on the Irish rebellion and another in which he explains (in mainly, but not exclusively, political terms) why there was no revolution in England. So the book is of considerable historiographical interest and, in certain respects, it breaks fresh ground. But it still strongly bears the mark of its times: each revolution is treated in isolation and there is no introductory or interlocking chapter that links the revolutions together or even one revolution with the next.[3]

In fact, apart from the Mazzinians and the Marxists (each of whom had international revolutionary connections), few writers were inclined to see these revolutions as part of a common pattern or to relate them to a common European context. And these few were likely to be those hostile observers, and later historians, to whom all such manifestations appeared as the outcome of an international conspiracy. The "conspiracy theory" of revolution is, of course, a familiar feature of conservative, or ultraconservative, historiography and has by no means been confined to the events of 1848. Sometimes it assumes a scholarly or sophisticated form, as in Edmund Burke's *Thoughts on the Revolution in France* or in Cochin's later study of the literary and secret societies which, he believed, played a large part in causing the Revolution of 1789. More often, it finds a vulgarly polemical, or even paranoiac, expression, as in the numerous lurid *exposés,* extending from medieval to modern times, of the alleged conspiratorial and antinational activities of *illuminati,* freemasons or Jews. Probably the French and Russian revolutions of the eighteenth

---

3. Edward Stillingfleet Cayley, *The European Revolutions of 1848,* 2 vols. (London, 1856).

and twentieth centuries have elicited a larger crop of these outpour-
ings than any others; but the revolution of 1848 has not been entirely
neglected. An example of this lunatic-fringe type of historiography of
revolution is that provided, some forty years ago, by the Vicomte
Léon de Poncins' *The Secret Powers behind Revolution: Freemasonry
and Judaism* (1929). Of the leaders of 1848, Mazzini, Garibaldi and
Kossuth are all said to have been masons, as are no fewer than nine
of the eleven members of the Provisional Government in Paris, who
enjoyed the particular support of "forty thousand masons, distributed
in more than five hundred workshops, forming between them but one
single heart and mind"! Jews and freemasons, moreover, the author
claims, were closely related; and "while studying Free Masonry we
have seen the Jew at work in all the secret societies which promote
revolutions"; and "during those years [after 1830] their bankers, their
industrial magnates, their poets, their writers, their demagogues
. . . strove for the same end."[4]

The conspiracy explanation of revolution dies hard and, even today,
it finds adherents and is apt to resurrect itself in a variety of guises;
but, at least, such crude extravagances as these have ceased, since
Nazi times, to command the respectful attention of any body of
professional historians. And, generally speaking, less attention is paid
to "plots" and more to the common ideological or economic and
social background out of which such revolutions as those of 1848
arose. "There was no plot," writes M. Charles Pouthas of the outbreaks of 1848, "and the revolutions were not concerted"; but, nevertheless, for all their diversity, he points as a link between them to a
similar revolutionary program and vocabulary and to the inspiration
of a common ideology. And this, it has been generally agreed, was,
in the first place, compounded of the two first of the *idées-force,* or
guiding principles, that we considered in an earlier chapter: liberalism
and nationalism. The liberalism of 1848, continues Pouthas, was of
the French rather than of the English or American kind and was
composed of three elements, each of which attracted differing groups

4. Vicomte Léon de Poncins, *The Secret Powers behind Revolution: Freemasonry and Judaism* (London, 1929), pp. 51, 65, 120–1.

of adherents: the liberal individualism of Benjamin Constant (popular in Switzerland and Germany), the liberal catholicism of Lamennais and *L'Avenir* (popular in Catholic Belgium, the Rhineland and Bavaria), and the Messianic republicanism which looked to Paris as the Mecca of international revolution (popular in France and Italy and in the south and west of Germany). Nationalism, on the other hand, Pouthas argues, was of two contrasting, and often contradictory, kinds: the French and the German. The French, deriving from the rationalism of the Enlightenment and 1789, "saw the nation as a spiritual community formed by the voluntary association of free men"; whereas the German, nurtured by Hegel's philosophy, Romanticism, philology and law, "saw the nation as a natural, primitive organism, endowed with specific genius that found expression in language, customs and history." The first conception inspired the Italians and the Irish, while the second found its firmest foothold in Germany and the Austrian Empire. The first was the natural ally of liberalism, the second its antithesis; as in Germany, where "the two movements were so far distinct that liberalism, inspired by the French example, was virtually a counterpole to nationalism, which was nurtured primarily on hatred of France."[5]

This "common ideology" of the revolutions of 1848 is stressed in their different ways by writers as diverse as Croce, Namier, Hobsbawm and Valsecchi. Croce terms them a "complex of liberal-national revolutions," in which "it seemed as though one and the same daemon were agitating the entire mass of Europe; and under this aspect 1848 was also one of those moments when the historical unity of European life, ordinarily concealed by the conflicts of the various states, leaps to the eye and seems to call for a political unity as well."[6] To Namier, though his picture of the events of 1848 is as far removed from Croce's as chalk from cheese, it appeared, too, that "the European Continent responded to the impulses and trends of the revolution with a remarkable uniformity . . . ; but then the common denominator was ideologi-

5. Charles Pouthas, "The Revolutions of 1848," in *New Camb. Mod. Hist.*, X, pp. 389–415.
6. Croce, *History of Europe in the Nineteenth Century*, pp. 168–9

cal and even literary, and there was a basic unity and cohesion in the intellectual world of the European Continent, such as usually asserts itself in the peak period of its spiritual development."[7] Hobsbawm does not dissent, though he stresses, more particularly, the importance of an international tradition: "This common outlook was strongly reinforced by the strong tradition of internationalism, which survived even among those separatist nationalities who refused to accept the automatic leadership of any country—i.e. of France, or rather Paris . . . The cause of all nations was the same . . . National prejudices . . . would disappear in the world of fraternity. Attempts to set up international revolutionary bodies never ceased, from Mazzini's *Young Europe* designed as a counter to the old Carbonari-masonic internationals—to the *Democratic Association for the Unification of all Countries of 1847* . . . Like fascism in the 1930s, absolutism in the 1830s and 1840s bound its common enemies together."[8] Valsecchi also links the common ideology of revolution with the attempt to forge closer bonds of international solidarity. He writes, "There is no doubt that there is a common ideological base which, everywhere, provides the primary impulse or motive force"; and to this there "responds an effective international solidarity among the revolutionary elements." And he instances the bonds established between the Italian Mazzini and the Hungarian Kossuth, between Ledru-Rollin and Mieroslawski, and between Louis Blanc in France and Hecker, Struve, Herwegh and Blum in Germany. "The Rhineland insurgents," he continues, "draw strength from the committees in France and Switzerland. Wandering champions of democracy, like the Hungarian Stefan Türr, appear on the revolutionary battle-fields of Italy and Germany; Vienna, in the delirium of newly won democratic rights, garlands with flowers the Hungarian delegation come to demand their national independence; and the people of Berlin secure the release of Polish patriots from their prisons. A single thread unites, in both thought and action, the revolutionary movement

7. Sir Lewis Namier, *1848: The Revolution of the Intellectuals* (New York, 1964), pp. 3–4.
8. Hobsbawm, *The Age of Revolution*, pp. 129–31.

spread over the Continent of Europe."[9]

There has, in fact, for many years been a wide consensus among historians over this common ideology of the revolutions of 1848. But, for some time now, it has also become increasingly evident to many that a European phenomenon that involved manufacturers, peasants and urban workers as well as liberal aristocrats and a professional *bourgeoisie* could not be explained in purely political or ideological terms. "The social problem," writes Pouthas, "was less immediate, but because it concerned the masses possessed overwhelming significance"; and Jean Dautry, a French Marxist, in writing of the economic crisis of 1847, notes the "ravages" that it caused among the commercial and industrial middle classes and the impetus given to the early workers' movements by low wages, rising prices and unemployment.[10] Contemporaries—Marx, Engels and Tocqueville among them —had not failed to appreciate the significance of these factors and the social antagonisms they engendered; but they were largely neglected by historians for the next eighty years. The first historical studies to pay serious attention to them appeared in the 1920s. Ervin Szabo, a Hungarian, published in 1921 a book on the social conflicts of 1848; and, in 1929, Halfdan Koht, a Norwegian historian and later Prime Minister, stressed the role of the peasantry in a pioneering study of Norwegian peasant movements from the sixteenth to the nineteenth centuries. It was only twenty years later, however, at the time of an international congress held in Paris to celebrate the centenary of the revolutions of 1848, that what had been only an occasional trickle became almost a flood. At that congress, papers were read by Polish, Czech, Hungarian and Roumanian historians, which stressed the need to go beyond the old ideological interpretations and to pay far greater attention to the economic and social aspirations of manufacturers, workers and peasants, and, in particular, to the ancient grievances over land, serfdom, tithe and feudal obligation that lay at the base of the great peasant insurrections of that year. Thus N. Gasirow-

9. Valsecchi, "L'évolution politique," in *L'Europe du XIXe et du XXe siècle*, I, p. 278.
10. Pouthas, *op. cit.*, p. 391; Jean Dautry, *1848 et la IIe République* (Paris, 1957), p. 33

ska, a Polish historian, insisted on the importance of such factors as the abolition of serfdom and the free sale of land to explain "the part played by the peasantry in the struggle for national liberation"; and Adolf Klima, a Czech, closely related the new sense of national consciousness among his people to "the upsurge of Czech industry and the birth of a new social class"; while the Roumanian Michael Roller wrote in the same year that "the revolution of 1848 opened up for Roumanians the prospect of becoming proprietors as well as citizens, without which liberty and equality would be only empty shadows; . . . it was a social revolution."[11]

These new preoccupations were by no means confined to the historians of Eastern Europe; Frenchmen, Italians, Americans and Englishmen also played a part; yet it is probably true that those influenced by Marxism did so more readily than others. At a conference at Perugia, also held in the centenary year, G. Luzzato and G. Falco read papers on "social classes" and "social aspects" of the Italian revolutions; D. Demarco wrote three "social" studies of the Roman revolution between 1944 and 1950; and Guido Quazza's *La Lotta soziale nel Risorgimento* was published at Turin in 1951. An earlier Marxist interpretation of the German events of 1848 by K. Kersten attributed the political fiasco of that year to *bourgeois* fears of a rising working class. Since then, and particularly in the last twenty years, similar studies have multiplied apace. In England and America, they are still comparatively rare; yet we can cite a number of examples. We have already noted Theodore Hamerow's work on Germany, in which he writes that in studying the causes and results of the revolution of 1848, "it became apparent that the Revolution was the expression not only of ideological forces like nationalism and liberalism, but also of deep-seated popular dissatisfactions engendered by the transition from agrarian manorialism to industrial capitalism." And, in England, even Namier, for all the importance he attaches to the role of "the intellectuals," concedes that "there was also an economic and social background to the revolution" and has given us some of the

11. Robert Demoulin, "Nationalité et équilibre," in *L'Europe du XIXe et du XXe siècle,* II, pp. 797–9.

most vivid pages written on the peasant outbreak in Galicia in 1846. Other English historians, possibly influenced by Louis Chevalier, have given the "social factor" a somewhat different twist by stressing the importance of demography, particularly the growth and size of cities. Thus A. J. P. Taylor, in his work on the Habsburg Empire, attributes a major role in the Austrian revolution to the rapid growth of Vienna, whose population almost doubled between 1815 and 1848. David Thomson, the author of *Europe since Napoleon*, extends the canvas to Europe as a whole:

The revolutions of 1848 were, in origin and impetus, the work of towns. Throughout the whole of Europe the course of events at first turned upon the actions of town dwellers: it was London and Birmingham, Paris and Brussels that set the pace ... It has been pointed out that in 1848 a revolution occurred in eastern Europe wherever there was a town with more than 100,000 inhabitants ... The increase came largely from immigration from the countryside, and industrial development was not sufficiently advanced to absorb the rapid increase. Before 1848 the labor supply grew faster than industry, with the result that towns experienced a declining standard of life and a phase of acute hardship and unemployment. The conditions bred the revolutionary spirit and provided the concentration of numbers and strength which a revolutionary movement needed in order to challenge established authority. Similar conditions existed in Milan, Florence and Rome, and to a lesser extent in Berlin; they did not exist in Budapest or Prague which were smaller and growing more slowly.[12]

Yet it is not so surprising, in view of current trends in French historical writing, that what is probably the most significant contribution to this whole debate should have come from France. The French economic historian C.-E. Labrousse also chose the centenary of 1848 to read an important paper: in this case on the part played by economic, rather than social or demographic, factors as a stimulus to revolution. As with the earlier revolutions of 1789 and 1830, Labrousse closely relates the outbreak of the revolution of 1848 to movements of prices and wages. In 1846–7, the price of wheat rose by 100 to 150% (compared with 50% in 1830), while wages fell (by 30% in

12. Demoulin, *op. cit.*, p. 799; Hamerow, *Restoration, Revolution, Reaction*, p. viii; Namier, *op. cit.*, pp. 4, 12–17; A.J.P. Taylor, *The Habsburg Monarchy 1809–1918*, p. 58; David Thomson, *Europe since Napoleon*, p. 206.

textiles alone). Yet he notes that while wages remained low, prices fell in early 1848 and were to stay low for several years to come. So it was not in the trough of the crisis, but during the slow upward movement that followed, that the political explosion erupted. "The wave of high prices had spread over the country like a flood, and, like a receding tide, it left behind it a ruined population." So the economic crisis, he insists, is due far more to "natural" than to "anthropomorphic" causes; yet the workers and middle classes, who suffer acutely from its effects, believe it is man-made and blame the government; so "the crisis arouses, intensifies, concerts and synchronizes all popular discontents." Politics thus follows in the wake of economics; there comes what Labrousse calls a *conjoncture* between the political and economic crisis; and the revolution results—a revolution to whose outbreak, in his view, the economic factor has made the principal, though by no means the only, contribution.[13] This "dualist" interpretation of the origins of revolution has made a considerable impression on Labrousse's fellow-historians in France; and he has subsequently edited a volume of a dozen papers on various aspects of the crisis and depression of the French economy between 1846 and 1851.[14]

By and large, this new orientation given by Labrousse and others to the study of revolution has, to some degree or another, left its mark on both the general histories and the monographs of 1848; and not many historians would now think it proper to omit from their accounts such factors as peasant land-hunger, wages and prices, or the financial and economic crisis of 1847. In fact, nearly all the historians we have cited, whether conservative, liberal or Marxist (Namier, Pouthas and Hobsbawm may serve us as examples), have balanced their presentation of the common ideology of revolution with factors such as these. Yet some historians in the West, though not entirely resistant to these developments, have thought the new trend has gone too far. Among them is E. L. Woodward, who, already in 1934, wrote

13. C.-E. Labrousse, "1848–1830–1789. Comment naissent les révolutions," in *Actes du Congrès historique du centenaire de la Révolution de 1848* (Paris, 1949), pp. 1–31; *cit.* J.-B Duroselle, *De 1815 a nos jours* (Paris, 1964), pp. 272–3.
14. C.-E. Labrousse (ed.), *Aspects de la crise et de la dépression de l'économie française au milieu du XIXe siècle 1846–1851* (La Roche-sur-Yon, 1956).

that "one must not exaggerate the importance of these economic causes. In the past they have been too much ignored by historians, but the pendulum was swinging too far in the other direction."[15] Valsecchi, too, while showing no inclination to return to the liberal idealism of Croce, has spoken up (in papers published in 1949 and 1959) against what he considers to be the "excessive" and "one-sided" materialism of certain of his Italian colleagues.[16] Another sceptic is Professor J. L. Talmon, of the Hebrew University at Jerusalem. Like Valsecchi, Talmon is by no means averse to striking a balance between the ideological and the socio-economic factors; and he writes at the opening of his book, *Romanticism and Revolt*, in terms which might have come from Hobsbawm: "It was the coalescence of two vast Revolutions, the French and the Industrial, that determined both the shape of things and the frame of mind of the age up to 1848." Yet, in his Foreword, he spells out his own personal preference more precisely:

My natural penchant has led me to dwell more on patterns of mind and behavior than on the substratum of social-economic relations. I have done this partly because of my reluctance simply to copy or paraphrase what others have already done on the basis of first-hand knowledge and with a competence much greater than I could aspire to. I am also convinced that the recent tendency to turn history into a statistical survey and sociological analysis— one might call it social geography—has gone far enough, and that it is time for a corrective in the direction of human drama.[17]

One may be inclined to give a sympathetic hearing to such a *cri de coeur:* it sounds like Edward Thompson's quarrel with the statisticians. Yet one may be tempted to enquire further as to what sort of "human drama" is intended. Is the "corrective" (not only in this case, but in others) to take the form of a return to the safe haven of the history of ideas and away from the "excessive" materialism of the 1950s? Is it to be a turn from the history of the people at large back to the history of the people "at the top"? Or is it simply, as in

15. E. L. Woodward, *French Revolutions* (London, 1934), p. 152.
16. Demoulin, *op. cit.*, p. 799; Valsecchi, *op. cit.*, pp. 276–8.
17. J. L. Talmon, *Romanticism and Revolt. Europe 1815–1848* (New York, 1967), pp. 10, 8.

Thompson's case, a plea for a social history of people in the place of abstract principles and institutions? Some historians will favor one, some another, and some perhaps a combination of two out of the three. And this is, of course, partly what the discussion of the revolutions of 1848, as of so many other questions in history, is all about.

27. The Revolution in France

French historians of the revolutions of 1848 fall into three broad categories: conservative monarchists, liberal republicans and Marxists. Of the three, there is little doubt that the conservative school, which has displayed such painstaking energy in discrediting the revolution of 1789, has, in the case of that of 1848, proved a disappointment and come off the worst. This may seem surprising in view of the excellent ammunition provided antidemocrats and antirepublicans by Alexis de Tocqueville's *Recollections.*[18] Yet Tocqueville, though a stern critic of democracy, has done little to inspire confidence among monarchists; and it may well be that, as Paul Farmer wrote some years ago, "French conservatives have preferred to direct their attack on 'the new regime' to its first great manifestation in 1789, and they have rather scorned to trouble with the smaller game of 1848."[19]

At all events, the traditional conservative historiography of 1848 began in the 1870s and virtually ceased in the 1880s. Apart from the general histories, in which it still makes a perennial incursion, it has confined itself to two two-volume works of substance: Victor Pierre's *Histoire de la République de 1848* of 1873–4 and Pierre de la Gorce's *Histoire de la Seconde République française* of 1887. Pierre, writing as a monarchist critic in the early unstable days of the Third Republic, looked back on the revolution of 1848 as another, and in this case futile, attempt by *bourgeois* republicans to upset the stability of France's traditional institutions; and (to quote Paul Farmer again) "he regarded the revolution of 1848 as the foredoomed work of men who had set out to found a stable government on the principles of popular

18. *The Recollections of Alexis de Tocqueville,* J. P. Mayer (ed.) (New York, 1959).
19. Paul Farmer, "Some Frenchmen review 1848," *Journ. Mod. Hist.,* XX, No. 4, December, 1948, p. 320.

revolution and who therefore had no means with which to defend their new regime against the chronic turbulence of the masses." La Gorce, like Pierre, was a constitutional monarchist, but his emphasis was different. Writing soon after General Boulanger's unsuccessful attempt to hoist himself to power, he was acutely conscious of the renewed dangers of Bonapartism. Thus to him the revolutionaries of 1848 stood indicted on a double charge; not only had they overthrown a monarchy of which the author approved, but they had paved the way for the dictatorial rule of the adventurer Louis Napoleon.[20]

The conservatives having so early vacated the field, it was taken over by their republican rivals—more often by moderates—towards the end of the century. Yet they, too, were slow to respond: they confined their observations to works of general history (such as those by Emile Bourgeois and Gabriel Hanotaux) and seemed inclined, like the conservatives, to view the events of 1848 as a poor replica of those of 1789 or 1793. They were, in fact, more inclined to direct attention to the evils of the monarchy of Louis Phillippe and to the villainies of the usurper, Louis Napoleon, than to the activities of their forbears of 1848, which, being so patently less glorious than those of the men of 1789, they treated with a certain ambivalence. Yet two works, which belong broadly to the republican tradition, are worthy of brief comment—the first by a socialist of the early twentieth-century Millerand school, the second by a typical Republican-Socialist of the First World War. Georges Renard's *La République de 1848* is the standard moderate socialist account of the events of 1848, contributed to Jean Jaurès' monumental socialist history of France; it appeared in 1907. Renard follows the republican tradition in his justification of the revolution of 1848 as a remedy for the ills of the monarchy of Louis Philippe and in the unflattering portrait that he paints of Louis Napoleon. Yet he departs significantly from the bourgeois-republican pattern in aligning himself firmly with the workers manning the June barricades: here he broadly follows the interpretation put forward by

20. Farmer, *op. cit.*, pp. 320–1. See also Gordon Wright, *France in Modern Times. 1760 to the Present*, pp. 264–5.

Marx in his two contemporary studies, *The Class Struggles in France* (*1848–50*) and *The Eighteenth Brumaire of Louis Napoleon Bonaparte*. It is also a work of considerable compassion. As a scholarly exercise, however, it is far outmatched by Charles Seignobos's *La Révolution de 1848—Le Second Empire,* which was published as part of Lavisse's *History of France* in 1921. Seignobos's account is the standard treatise of the republican school of historians and presents a solid *apologia* for the successive Republics of 1848 and 1870. But it is more than this; it is also (even more than Renard's and far more than those of his conservative predecessors) a *social* history and is a mine of information on French industry and agriculture, on the growth of Paris, and on the whole complexity of the socio-political events of 1848.[21]

But the really decisive turn to the new social history of 1848 was given, as we noted earlier, by the centenary celebrations of 1948. They released, as we have said, a flood of new studies; Mr. Paul Farmer notes a dozen of them in his review article of the same year in the *Journal of Modern History,* which we have cited above. Among them is Gaston-Martin's slim volume in the *"Que sais-je?"* series, *La Révolution de 1848.* It is, like Seignobos's earlier work, solidly Republican-Socialist (or moderate republican) in both tone and content, and its method is more narrative than analytical. Yet, like most other authors of the centenary year, Gaston-Martin firmly sets out to write a "social" history of these events. For the revolution, he insists, "was, in truth, a social revolution which strove toward something quite other than the political conquest of the universal right of suffrage." So this is a history of the months of February to July, for with the defeat of the Paris workmen and all hopes of the "democratic and social Republic" in June, all that was significant and original in the revolution was completed. "The day that General Eugène Cavaignac handed back to the National Constituent Assembly the dictatorship

---

21. Georges Renard, *La République de 1848* (*1848–1852*), vol. IX of *Histoire socialiste* (*1789–1900*), J. Jaurès (ed.) (Paris, 1907); Charles Seignobos, *La Révolution de 1848* —Le Second Empire (*1848–1859*), vol. VI of *Histoire de la France contemporaine,* E. Lavisse (ed.) (Paris, 1921).

entrusted to him . . . the social Revolution was finished and the Republic was already in decline."[22]

In fact, a result of the centennial celebration has been to lead historians to take a more sympathetic view of the June insurgents, and therefore a more critical view of the liberal and liberal-conservative leaders; moreover, the whole historiography of the revolution of 1848 has taken a turn to the left. Indeed, several of the more recent works conceived in the republican tradition have been by Marxists: among them are Jean Bruhat's *Les journées de février 1848*, E. Tersen's *Le gouvernement provisoire et l'Europe* (both of 1948), and Dautry's impressive *1848 et la IIe République* (1948; reprinted in 1957). So there is a solid substance of truth in Professor Gordon Wright's observation, in discussing the "varieties" of French history between 1814 and 1870, that "interpretations of the 1848 revolution and the Second Republic have gone through a complete cycle during the last century, beginning with Karl Marx's *The Class Struggles in France* . . . and ending with a return to the Marxist viewpoint in many of the books written for the centennial celebration in 1948." Nor is this surprising in view of the deep deceptions caused by the Third Republic; in view, too, of the solid tradition left by Marx in his two penetrating studies of 1848–1850—two works that (Wright tells us) "contained such a remarkable combination of insight and plausibility that his analysis continues to be widely accepted in our day."[23] Yet that is not the whole picture. If conservatives have dropped out of the race, there are still a few others besides Marxists and new-style republicans whose views have to be considered. We have, for example, to take serious account of Tocqueville, even if traditional conservatives have tended to ignore him and he has left no school. There are others besides, like Georges Duveau and Rémi Gossez, who, while clearly leaning towards Marx, have probably been as much influenced by Proudhon or Jaurès and cannot be given neat ideological labels. Let us now look a little more closely at some of these historians' views on

22. Gaston-Martin, *La Révolution de 1848* (Paris, 1948), pp. 5, 116.
23. Gordon Wright, *op. cit.*, pp. 264, 167.

the February and June events, on Louis Napoleon, the "men of 1848," and on whether there was or was not a peasant as well as an urban revolution.

It has often been said that the February revolution came as a bolt from the blue. "The old society," writes Marx, "was taken by surprise"; and he writes of the people's *"coup de main"* as an "unexpected achievement."[24] And Tocqueville, for all his earlier "prophesy" of a pending revolution, does not disagree. Consistent with this view of a spontaneous and unexpected *coup* was the further view, long held, that Louis Philippe might have saved his throne if he had made some effort of resistance. Another, also related, view presents the famous *fusillade* of the Boulevard des Capucines as an entirely fortuitous event which, almost single-handed, transformed riot into revolution. Minor correctives have been made to this traditional picture of the February "days," mainly by specialists who have made them their particular field of study. A. Crémieux, for example, a descendant of one of the "men of 1848," showed, in *La Révolution de Février* (a Paris doctoral thesis of 1912), that Louis Philippe put up more of a fight than had generally been supposed. Subsequently, Jean Bruhat, in a study of the February events contributed to the centenary year, "played down" the unique importance of the drama in the Boulevard des Capucines by insisting that there had been no relaxation of activity in the workers' districts after Guizot's dismissal earlier that day. And Duveau, in turn, has argued that Louis Philippe, far from abdicating in a fit of sudden panic, had already lost control of events by his dismissal of Guizot, which had shown him unfit to rule.[25]

Who were the heroes, and who the victors, of the February barricades? Orleanist historians, like Victor Pierre and Pierre de la Gorce, were naturally inclined to see as the main agent of revolution the "conspiracy" hatched in the offices of the newspapers, *La Réforme* and *Le National,* while the Paris workmen and tradesmen were a

---

24. K. Marx, *The Eighteenth Brumaire of Louis Bonaparte* (New York, 1963), p. 27.
25. Droz, *L'époque contemporaine*, I, pp. 119, 121; G. Duveau, *1848. The Making of a Revolution* (New York, 1967), p. 29.

mere passive "rabble" who came onto the streets at the conspirators' behest. But Tocqueville, though his sympathies lay on the other side of the barricades, agreed with Marx that "the people" played a principal part in bringing the dynasty down; and this has been the general view of both liberal-republican and socialist historians since. Duveau, who shares the view, presents it vividly and dramatically in the persons of his three typical Paris tradesmen: the hosier of the Faubourg St. Denis, the cabinetmaker of the Faubourg St. Antoine, and the mechanic of La Chapelle. The three tradesmen not only follow different occupations and live in different districts, but they differ considerably from one another in their political affiliations and in the newspapers they read. The hosier is the most prosperous and conservative and reads the more moderate of the opposition papers, *Le National* or *Le Siècle*. The cabinetmaker is an old-style Jacobin of the old revolutionary Faubourg, who reads *La Réforme*, is a follower of Cabet, and reveres the memory of Robespierre. The mechanic alone is a "new" man, bred in a new industry and a new industrial suburb, a follower of Blanqui, and already won for socialist ideas. Such men were naturally inclined to pursue different ideals and follow different paths and, as Duveau explains, it needed the universality of the crisis of February to bring them together in a common enterprise. They all agreed, for one thing, that Guizot must go; and he adds: "It augured ill for the monarchy that on the morning of February 22 the hosier, the cabinetmaker, and the mechanic should meet before Durand's wineshop as brothers in a common cause."[26]

The republican tradition has gone further and generally presented this concord and "fraternity" of the February "days," once the initial victory was won, as embracing the widest sections of the people. Duveau, for instance, like Michelet in his famous picture of July 1789, suggests that not only the classes most actively engaged—the Paris tradesmen and liberal *bourgeoisie*—but the nation at large had won a victory; and he cites as evidence the rallying to the Provisional Government of the Church, the army, the old bureaucracy, and even many of the former royalist politicians. This atmosphere of harmony

26. Duveau, *op. cit.*, pp. 17–19.

and "kiss-and-make-up" has been made familiar by Louis Blanc in his picture of the armed workers mounting guard over the properties of the rich:

One hundred thousand workers, armed from head to foot yet starving, guarded Paris with heroic devotion. The blood-thirsty followers of the red flag who were then in control of the streets made sure that no one would so much as lose a hair. The homes of the rich were guarded by the poor and men in rags stood watch at the doors of those who slandered them.[27]

Marxists, though subscribing to much in the main republican tradition, have generally rejected this rosy presentation of events. Seeing history in terms of a struggle of opposing classes, they have naturally looked for "contradictions" among the allies of February and, having found them, have not been inclined to see the blood-bath of June, which followed four months later, as a sort of accident or aberration, or the outcome of the evil machinations of a few. Marx himself recognized the February revolution as a "common uprising" in which the workers and *bourgeoisie* had temporarily joined forces; but he referred to "its illusion, its poetry, its imagined content, and its phrases," and he looked on the harmony of classes, with its visible expression in the Provisional Government, as a fraud, an illusion that blurred the realities of the struggle between classes. This may help to explain why, though he shared Tocqueville's view of the origins of the French revolution, he differed from him over its outcome and significance. To Tocqueville, the champion of property, it "seemed that the revolution had been made entirely outside the bourgeoisie and against it," that the workers were at least the potential victors, and that "socialism will always remain the essential characteristic and most redoubtable remembrance of the Revolution of February." Nassau Senior, the English economist, who was visiting Paris at this time and disapproved of much that he saw, wrote that "the theory to which we attribute the revolution of 1848 is a disguised Socialism." To Marx, however, the essential outcome of February was the creation of a "bourgeois republic," though one temporarily "surrounded by social

27. *Cit.* Peter Amann, "The Changing Outlines of 1848," *Am. Hist. Rev.*, LXVIII, No. 4, *July, 1963, pp. 938–53.*

institutions"; and the real victors were the middle classes, who had only made concessions to the workers under pressure from the streets.[28]

A modern, and somewhat different, criticism of the "fraternity" thesis is that made by Peter Amann, an American historian. He instances the expulsion of English skilled workers from the Rouen area to cries of "Long live the Republic!" and the agitation against the unskilled Flemings in the Nord. "In sum, virulent xenophobia, feeding on economic insecurity, was more characteristic of the urban masses than was any sentiment of international fraternity." He points, further, to the desperate, Luddite-style outbreaks of machine-breaking and railroad-burning by printers, teamsters and textile workers in Paris, Normandy and along the Belgian frontier, released by the February revolution. And he concludes:

The Revolution of 1848 was more than a fraternal banquet: it unleashed a wave of violence that sought to redress social grievances which had nothing to do with revolutionary ideology. It would indeed have been astounding if, after two years of bread shortage and unemployment, the "people" had really played the role of plaster saints *en blouse* assigned to them by republican mythology.[29]

If the "people" have generally been treated by historians with compassion or respect, the same can hardly be said of the leaders, the ill-starred "men of 1848." Both contemporaries and historians have tended to present them either as poor imitations of their forbears of 1789 or, at best, as well-intentioned idealists and romantics, but ill-fitted for the tasks that were thrust upon them. Typical of such views were those expressed by French historians at the time of the centenary celebration of 1948. On this occasion, Georges Lefebvre, in a commemorative article in the *Revue historique*, considered that the men of 1848 had been sadly lacking in the rationalism of the men of 1789; and C.-E. Labrousse, writing in the *Revue socialiste*, observed that

28. Nassau William Senior, *Journals kept in France and Italy from 1848 to 1852,* 2 vols. (New York, 1871), I, p. 1; Marx, *Class Struggles,* p. 59; Tocqueville, *Recollections,* pp. 78 ff.
29. Amann, *op. cit.;* cited in. *The Shaping of Modern France,* Friguglietti and Kennedy (eds.), pp. 249–50.

"the new industrial economy presented problems to men incapable of understanding them." Duveau alone is inclined to be sympathetic, even indulgent, in regard to them; yet, even for him, there are exceptions: Crémieux, for example, who only broke with Louis Philippe at the last moment to become one of the despised number of *Républicains de lendemain;* and Flocon, another turncoat, who drifted from the republican left into the moderate camp of *Le National* and became a minister under Cavaignac in June. He finds little to admire, either, in Marie or Garnier Pagès, who soon found themselves in the conservative "party of order." But he puts in a kind word for Lamartine, who, for all his high-sounding phrases and theatrical postures, played a positive role in the February events; and for Blanc whose schemes, he believes, were practical and realistic, though ill-suited to the romantic atmosphere of the time.[30]

The views of contemporaries, though they naturally varied with political commitment, had not been so very different. The Marquis of Normanby, who kept a journal during his residence in Paris, was conservative rather than liberal and found little good to say of France's new rulers; yet he shows a certain regard for Lamartine. Nassau Senior, who was more of a liberal than a conservative, again singles out Lamartine for particular praise.[31] This was not the case, however, with Marx and Tocqueville. Marx gives the leaders the collective title of "republican duffers" and sees them as mere "ghosts" of the earlier revolution—"now in the form of Marrast, the Republican in yellow gloves, dressed up as Bailly; and now in the form of the adventurer who hid his commonplace and unpleasing physiognomy behind the iron death-mask of Napoleon." Tocqueville, for his part, thought that there had been "more wicked revolutionaries than those of 1848"; but he doubted "if there were ever any more stupid." For Ledru-Rollin, probably next to Lamartine the most influential leader of 1848, he has a certain affection mingled with contempt; but his view of Lamartine is almost entirely unflattering. He allows him personal courage, a

---

30. Droz, *op. cit.,* p. 121; Duveau, *op. cit.,* pp. 182–202.
31. Marquis of Normanby, *A Year of Revolution; from a Journal kept in Paris in 1848,* 2 vols. (London, 1857), I, p. xix; II, p. 382, Nassau Senior, *Journals,* I, pp. 6–8.

lively imagination, and a talent for oratory, but precious little else. "I do not know that I have ever met . . . a mind so void of any thought of the public welfare as his . . . Neither have I ever known a mind less sincere, nor one that had a more thorough contempt for the truth. . . .When speaking or writing, he spoke the truth or lied, without caring which he did, occupied only with the effect he wished to produce at the moment."[32] Later writers have not been as severe; but, following Tocqueville, they have generally presented Ledru-Rollin as a good-natured and courageous, but somewhat boneheaded demagogue, and Lamartine as a reincarnated Girondin of 1793, romantic, vain, insincere, unused to practical affairs, and self-consciously playing a role in a historical drama.

Historians' views have differed more widely over the nature and significance of the June events. The division has tended, among Frenchmen at least, to fall along party lines: traditional republicans seeing them as an unfortunate diversion in a year of liberal revolution; "social" republicans, socialists and Marxists as marking a decisive stage, if not the climax, of the revolution as a whole. Marx and Tocqueville saw June in somewhat different terms, though both agreed that it was the almost inevitable result of February: Marx because he believed that the "bourgeois republic," begotten in February, was not yet secure; Tocqueville because he "saw society cut into two" and "had always believed that it was useless to settle the movement of the Revolution of February peacefully and gradually, and that it could only be stopped suddenly by a great battle in the streets of Paris." In fact, both understood (and Tocqueville could almost as easily have written the words as Marx) that "a second battle was necessary in order to sever the republic from the socialist concessions" and that "the bourgeoisie had to refute the demands of the proletariat with arms in their hands." To both, therefore, the workers' defeat was equally inevitable and one that marked a new stage in the struggle of opposing classes. But, beyond this, there could be no agreement. To Tocqueville, the conservative, the workers' defeat was a kind of naturally ordained punishment for their presumption in February, which

32. Marx, *Eighteenth Brumaire*, p. 25; Tocqueville, *Recollections*, pp. 111–12, 123–6.

restored the proper *status quo*. To Marx, the revolutionary socialist, its significance was two-fold: on the one hand, it restored the "bourgeois republic" on more secure foundations; but it was also "the first great battle . . . between the two classes that split modern society" and from now on revolution (and not only in France) meant "overthrow of bourgeois society, whereas, before February, it had meant overthrow of the form of state."[33] And, broadly, this is still the issue dividing historians, with conservatives and traditional republicans ranged on the one side and new-style republicans and Marxists on the other.

Was the closure of the National Workshops in June a deliberate act of provocation to stir the workers to revolt? Tocqueville appears to have hoped for something of the kind; for, when prophesying (in April) the "inevitability" of a battle in the streets, he added that "it would be well to seize the first opportunity to deliver it." Moreover, Emile Thomas, while still director of the workshops, warned the government (in May) that their closure would precipitate an insurrection. So there was ample provocation, as was widely understood; but was it deliberately planned with the workers' inevitable defeat in view? Some historians have argued that it was. H. Guillemin, for example, a left-wing Catholic, argued, in *La tragédie de quarante-huit* (Geneva, 1948), that the Comte de Falloux persuaded his colleagues to provoke a civil war by closing the workshops, with the deliberate intention of bringing the workers to heel. John Plamentaz, an English political historian, demurs. He concedes that the government, in not heeding Thomas's warning, took a calculated risk; also that there was a suspicious delay between the building of the first barricades on the evening of 22 June and the assault made on them by the troops the next day. But, on the other hand, he argues that this can be explained by the authorities' desire to avoid dealing with the insurrection piecemeal and that their decision to continue to pay the unemployed a franc a day for another three months showed that they were trying to appease the workers rather than to provoke them.[34]Neither set of arguments

33. Marx, *Class Struggles*, pp. 84–9; Tocqueville, *Recollections*, p. 150.
34. Tocqueville, *op. cit.*, p. 114; Droz, *op. cit.*, p. 121; John Plamenatz, *The Revolutionary Movement in France 1815–71* (London, 1958), pp. 76–8.

is conclusive, so the mystery remains.

Further questions have been asked about the nature of the June conflict itself. Was it a struggle of "proletariat" and "bourgeoisie," as Marx defined it, or one of "class against class" or "a servile war," as seen by Tocqueville (which amounts to much the same thing)? Marx's definition is certainly the one most commonly adopted by the more recent school of republican historians, whether Marxists or not. But Mr. Peter Amann, in an article in the *American Historical Review*, is inclined to dismiss it as another piece of "historical folklore."[35] To prove his case, he rightly points to the early stage reached by industrialization in France: Paris was still a city of small workshops and crafts that had changed comparatively little since the revolution of 1789; and he might have added that the occupations of the great majority of those arrested in June bore a remarkable similarity to the trades of those who stormed the Bastille and captured the Tuileries sixty years before. Quite properly, too, Mr. Amann calls to his aid (as others have done as well) the authority of M. Rémi Gossez, who has studied the question far more deeply than anyone else. M. Gossez's researches, as we noted in an earlier chapter, have not yet been completed and their results have only been published in part. But, as far as they go, they appear to support the view that, on balance, the conflict was one of "poor" against "rich" rather than of industrial workers against an industrial *bourgeoisie*. He suggests, in fact, that there was no clearcut class division between the two opposing forces: workers served in the National Guard alongside property-owners, shopkeepers, clerks and professional men; the Mobile Guard (which fought on the government side) was largely composed of young workers—many of whom had fought on the February barricades; and, of industrial employers, most remained neutral in the fighting in order to guard their factories and shops, while several fought with their employees in the insurgents' ranks. From this he concludes that while the *social* conflict was genuine enough, it was one that ranged small producers, lodgers and sub-tenants (and not only wage-earners) against shopkeepers and merchants, and against landlords and "principal" tenants (often shop-

35. Amann, *op. cit.*, pp. 251–2.

keepers), rather than against factory owners, masters and industrial employers. Yet, elsewhere, he adds that building workers, railwaymen (a new trade), port and riverside workers were among the most highly organized and militant in the capital; and many of these he describes as forming "the vanguard of the insurrection."[36] So this was something new and showed that a modern "proletariat," if not yet fully developed, was already in the making.

The constitution-making that followed June has not commanded the attention of many historians—except in so far as it has had some relevance for Louis Napoleon's election as President of the Republic. For once the June "days" were over and Cavaignac had handed back his powers, Napoleon became the man of the hour, and it is on him that historians' attention has become fixed. Generally, he has had as bad a press as the "men of 1848," though for entirely different reasons. Where they have been considered ineffectual though (possibly) well-meaning, he has most often been considered a master of duplicity. Marx, as we have noted, saw him as a grotesque caricature of his more illustrious uncle. To Tocqueville, he was the living embodiment of the "despotism" that was the direct antithesis of the aristocratic "liberties" that he cherished; and the experience of Napoleon colored his whole presentation of the two revolutions (that of 1789 as well as of 1848) that he wrote about. We saw, too, that the Orleanist historians, Pierre and La Gorce, were as contemptuous of the "usurper" Louis Napoleon as their Legitimist colleagues were, in another context, of the "usurper" Louis Philippe. Moreover, republicans, whether of the Third Republic or the Fourth, have not been likely to feel any affection for the man who overthrew the earlier Republic of 1848. So French historians, whether conservatives, republicans, moderate socialists or Marxists, have been fairly solidly united in a common dislike of Victor Hugo's "Napoleon the Little." Of course, there have been exceptions. Among the Prince-President's admirers has been an Englishman, F. M. Simpson, author of *The Rise of Louis-Napoleon*

---

36. Rémi Gossez, "Diversité des antagonismes sociaux vers le milieu du XIXe siècle," *Revue economique*, I, 1956, pp. 439–58; and "L'Organisation ouvrière à Paris sous la Seconde République," *1848. Revue des révolutions contemporaines*, XLI, 1949, 31–45.

(1925); and, as Emperor, he has received praise, ranging from adulation to friendly accolades, from Albert Guérard (1943), Georges Pradalié (1963), and Theodore Zeldin (1958). But all but the first of these deal with a period of his life with which we are not concerned at present.

Mr. Amann has drawn attention to another problem: was there a peasant revolution in 1848? He takes issue with traditional historians who have presented the revolution of 1848 as a strictly urban and largely Parisian affair, in which the peasants are neglected or presented in the context of the towns. The older history, it is true enough, tended to ascribe to the peasants a purely negative, or counterrevolutionary, role. Their intervention was generally confined to two familiar episodes in 1848: their support for the government's forces in the June insurrection (graphically related by Tocqueville, who approved it), and their massive vote for Louis Napoleon in December, which Marx unkindly termed "the *real* peasant revolution." Thus their role was seen as being purely negative and antiurban, and generally, or solely, attributed to their anger over the 45-centimes tax. This, argues Mr. Amann, is to ignore three distinguishable waves of agrarian revolution. The first, sparked off by news of the fall of the monarchy, took the form of widespread peasant attempts, particularly in the southwest, to recover traditional collective rights which had been taken from them since the revolution of 1789. A second wave, provoked by the imposition of the 45-centimes tax, began in March and involved, in order to suppress it, an army of 50,000 regular troops. Third, and more significant of a growing peasant radicalism, was the considerable peasant vote recorded for the democratic-socialists in 1849, who gained a clear majority in eighteen departments and a 40 percent vote in twenty-three others, most of them agricultural departments in the southeast, center and southwest. And Mr. Amann adds: "Peasant radicalism dies hard: the 25–30,000 peasants of the Alpine departments who resisted Louis Napoleon's *coup d'état* by force of arms did so, not in support of an alien constitution, but in behalf of a revolutionary republic in the making."[37]

37. Amann, *op. cit.*, pp. 252–5.

The point is well made, though perhaps the author protests too much. Even among the older republican histories there was, as a balance to the purely urban Parisian presentation of 1848, A. Charles's study of the revolution at Bordeaux and in the department of the Gironde (1945); there were also studies by E. Gossez on the Nord (1904), E. Dagnan on the Gers (1932), and Privas on the Ardèche (1948). The centenary year has brought several more: among them studies on Toulouse and the Haute-Garonne, the Aude, the Jura, and the Isère, as well as articles by Albert Soboul and P. de Saint-Jacob on peasant grievances in the Nord and elsewhere.[38] And Mr. Amann himself has, in the *Journal of Modern History,* discussed a number of more recent works of this kind, including René Lacour's study of the Lyonnais (1955), Christianne Marcilhacy's on the Loiret (1959), and Philippe Vigier's on the southeastern Alpine region (1960).[39] Moreover, the *Société d'histoire de la Révolution de 1848* has, over the past fifteen years, opened up a wide field of enquiry into the revolution in the provinces. Among its products have been closely documented articles and maps by Rémi Gossez, charting the course and incidence of the varied peasant disturbances of 1846–7 and the resistance to the 45-centimes tax of 1848.[40] So there is just a possibility that a new synthesis of the revolution, which takes account of the more recent research and brings the village into focus, will soon be on its way.[41]

28. The Revolution in Germany

The German revolution of 1848 was a far more complex and a far more *unique* affair than the French. It was more complex because in Germany more or less simultaneous revolutions erupted in a multiform community of thirty-nine self-governing states at different lev-

---

38. Droz, *L'époque contemporaine,* I, pp. 120–1.
39. P. Amann, "Writings on the Second French Republic," *Journal of Modern History,* XXXIV, 1962, pp. 409–29.
40. R. Gossez, "La résistance à l'impôt. Les quarante–cinq centimes," in *Etudes,* Bib. de la Révolution de 1848, XV, 1953, pp. 89–132; and "Carte des troubles de 1846–47," in *Aspects de la crise,* C.-E. Labrousse (ed.), 1956.
41. A brief foretaste is provided in the "Que sais-je?" series, by Philippe Vigier's *La Seconde République* (Paris, 1967).

els of development; and more unique because where France has experienced and accommodated a long series of revolutions since 1789, apart from her socalled "national revolution" of 1933, Germany's only really nationwide revolution was in 1848. Moreover, it was a particularly traumatic experience and a parting of the ways, which has haunted her whole history ever since. For while German nationalism, very much alive and kicking in 1848, led on through Bismarck to national unification, German liberalism, a far more tender plant, was dealt a blow from which most historians have agreed that it has never fully recovered. It was this blow to liberalism, this sense of the intrinsic failure of 1848, that has led succeeding generations of German historians—whether Marxists, liberals, nationalists, or what Mr. Hamerow calls "Revisionists"—to come back again and again to the familiar question: what went wrong in 1848? The answers have inevitably been strongly colored—perhaps even more than in other countries—by current political trends and the ideologies of the disputants; and Mr. Hamerow cites from Hermann Oncken, a German historian from the turn of the century, the view that "nothing is more certain than that the political and spiritual heirs of the parties of 1848 still look today upon these events with the eyes of their fathers and . . . maintain their views as shibboleths of the orthodoxy of their political ideologies."[42]

Once more, it was the Marxists who were the first in the field. Both Marx and Engels were in Germany during the revolution and played an active part in it: Marx in the Rhineland, where (from June 1848) he edited the *Neue Rheinische Zeitung,* and Engels in Baden. Whether their influence was of moderate or insignificant account on the course of events has been debated by historians;[43] but this need not concern us further here. What is more to the point is to consider briefly their analysis of what took place, as later recorded by Engels (though in

42. See Theodore S. Hamerow, "History and the German Revolution of 1848," *Am. Hist. Rev.,* LX, No. 1, October, 1954, pp. 27–44. I have made extensive use of Mr. Hamerow's article in this part of the chapter.
43. See, for a *positive* view, J. Droz, "L'influence de Marx en Allemagne pendant les révolutions de 1848," *Etudes,* XVI, 1954, pp. 3–16; and, for a *negative* view, Hamerow, *Restoration, Revolution, Reaction,* pp. 66–7.

Marx's name) in his book, *Revolution and Counter-Revolution in Germany* (first published from newspaper articles in 1852). From the outset, they had no illusions about the maturity of the German working class, which might at best become a junior, though an important, partner of the middle class whom they looked to as the only possible leaders of the revolution; and, in view of the prevailing discontents, the antiquated forms of government and the divisions among Germany's rulers, they believed the political opportunities of this middle class to be particularly favorable. "Was there ever a more splendid position for the middle class of any country, while it struggled for power against the established Government?" Yet, as is known, the German middle class proved a dismal disappointment and surrendered ignominiously to the conservative forces of the landed aristocracy and royal government. To Marx and Engels the explanation was simple enough. Although they railed at the "childish conduct," the "tomfoolery" and futility of the "old women," the "wiseacres" and "humbugs" who sat in the Parliament at Frankfurt, it was not just weakness, or even corwardice, that led to their surrender, but a deliberate and gross *betrayal* of the people's interests, prompted by their fear of a revolution "from below." So the liberal middle class sold out on the revolution, betrayed the workers and peasants and the Polish and Bohemian patriots, and joined the Prussian army, the landed classes and bureaucracy in restoring law and order. But at least the whole experience, Marx and Engels believed, would teach the workers a useful lesson for the future: to distrust the *bourgeois* liberals and build up their own resources.[44] And this, broadly speaking, has been the interpretation placed on these events by Marxist historians, both in Germany and other countries, up to the present day.[45]

For quite different reasons, the Liberals of the Frankfurt Parliament were also to receive a rough handling from the next generation of historians that grew up in Bismarck's new national Germany. The

---

44. F. Engels, *Revolution and Counter-Revolution in Germany* (London, 1933), esp. pp. 31–2, 50–3.
45. See, for example, K. Kersten, *Die deutsche Revolution* (Berlin, 1933); Roy Pascal, *The German Revolution of 1848* (London, 1948); and Alfred Meusel, "Die deutsche Revolution von 1848," *Neue Welt*, III, No. 6, 1948, pp. 3–14.

"Prussian School," as Mr. Hamerow terms them, was given its cue by Bismarck himself when, in the Prussian Diet of 1862, he substituted his own policy of "blood and iron" for the futile "speeches and majority resolutions" of the Frankfurt Liberals of 1849. The principal spokesmen for this Prussian School were, with their very different styles and points of emphasis, Heinrich von Treitschke and Heinrich von Sybel, whose works we have discussed in an earlier chapter. As we then noted, Treitschke's *History* ends with the eve of the "spring revolution"; but it needs little imagination, having seen what he wrote of Jews, Liberals, foreigners, and Frenchmen in the period up to 1847, to realize what construction his Prussian-nationalist and antiliberal bias would have led him, had his *History* been continued, to place on the events of 1848 and 1849. Sybel's nationalism, we saw, was far more muted and restrained than Treitschke's; and his criticism of the "professors' revolution" is by no means a sweeping condemnation and is tempered with faint praise. He notes, somewhat regretfully, the Liberals' hesitations and "mistakes" which, he believes, contributed to "such a pitiable result." But he gives them credit for their patriotism and good intentions and for setting before the people "the true goal of the nation—the maintenance of Freedom among its members, and of Union in its attitude to foreigners."[46]

With Bismarck's departure in 1890, there came a more charitable attitude towards the middle-class revolutionaries of 1848. The achievements of 1871 no longer remained unquestioned and, up to the First World War, German Liberalism enjoyed a fresh lease of life. In 1892, Karl Binding of the University of Leipzig, in an academic address, called for a new, and a more objective, evaluation of the March "days" in Berlin and the work of the Frankfurt Parliament; and, for some years to follow, there appeared historians who were generally sympathetic to the old Liberals' ideas. Even conservatives reared in the Prussian School, such as Max Lenz and Erich Marcks, followed Sybel in according recognition to their patriotism and idealism; and the immediate prewar years saw the appearance of important works by Friedrich Meinecke and Erich Brandenburg, which gave a

46. H. von Sybel, *The Foundation of the German Empire by William I,* I, pp. 365–6.

new historical, and generally sympathetic, perspective to the ideas put forward in 1848. Brandenburg, in particular, in his *Die deutsche Revolution* and *Die Reichsbegründung* (the first published in 1912, the second in 1916), attempted to assess their importance for the evolution of the German state. He denied that these Liberals were demagogues who had provoked a revolution without solid popular support. He also denied that the Frankfurt Parliament had been a total failure, that its proceedings were dilatory, and that its members—as had so long been stated—were unpractical doctrinaires. In fact, he acclaimed the Constitution of 1849 as an important stepping-stone towards the unity of Germany, and insisted that the ideas of 1848 were not only excellent for their times but highly relevant to present-day German needs.[47]

It was natural that this new, liberal interpretation of the past should, after a brief wartime intermission, have revived with even greater vigor with Germany's defeat and the collapse of the Bismarckian Empire. For there were obvious similarities between the problems of 1848 and 1919, and now for the first time the liberal view could enjoy the blessings of government approval. In 1923, Professor Alfred Weber was offered the Paulskirche itself, the scene of the old Frankfurt Assembly, to deliver an address which hailed the Parliament of 1848 as the true progenitor of the Weimar Constitution; and between 1918 and 1933 there was more literature published on 1848 than in all the years before and since.[48] Among much that was indifferent and ephemeral there was at least one work of solid scholarship: Veit Valentin's *Geschichte der deutschen Revolution*, which was published in two volumes in 1930–31. (A condensed English translation appeared in London, under the title *1848: Chapters of German History*, in 1940.) Valentin's style and approach, as we saw in a previous chapter, are entirely those of an old-style liberal of the 1920s. He might almost, in fact, be called a German Croce: he uses a similar vocabulary, as when (in *The German People*) he writes of the German

47. John A. Hawgood, "The Frankfurt Parliament of 1849–49," *History*, XVII, July, 1932, pp. 147–51.
48. Hamerow, "History and the German Revolution of 1848," p. 32.

people first "becoming aware of itself as a nation through German mind and soul." So he could hardly fail to be an enthusiast, and an often undiscriminating apologist, for the German Liberals of 1848. Yet for all its effusiveness and lack of method, the *Geschichte* is both a scholarly and original book. It is, for one thing, an encyclopedia of information, both on the revolution itself and on all that had been previously written about it. Moreover, it treats the revolution as a whole, not limiting its scope to Berlin or Frankfurt on which so much earlier work had been focused. Yet, like Brandenburg, he attributes to the Parliament a significant place in the history of German political ideas and bestows particular praise on its *Grundrechte,* or "Fundamental Rights of the German People," which had been the target for so much ridicule by the nationalist historians of the past.[49]

Hitler's Third Reich followed soon after and, for a dozen years, the revolution of 1848 was either relegated to the shades as a matter of no importance or presented as a conspiracy against the German people and nation. There were, it is true, a few old-style conservatives like Erich Marcks and Heinrich von Srbik, whose work, while not conceived in the spirit of National-Socialism, was tolerated as being sympathetic to Germany's national ideals. But the genuine practitioners of the Nazi interpretation of the past were not just old-fashioned, timid conservatives reared in the school of Sybel, or even of Treitschke. In the works of Klaus Besser and Kurt Neumann, the revolution of 1848 was pictured as the outcome of an international conspiracy, or witches' cauldron, to which not only Jews but Jesuits, communists and freemasons had contributed their offerings. Happily, it was argued, this sinister plot to ensnare the honest Germans was foiled in time; yet it revived and destroyed the Kaiser's Reich in 1918, and was only finally defeated by the "national revolution" of 1933.[50]

It was natural that the end of the Second World War, with the defeat of the Nazi regime and the eclipse of its ideology, should have evoked a new spate or rewriting of Germany's past. Within Germany, after an understandable delay and readjustment, the centenary of

49. Hawgood, *op. cit.,* p. 150; Hamerow, *op. cit.,* p. 33.
50. Hamerow, pp. 34–5.

1848 occasioned a new crop of literature, divided between Germans East and West, between Marxists and Weimar-style liberals. In the East, Jürgen Kuczinski, to whose labor histories we have already referred, broke fresh ground with a study of the economic and social problems of 1848–9; while, in the West, the old political debate opened up again, with Wilhelm Mommsen and Theodor Heuss (a future President of the Republic) praising the liberal-national heritage bequeathed to their generation by the men of 1848, and with Rudolf Stadelmann, while restating the liberal view, adding a note of impatience with the political naïveté and timidity of the German middle class.[51]

But the sharpest reaction came from outside Germany itself, from those whom Mr. Hamerow has called the "Revisionist School." They include, among Englishmen, such distinguished writers as Sir Lewis Namier and A. J. P. Taylor; among Frenchmen, Edmond Vermeil; and a number of German and Austrian expatriates resident in the United States. It was no longer merely a case of bewailing the failure of liberalism in 1848: its inevitable defeat and the consequences that flowed from it could now be traced far back into Germany's historical past, to the Teutonic tribes, Martin Luther or the militaristic paternalism of Frederick the Great. Hot on the heels of Nazi Germany's defeat, Taylor wrote in his *Course of German History:* "It is unnecessary for any individual to indict the Germans . . . They have indicted themselves by their own acts. No civilised nation has such a record of atrocity." And of 1848 he adds; "For the first time since 1521, the German people stepped on to the centre of the German stage only to miss their cues once more . . . this was the fateful essence of 1848."[52] It was two years earlier that Namier, in his British Academy lecture, *The Revolution of the Intellectuals,* insisted that it was nationalism far more than liberalism that motivated the German revolutionaries of 1848; and, elsewhere, he writes: "With 1848 starts the German bid for power, for European predominance, for world dominion: the national movement was the common denominator of the German revolution

51. *Ibid.,* pp. 38–9.
52. A.J.P. Taylor, *The Course of German History* (London, 1951 edn.), pp. 7, 68.

of 1848, and a mighty Germany fit to give the law to other nations, its German aim."[53] To Edmond Vermeil, the French historian, the explanation for "the disastrous climax" of 1848 and 1849 lay "not so much in external causes as in the mentality of the German people"; and, like Namier, he considered that "the tragedy of 1848 already foreshadowed Europe's tragedy in the twentieth century."[54] And Monty Jacobs, a German expatriate, meets the question: "Why was the play [of 1848] bound to end tragically?" with the answer: "Because it was a German play and because the German people, to quote the words of young Fontane, had not been brought up in liberty."[55]

Such views are, in Mr. Hamerow's words, at best "one-sided"; and they were not, even in the immediate postwar years, the only ones professed among Germany's former opponents. Some Englishmen, for example, took a less catastrophic view. Alfred Cobban, in his *The Nation State and National Self-Determination* (the first edition of which appeared under a shorter title in 1945), wrote that Germany, in 1848, "did not remain uninfluenced by the democratic current of opinion"; though he adds, it is true that "the democratic and liberal elements in the nationalism of the 1848 Revolution were very limited, and collapsed without great resistance when the task of achieving political unity was taken over by the Prussian monarchy."[56] Roy Pascal, like Taylor and Namier, also wrote a book on Germany immediately after the Nazis' military defeat. But being a Marxist, he was less inclined to impute the sins of German governments to the German people as a whole and to see Germany as a sort of congenital villain of the piece. In the preface to his book, *The Growth of Modern Germany* (New York, 1946), he is conscious enough of the pressures of the present on the record of the past. He writes:

In the case of Germany, it was only too inviting, in the period of the Weimar Republic, to see German history as the development of democracy; and today,

53. Namier, *The Revolution of the Intellectuals, passim;* and *Vanished Supremacies* (New York, 1963), p. 28.
54. Edmond Vermeil, "An Historical Paradox: the Revolution of 1848 in Germany," in F. Fejtö (ed.), *1848. The Opening of an Era* (London, 1948), pp. 223–52.
55. Hamerow, *op. cit.,* p. 36.
56. A. Cobban, *The Nation State and National Self-Determination,* p. 45.

after authoritarian leaders have once again led an enthusiastic people in a war of expansion, German history may seem to be the history of aggressive nationalism.

To avoid the pitfall, he attempts "to show the changing character of German nationalism and the circumstances which made aggressive imperialism dominant in Germany." These circumstances, he adds, were created not only by what was going on in Germany herself, but also by "the influence of other empire nations." Nor can the failure of 1848 be attributed (as Namier and others would have it) to any congenital weakness of the German people but, more simply, to the fact that the middle class "failed to strike at the real seat of power."[57] In *The Origins of Modern Germany,* which appeared in the same year, Geoffrey Barraclough also uses the argument of circumstance rather than heredity to explain the Germans' weakness in 1848. But, unlike Pascal, he returns to the old liberal view that the Frankfurt Parliament was not so mistaken or so foolish after all; for "it may be doubted . . . whether a genuine attempt to 'go with the masses' offered any real prospect of success; in which case the failure of the Frankfurt Parliament was due rather to circumstances beyond its control than to the deficiencies of its members and the dilatoriness of its procedure."[58]

So far, the reader may note that all the debates we have recorded have been carried on in a "little German" (*kleindeutsch*) or Prussian context, while Germany's relations with Austria, which profoundly influenced the outcome, have been entirely omitted from the score. It was natural, however, that some Austrian historians, concerned with the history and future of a "Greater Germany," should have seriously questioned the assumptions on which such a one-sided discussion was based. Heinrich von Srbik, for example, in his *Deutsche Einheit* 4 vols. (Munich, 1934–49), finds a new cause for failure of the revolution in the Frankfurt Parliament's decision to exclude the Austrians and to attempt a *kleindeutsch* solution under Prussia. The Frankfurt leaders,

57. Roy Pascal, *The Growth of Modern Germany* (New York, 1969), pp. 3, 40.
58. Geoffrey Barraclough, *The Origins of Modern Germany,* rev. edn. (New York, 1963), pp. 415–16.

he maintains, were mesmerized by Prussia's cultural and military tradition and failed to appreciate the historic services rendered by Austria to the whole community of Germans. So he sees the tragic turning point of the whole revolution in the Frankfurt Parliament's decree of October 1848, excluding the non-German Austrians from its deliberations. This conservative *grossdeutsch* interpretation, which also "rehabilitates" Prince von Schwarzenberg (the villain of the piece at Olmütz), has been challenged in turn by German apologists for the *kleindeutsch,* or Prussian solution, with Erich Marcks voicing the conservative and R. Stadelmann the liberal view. Other historians have debated the virtues and vices of Frederick William IV and the alternatives to the Prussian "surrender" at Olmütz.[59] But such discussions, Mr. Hamerow wrote in his review article of 1954, had already become sterile; and "so thoroughly have these problems been explored that there is evidence that the spring is beginning to dry up." And he welcomed the new turn, already long overdue, that was being made towards the study of the social and economic problems of the revolution.[60]

The need for such a new direction had long been felt. It was, of course, implicit in the analysis made by Marx and Engels a hundred years before; but such approaches had been swept under the carpet by the passionate ideological debate, successively carried on by nationalists and liberals, that followed the unification of 1871. In 1884, a first tentative voice was raised in favor of a social-economic interpretation by Konrad Bornhak, who saw behind the political revolution a conflict between industrial capitalism and feudal agrarianism. Thirty years later, Erich Brandenburg, the liberal historian, raised the matter more sharply. In his *Reichsgründung,* he contrasted the Liberals' demand for political change with the economic advantages demanded by the "lower classes" as the price of their support. "When their economic demands were met, or when they saw that the system sought by the liberals promised them as little satisfaction as the old system, then these classes lost all interest in the political movement." This all sounded as if Brandenburg had adopted (as indeed he had)

59. Droz, *op. cit.,* pp. 181–2.
60. Hamerow, *op. cit.,* p. 41.

something of Engels' old interpretation; so it is not surprising that his views should have been challenged—in the first place by Meinecke, who, towards the end of the First World War, engaged him in a spirited debate in the columns of the *Historische Zeitschrift.* During the Weimar Republic, however, other historians rallied to Brandenburg's cause; but the Nazi interlude put a stop to all that, and as late as 1949, Oscar J. Hamann, writing in the *American Historical Review,* could complain that "aside from a number of special studies by German historians, the standard accounts of the Revolution of 1848 place an almost exclusive emphasis upon the political aspects of the movement and upon the constitutional and national strivings of the liberal middle class." Yet, by this time, even Meinecke had made his peace with the shades of his old antagonist. In the centennial year, he boldly abandoned his old position and declared that "the German revolution . . . shows not only an all-pervading spirit of idealism . . . it also brought to bear what in actual effect was more powerful—the reality itself, the massive and elemental interests of individuals and social groups."[61]

Since then, there has been a steady turn in this direction, but it has been slow and on a far smaller scale than it has been in France since 1948. It has been distinctly more marked in East Germany than in the West: We have already noted briefly the work of Jürgen Kuczinski, but, in West Germany, too, there appeared in the centennial year R. Stadelmann's social and political history of the revolution of 1848; followed a year later by W. Mommsen's study of German middle-class properties and policies in 1848 and 1849—though neither of these are "social" histories in the strict, or "French," sense of the term.[62] Some of the more significant contributions have, in fact, come from outside Germany itself; from two authors in particular: Jacques Droz, the French historian, whose *Les révolutions allemandes* appeared in 1957, and Theodore Hamerow, whose *Restoration, Revolution, Reaction* (only related in part to the revolution of 1848) was published at Princeton in 1958.[63]

61. *Ibid.,* pp. 41–4.
62. Droz, *op. cit.,* pp. 181–2.
63. Droz, *Les révolutions allemandes de 1848* (Paris, 1957); Hamerow, *Restoration, Revolution, Reaction.*

Mr. Hamerow's book has been discussed in an earlier chapter and we do not need to return to it here. Mr. Droz's theme, though it is stretched over a far larger canvas, is similar to Professor Pascal's of fifteen years before. He, too, firmly lays the blame for the failure of revolution on the Liberals of the Frankfurt Parliament; but, like him, he is disinclined to seek the explanation for it in the German national character. "The spirit of servitude and obedience," he writes, "that is so readily ascribed to the German people does not appear, at least, in the events of 1848." The explanation must, in fact, be sought largely in the circumstances of Germany's economic development and the strains and fears that these imposed on the German middle class. He continues:

It was Germany's misfortune that, because of the slow economic growth imposed on her by her territorial division, she was able to devise liberal institutions only at the moment that large-scale industry was facing her with the challenge of a militant proletariat. Germany was, therefore, denied the opportunity, essential for a democratic country, of experiencing a parliamentary form of government.[64]

So, as in Hamerow's book, economic factors are made to form a solid base for the political conclusions that follow.

Of course, such work as this leaves plenty over for Germany's own historians to explore. And maybe researches carried out along similar lines will help to revive the debate on the revolution of 1848 in a new and more vigorous manner.

29. The Revolution in the Austrian Empire

If the revolution in Germany was more complex than the French, the revolution in the Austrian dominions was undoubtedly more complex than the German. For the Austrian Empire was not merely a politically multiform but a multinational state, with eleven peoples— at differing stages of development towards nationhood—ruled by the same central government at Vienna. So the revolution, in addition to the issue of liberalism and freedom from autocracy, voiced in the first

64. Droz, *Les révolutions allemandes,* pp. 639–40.

place in Vienna itself, raised even more sharply questions of self-government and national independence, ranging from the mild forms of autonomy demanded by Croats and Czechs to complete separation from the Empire, as briefly practiced by the Hungarians. And there were other centrifugal forces at work besides, drawing the Emperor's subjects into closer association with their fellow-"nationals" across the Imperial borders—Transylvanians towards Roumanians, Southern Slavs towards Serbians and Montenegrins, Galician Poles towards the Poles in Poland, and Austrian Germans (by far the most privileged group) towards their fellow-Germans in the other thirty-eight German states. To add to these complexities, the revolutions in Paris and Vienna touched off similar revolts in the Austrian dominions in Italy—among Tuscans, Parmese, Lombards and Venetians. So the central problem for Austria's rulers was not so much how to restore the central government in Vienna as how to prevent the whole Habsburg Empire from falling apart; and this, as far as they were concerned, was what the revolution was mainly about.

It is, of course, appropriate that the literature on the subject should have a similar complexity, ranging from the comparative simplicity of the March-to-October revolution in Vienna to the intricate relations within and between the separate national groups. Yet, perhaps not surprisingly, a comparatively small proportion of this literature has appeared in French or English; and it is unfortunate that, whereas the English-speaking reader is reasonably well served by books on the French, German and Italian revolutions, he has to depend on a rather indifferent assortment in the case of the Austrian.[65] Moreover, much of what has been written in English has been strictly narrative, unthematical and unanalytical: A case in point is Professor C. A. Macartney's recent work, *The Habsburg Empire 1790–1918* (London, 1968), which contains a long and highly readable chapter on 1848, preceded by two further chapters on the *"Vormärz"* and "Before the Storm." These qualities will be welcomed by the general reader, but

---

65. See F. R. Bridge's critical bibliography, *The Habsburg Monarchy 1804–1918: Books and pamphlets published in the United Kingdom between 1818 and 1967* (University of London, 1967), School of Slavonic and East European Studies. 22 items of very uneven merit relate to the general history of 1848–9.

they pose problems for those who, like the present writer, are searching for distinctive trends! But, nevertheless, an attempt will be made, as far as the literature permits, to see how certain commentators and historians have discussed a number of problems relating to the liberal revolution in Vienna and the national movements in the provinces.

To begin with the outbreak in Vienna, which, on 13 March (following a casual salvo before the *Landhaus*), toppled Metternich from power with a minimum of noise and trouble. This, then, both as to the *fusillade* and the overthrow of an unpopular minister, bears a remarkable resemblance to what had taken place in Paris a little over a fortnight before. But, in Vienna, the consequences (and possibilities) were more dramatic; for here it was not just a matter, as in the case of Guizot, of toppling a minister who, for all his qualities, was not considered altogether indispensable; but the great master-manipulator of the European System, Metternich himself. So why, it has been asked, did he fall so easily from power at the first rumble of a students' and workers' demonstration? One of the most recent accounts of the event—in a short textbook by Barbara Jelavich—states quite simply that "in Vienna an uprising led by students, workers and middle-class men of liberal, socialist and radical tendencies first *forced* the Habsburg Government to dismiss Metternich"; while M. Pouthas, in the *New Cambridge Modern History,* writes more obliquely, but what in terms of cause and effect amounts to much the same: "The Court gave way in fear. Metternich fled." Mr. Macartney, on the other hand, as is his wont, merely records the event.[66] But was it just a simple matter of cause and effect? About this some historians have been more in doubt than others. Goetz von Poelnitz, for example, shows himself to be uneasy about some of the answers given in a paper he wrote in 1959. Poelnitz argues, first, that the protests in the Empire had already gone so far that no means of accommodation appeared possible as long as Metternich remained in office; secondly, that, quite apart from the Vienna demonstrations, there was already sufficient animosity to the minister at Court to make him a convenient scape-

---

66. Barbara Jelavich, *The Habsburg Empire in European Affairs 1814–1918* (Chicago, 1969), p. 57 (*my italics*); Pouthas, *op. cit.,* p. 396; Macartney, *op. cit.,* pp. 329–30.

goat; and, thirdly, that it was believed that he would be willing to accept the role without demur in order to save the Imperial Crown —a calculation that proved, in the event, to be quite justified. Poelnitz writes:

The fact that the Chancellor had held power for over thirty years had so far removed the possibility of any return from the revolution already developing in Central Europe that the first outbreak on 13 March sufficed to sweep from power a man hitherto believed invincible with the speed of a surprise attack ... [and] the prince assumed the sole responsibility for all the past errors of commission and omission in order once more to save the crown and monarchy from the destructive waves of revolution.

Yet, in spite of all, the question remains whether the Hofburg acted wisely in literally sacrificing its most powerful leader with such little hesitation. It may be that personal enmities, as well as immediate fears, prompted a decision that gave satisfaction to the large and varied body of opinion that held Metternich in detestation ... But who then could assume the direction of the ship of State in such a raging sea, after the pilot, too aged perhaps but familiar with all the shoals and reefs, had been dropped from its side?[67]

Among those who watched developments in Vienna, as they watched them in Berlin, Frankfurt and Baden, were Marx and Engels. In his account of the Austrian revolution (he is mainly concerned with Austrian Germany), Engels related its inception, development and ultimate collapse in the familiar terms of a balance and struggle between classes. "The Revolution of Vienna," he wrote to the *New York Daily Tribune* from London in October 1851, "may be said to have been made by an almost unanimous population. The bourgeoisie (with the exception of the bankers and stock-jobbers), the petty trading class, the working people, one and all arose at once against a Government detested by all, a Government so universally hated, that the small minority of nobles and money lords which had appropriated it made itself invisible on the very first attack." But Engels adds, "it is the fate of all revolutions that this union of different classes, which in some degree is always the necessary condition of any revolution, cannot subsist long." Such division may obviously prove a weakness (as, in this case, it undoubtedly proved to be in the long run), but,

67. Goetz von Poelnitz, "L'Autriche," in *L'Europe du XIXe et du XXe siècle*, I, p. 565.

temporarily, it may help the revolution along by providing a balance to the aims of any single group. So, in Vienna, Engels argues, the *bourgeoisie* should have emerged as the single dominant group; and, in fact, it would inevitably have become so if the revolution had lasted long enough and the concessions made (mainly to the middle class) had had time to be consolidated. But, in practice, there emerged, from the balancing of classes, a sort of dual authority. On the one hand, the middle class and petty tradesmen formed their own militia, the National Guard, and exercised local political authority through the Committee of Public Safety that appeared in May. But the students had a militia of their own—the Academic Legion—and through the "Aula," and, with the aid of the workers (many of whom, being unemployed, were still under arms), were able to exert constant pressure on the *bourgeois* city authorities. Moreover, when the new central government—dominated by the manufacturers and trading interests—attempted, in May, to withdraw some of the concessions made in March (a constitution, trial by jury, freedom of the press, etc.), there was a fresh uprising and the old allies—tradesmen, students and workmen—joined forces again to bring the government to heel.

So the revolution was kept going and won considerable concessions; and not only in Vienna, for, throughout Austria, the peasants were left free to throw off the last vestiges of serfdom. But how and why did it collapse? In the first place (and here Engels's view is no different from anybody else's), because once the Court and the army had reestablished their old authority in Prague and Italy (though not yet in Hungary), the middle classes, even with the uncertain aid of other classes, were not strong enough to hold the fort; and, on 30 October, Vienna fell to Windischgrätz. And, Engels adds, there was also confusion, mistrust and recriminations among the Viennese themselves, engendered by conflicting loyalties, class weaknesses and class divisions. He sums up the final *débâcle* as follows:

Outside, the reorganised Austrian army, flushed with the victories of Radetzky in Italy; sixty or seventy thousand men well armed . . . Inside, confusion, class division, disorganisation; a National Guard part of which was resolved not to fight at all, part irresolute and only the smallest part ready to act; a proletarian mass, powerful by numbers but without leaders, without any political education, subject to panic as well as to fits of fury almost without cause, a prey to every false rumour spread about, quite ready to fight, but unarmed at least in the beginning, and incompletely armed, and barely organised when at last they were led to battle; a helpless Diet, discussing theoretical quibbles while the roof over their heads was almost burning; a leading committee without impulse or energy. Everything was changed from the days of March and May, when, in the Counter-Revolutionary camp, all was confusion, and when the only organised force was that created by the Revolution.[68]

Since Engels wrote, few writers have appeared, even in Austria, to give a comprehensive account of the Viennese revolution. The longest and earliest account is that by Freiherr von Helfert, whose *Geschichte Oesterreichs vom Ausgange des Wiener Oktoberaufstandes 1848* was published in six volumes, in Prague and Leipzig, in 1869–76. It is a conservative history, sympathetic to the Court and army and hostile to the revolutionaries. More recent accounts appear in two works by socialist historians: E. Fischer's *Oesterreich 1848* (Vienna, 1946), and R. Endres's *Revolution in Oesterreich* (Vienna, 1947). Both take up Engels's old question: why did the revolution collapse? Endres underlines the weakness and immaturity of the Viennese working class, which was incapable of absorbing the new socialist ideas and wasted its energies on the destruction of machinery, thus aggravating an economic crisis which had already begun. Fischer explains the failure mainly in terms of the divisions among the non-"privileged" classes and between the national groups within the Empire. Like Engels, he considers the revolution to have been, at its inception, a revolt by virtually all classes in society against feudalism and absolute government. And he believes that it suffered eventual defeat from a succession of betrayals: from May onwards, by the *bourgeoisie* and, in the autumn, by the peasants and lower middle class; so that, in October, workers and peasants both found themselves in isolation. Moreover, at the national level he believes that the advance of capitalism had turned each national group against its neighbor, so that it became impossible for democrats to unite against their common enemy: he

68. Engels, *Revolution and Counter-Revolution*, pp. 33, 40–3, 70–1.

instances the case of the poet Grillparzer, who, from fear that democracy would act as a disintegrating force, abandoned it for the greater security of the counterrevolution centered on the Court in exile.[69] Poelnitz, who might perhaps be termed a liberal conservative, gives a slightly different sequence to the stages leading up to the October collapse. It was, he believes, the countryside in German Austria that was the first to be impressed by the new strength acquired by the Court after Radetzky's early victories and to desert the revolution. Next, the Vienna *bourgeoisie,* faced with growing economic crisis and fearing for its properties, began to abandon the city, with the remnants of the new central government, after the May insurrection. So Vienna became a "boiling witches' cauldron," progressively deserted by tradesmen and property owners, large and small, and thus fell an easy prey to the advancing Imperial army.[70]

Other historians have considered the internal events in Hungary and Bohemia. Much of this work has, of course, been done by the postwar generation of historians who have emerged under the socialist governments of Eastern Europe; so it has tended to be Marxist and to be concerned with socio-economic as much as with purely political factors. In Hungary, however, this trend was already in evidence some years before the war. Mention has already been made of Ervin Szabo's study of 1921, which revealed a conflict of social classes behind the national independence movements of the 1840s. Work of a similar inspiration was contributed by Hungarian historians to mark the centenary year: among them D. Kosary, whose paper on "the social aspects of the revolution of 1848" was published in the proceedings of the Paris congress. Kosary argues that the role of the Third Estate in Hungary fell to the middling ranks of the nobility, who sought a solution for the current crisis of the feudal economy in the abolition of the old social system. But to the left of them was a group of petty noblemen, who, with the completion of their university studies, found themselves reduced to an intellectual proletariat; these looked to more radical solutions and became the main body of Kossuth's supporters.

---

69. Droz, *L'époque contemporaine,* I, pp. 251–2.
70. Poelnitz, *op. cit.,* pp. 567–8.

Thus, while a majority of the nobility were united behind a common demand to destroy feudalism, political divisions arose between the petty and middling nobility, which would have assumed a more destructive and violent character if the compelling necessity had not arisen to unite behind Kossuth's national leadership in September 1848. Yet the divisions served as a barrier to progress, for Kossuth's need to appease and manipulate the nobles prevented him from completely abolishing the old feudal order. Among other historians, C. Benda (in a paper published in Paris in 1949) has argued that the reforms of April 1848 were inadequate, as they distinguished between the "serf" lands, which were declared free, and the lords' private demesne-lands, which had become progressively more extensive and on which the peasants were not given ownership of the plots they cultivated. A situation, he adds, that was further aggravated by the lords' appropriation of common pastures and other traditional rights of the village community. In a somewhat different field, Francis Fejtö has written of the spread of socialist and revolutionary ideas from France; and, in particular, of the impact on the Hungarians of the ideas of Cabet, Fourier and Lamennais. [71]

The revolutionary situation in Bohemia has been discussed by a number of Czech historians. Among the older writers, M. Kazbunda and F. Roubik both published accounts, between the wars, of Bohemian industrial development, of the economic crisis of 1848, of machine-breaking by angry workers and the spread of socialist ideas. More recently (in 1945), a work by B. Mendl has dealt with the attitude of the working class to the events of 1848 in Prague. It appears that workers took part in the first great demonstrations held in the St. Wenceslas Baths, but that the conservative middle class soon edged the radicals aside, took over the direction of affairs and, from hostility to the Germans, entered into early negotiations with the Court. Another short study by L. Gogolak, published in the same year, deals with the relations between· Bohemia and the Imperial government. Gogolak shows that even radical leaders like Havlicek had no intention of breaking with Austria before 1848. It was the

71. Droz, *op. cit.,* pp. 252–3.

claims of the Frankfurt Parliament that gave birth to the political movement in Bohemia, which quickly adopted the "Austroslav" cause. In reply to the Frankfurt invitation, the Czech national leader Palacky declared that the integrity of Austria and her independent existence outside a united Germany were the guarantee of the future of both the Czech nation and of every other nation within the greater Austrian community. This Austroslavism of the Czech national leaders accounts for their moderation in the spring of 1848, as well as for their loyalism even after the bombardment and subjugation of their city in June, and for their accommodating attitude in the Parliament at Kremsier, when Palacky argued the case for national equality within the Austrian Empire. So the attitude of the Czech leaders was crucial to the salvation of the Empire from disintegration in 1848.[72]

Most historians have, in fact, agreed that the outcome of the revolution in Vienna, Prague and Budapest ultimately depended not so much on the internal conflicts and events within those cities (not even within Vienna itself) as on the relations between the nationalities and national groups within the Empire. The essential question soon became evident: could the Court and Chancellery, after their initial defeat, recover sufficient strength to resume their old game of "divide and rule" by playing off one national group against the next? (As Metternich is reputed to have said: "If the Hungarians revolt, we'll turn Bohemia against them—they hate each other; then the Poles or Germans or Italians.") For, it has been widely held, in that possibility lay the key to the eventual success of counterrevolution, whether in Vienna or elsewhere. A French historian of the late-nineteenth century, Louis Léger, in his *History of Austro-Hungary*, put the problem quite succinctly: "Within this Empire three great races felt simultaneously the sudden shock, and rushed towards liberty by three different and opposite paths, and their various interests and old rivalries led to conflicts among themselves, which rendered their generous efforts of no avail and for a long time destroyed their hopes."[73] Namier, writing

72. *Ibid.*, p. 253.
73. Louis Léger, *A History of Austro-Hungary from the Earliest Time to the Year 1889* (London, 1889), p. 524.

seventy years later, says much the same thing, though less charitably and with greater accuracy and precision:

There were four dominant nationalities within the Habsburg Monarchy whose upper and middle classes covered also the territories of the subject races: Germans, Italians, Magyars, and Poles, *versus* Czechs, Slovaks, Yugoslavs, Ruthenes, and Rumans. The four master races demanded a united Germany, a united Italy, an independent Hungary, and a reunited Poland, including between them all the territories of the subject races inhabiting the Monarchy.

Such aims, had they been realized, would of course have ripped the Austrian Empire apart and were, therefore, sternly resisted by the dynasty, as well as by "those among the Austrian Germans who were more Austrian than German." "The subject races, too," adds Namier, "desired national unity and independence, but they preferred the rule of the non-national Habsburgs to that of the master races."[74] And it was out of this welter of national antagonisms and affinities, which ultimately served the dynasty so well, that there followed the bombardment of Bohemians by Slovaks and Croatians, the disruption of Kossuth's Hungarian Republic by Slavs and Roumanians, the refusal of Czechs to go to Frankfurt, and the tragi-comedy of the Slav Congress held in Prague in June 1848.

It is the Slav Congress, in particular, that has attracted the attention of historians. Most have been critical, contemptuous or frankly hostile, while a few—Slavs for the most part—have rallied to its defense. Among the defenders has been A. Fischel, whose scholarly work, *Der Panslavismus bis zum Weltkrieg*, was published at Stuttgart in 1919. Although by a German liberal, it offers a balanced *apologia* for the Congress's intentions; and, among other more important matters, it disposes of the legend (repeated, among others, by Engels) that such was the Babel of Slavonic tongues that the delegates were forced to speak in German! Among Czech historians, J. Macurek contributed a paper to the 1948 centenary on the "Achievements of the Slavonic Congress." The writer insists that, whereas the Germans and Magyars would recognize among them no other nationality than their own, the

74. Namier, *Vanished Supremacies*, p. 27.

"Manifesto to the Peoples of Europe" issued by the Congress demanded equal rights for every national group. Thus the Slavs, far from seeking revenge for the many affronts they had suffered, placed themselves at the head of a struggle for human and national rights.[75]

Others, as we have noted, have taken a far less charitable view. Among contemporaries, Marx and Engels, as is known, adopted a sternly hostile and critical attitude. In the conditions of 1848, they argued, some nationalities played a progressive and some a reactionary role. Among the former were Hungarians and (generally) Poles and (sometimes) Germans, and among the latter Czechs and Croats, neither of whom were strong enough to form nations of their own and (in Engels's words) "could only hope to be restored to anything like independence by an alliance with the Slavonic nations." So why not form an alliance of 80 million Slavs by joining with Poles, Russians, Serbs and Bulgarians, and thus "drive back or exterminate the intruder upon the holy Slavonic soil, the Turk, the Hungarian, and above all the hated, but indispensable *Niemetz,* the German"? This theory, Engels argues, was not only "ludicrous" but dangerously reactionary; for it could only redound to the greater glory of the arch-enemy of all the revolutionaries of 1848, the Russian Tsar; for behind the theory "stood the terrible reality of the *Russian Empire.*" Thus the Bohemians and Croats, who convened the Congress, "some intentionally, some without knowing it, worked in the direct interest of Russia; they betrayed the revolutionary cause for the shadow of a nationality which, in the best of cases, would have shared the fate of the Polish nationality under Russian sway." But, unfortunately for "the poor Slavonic enthusiasts," Engels adds in his most bitterly sarcastic vein, "another Slavonic Congress was assembling in Prague" in the shape of Windischgrätz with his army of Croats, Slovaks and Galicians, who, "in less than twenty-four hours, drove the founders of an imaginary Slavonic supremacy out of the town, and dispersed them to the winds.' [76]

The English historians, A. J. P. Taylor and Sir Lewis Namier, have adopted a contemptuous rather than a hostile attitude towards the

75. Droz, *op. cit.,* p. 253.
76. Engels, *op. cit.,* pp. 58–9.

Slavs and their aspirations. They agree that they were inspired, in part at least, by hatred or suspicion of the Germans. But, being products of the twentieth and not of the nineteenth century, they reject the "Russian bogey" theory that was so widely held, not least in England, on the eve of the Crimean War; and, in its place, they advance another factor, that of "Austroslavism." So there are shown to have been two Slavisms at work in the confused proceedings of the Slavonic Congress: not only Panslavism (on which Engels concentrated) but Austroslavism as well, the first promoted by Slovaks and Poles, the second by Palácky and the Czechs and Slovenes. Some of the leaders of the "subject races," Namier remarks, "especially among the Czechs, went the length of developing a program of 'Austro-Slavism'—of an Austria reconstructed on a Slav basis"; but this, he adds, was a "phantasm," as it threatened the survival of the very Empire that Palácky was anxious to preserve. So the Slav Congress, when it assembled at Prague in June, was not so much a reactionary body (as in Engels' view) as a hopeless and illassorted medley—"a mixture [in Taylor's words] of Austroslavism and Slav nationalisms, spread over a vague Slav solidarity." And so, adds Taylor, it is not surprising that it produced two "contradictory" programs—a revolutionary manifesto to the peoples of Europe, mainly inspired by the Poles, and a conservative address to the Habsburg Emperor, promoted by the Austro-Slavs and firmly rejecting any union with Germany. Professor Macartney is less contemptuous than Namier or Taylor, but he only gives the Congress a single page in his book, and observes mildly that "it did not work out according to plan."[77]

This judgment, at least, among all the other contentious judgments that the events of 1848 have provoked, is beyond dispute.

30. The Revolution in Italy

The Italian *Risorgimento*, as we saw, while tracing its origins to Napoleon's occupation, if not to the eighteenth-century Enlightenment, was not completed until 1870. In Italy, therefore, the revolution

---

77. Namier, *op. cit.*, p. 27; A. J. P. Taylor, *The Habsburg Monarchy 1809–1918*, pp. 68–9; Macartney, *op. cit.*, p. 364.

of 1848, even more than in Germany, has been seen as an important episode in the long history of national unification. We have already considered historians' opinions on the wider aspects of the *Risorgimento;* so here we shall be concerned, more particularly, with the problems relating to the years 1848 and 1849.

In this case, too, we find that the older historians (and the term does not exclude some of those still living) were mainly preoccupied with the battle of ideas, with political problems of unity and independence, and, above all, with the virtures and vices of the "great men" or founding fathers who acted as prophets or creators of the new united Italy. But whereas to many patriotic Germans, looking back on the events of 1848, it has seemed an age of shame and failure, to Italian liberals it has been one of pride and heroism, "a generation of giants," as Settembrini termed it in recalling the recent past in the late 1870s. "The men of the Risorgimento," Adolfo Omodeo, a more recent liberal, wrote half-a-century later, "acted for the people. They made themselves the nation, as the seven thousand Israelites, who at the time of Elias refused to bow to Baal, became the true Israel." There was also a sense of deep pride in the achievement of the Italian people as a whole, who appeared, almost overnight, to have awoken to a sense of nationhood. "This generation," wrote Settembrini, "made Italy"; and he evokes "the point at which we became Italians, felt ourselves united and gathered together under a single standard."[78] Nor have such effusions been confined to Italian liberals alone. In Britain, for example, Italy could, like Greece, generally count (until Mussolini's time at least) on the generous sympathies of liberal, and even conservative, historians. So we find, in the translator's preface to Pietro Orsi's *Modern Italy* (published in London in 1899), the "makers" of Italy compared to the "picturesque heroes" of Roman times: "Charles Albert, that most noble and pathetic of kingly figures"; "Cavour ... the pilot who steered the bark of Italian independence safely home to port, between the rocks of absolute reaction and the whirlpool of revolutionary fanaticism—and many more."[79] And G. M. Trevelyan,

78. S. J. Woolf, *The Italian Risorgimento,* pp. 69–74.
79. Pietro Orsi, *Modern Italy 1748–1898* (New York, 1903), p. xi.

whose eulogy of Cavour as possibly the greatest of all European statesmen we noted in an earlier chapter, remained all his life a passionate devotee of Garibaldi. In his epilogue to *Garibaldi's Defence of the Roman Republic,* one of three books that he devoted to his hero, the great "Captain" is thus described during the years of exile that followed his defeat in 1849:

He was never more noble than during the obscurity of the years that followed. He acquired none of the faults and habits characteristic of the exile, but cheerfully set about the task of earning his bread, first as a journeyman candle-maker, then as a merchant captain, and finally as a farmer, until the time came round for him to deal in the manufacture of kingdoms, and to be hailed by his countrymen as 'Captain of the People.'[80]

Yet, once the first flush of enthusiasm was over, the more or less undiscriminating adulation of the "makers" became short-lived. For one thing, the "great-man" type of history was, slowly but surely, beginning to go out of fashion; and, even before this happened, historians and biographers were becoming more selective. While Cavour, until long after his death in 1861, enjoyed almost universal veneration, the time soon came when, with some at least, Mazzini and Garibaldi found greater favor; even Pius IX, long seen as a traitor to the national cause, was recast in a more heroic mold. We noted the case of the Englishmen, G. F. H. and J. Berkeley, for whom Pius was "Gioberti's Pope come into being," a genuine liberal reformer, who made an important contribution to the regeneration of Italy. They admit, however, that he failed to live up to his promise when confronted with the crisis of 1848. Yet his conduct is condoned, as the war with Austria faced him with an intractable dilemma. For, as he told the liberal Giuseppe Montanelli, "as an Italian he wanted to see the foreign invaders driven out of his country, but as Pope—as the universal Father—he could never declare a war of independence against Austria." E. L. Woodward, whose portrait of Pius is almost uniformly unflattering, makes no such allowances. Moreover, he sees the real dilemma in different terms. "How could the 'Sovereign Pontiff' be-

80. G. M. Trevelyan, *Garibaldi's Defence of the Roman Republic 1848–9* (London, 1920), p. 314.

come a constitutional ruler? . . . Who could be responsible for the
actions of the Vicar of God on earth?" So Pius's liberalism was, from
the start, a fraud or, at least, beset with insoluble contradictions; and,
as Rome falls to French arms and the Pope returns after a brief period
of exile, the author concludes: "To men of little mind in Rome the
revolution was defeated when those who had been willing to die for
it had given their lives. Pius IX turned to other fields for popularity
and success."[81]

Others among the earlier historians who were inclined to distribute
their praise with a certain discrimination were Bolton King and Sir
John Marriott. King, whose liberalism was certainly more in evidence
than Berkeley's, made no attempt to disguise his preference for some
and his antipathy to others. "I have done my best," he writes in his
preface, "to do justice to all sides, though I have not attempted to
disguise my sympathies. I make no apology, if I have said hard things
about the Papacy." Among the founders his particular hero was
Mazzini, and his book has been called "the classic Mazzinian interpretation."[82] Nevertheless, as reaction closed in after 1849, he sees
Piedmont rather than Mazzini's liberal republicanism as the main
hope for Italy's future. "The governments were too rotten for good
rule, and the ideal of a benevolent absolutism vanished into mockery
at Rome or Parma or Milan. And between the Ticino and the Alps
Piedmont was gathering her forces for the immediate struggle, whose
victory meant annihilation alike for Austrian domination and the
Temporal Power." Sir John Marriott, too, having bestowed his praises
in turn on Mazzini, the Neo-Guelphs and Garibaldi, ends by firmly
placing his money on Piedmont and Cavour. He writes of Italy in
1850:

More than one lesson had been taught by the events of the last few years. It
was vain to look for political salvation to a reformed or reforming Papacy.
The Neo-Guelph ideal was shattered. Republicanism nurtured on civic patriotism was unequal to the task of national emancipation. A unitary Republic
was as impracticable as Papal Federation. Mazzini's ideal, like Gioberti's, was

81. G. F. H. and J. Berkeley, *Italy in the Making*, III, pp. 4–5; E. L. Woodward, *Three
Studies in European Conservatism*, pp. 286, 292.
82. Woolf, *op. cit.*, p. 115.

shattered . . . For modern Italy to live it was necessary that Mazzini's immediate ideal should die . . . Thus the hope of all patriotic Italians began to be concentrated on the House of Savoy.[83]

Recently, it has become more fashionable either to damn the leaders with faint praise, to consider them more coolly "warts and all," or merely to relegate them to a less dominating perch in the presentation of events. Among this more realistic, "warts-and-all" school of historians we may cite the case of Denis Mack Smith, whose treatment of the "makers of modern Italy" is far less fulsome than that of Trevelyan, Marriott, or Bolton King. Mack Smith certainly gives an air of greater impartiality and he is as willing to be tough with any one of his subjects as with any other; yet he has a particular regard for Camillo Cavour. Mazzini's success, he tells us, lay in "defining the goal and arousing enthusiasm among more practiced soldiers and statesmen"; but he was intractable and distrustful of compromise, incurred the enmity and ingratitude of both Garibaldi and Cavour, and died, an unhappy and disillusioned fugitive, two years after unification had been completed. Garibaldi had a "single-minded and disinterested love of Italy"; but though "he genuinely believed in what he called liberty," he was "all for a dictatorship modelled on Caesar's and "thought it should be forced on people for their own good." Looking forward into the 1850s, he sees Cavour as "the most interesting and important figure in modern Italian history, who had "a novel and invaluable spirit of enterprise." But, "far more amiable and sympathetic than Bismarck," he "was no less sure of touch, no less self-confident, and almost as unscrupulous when occasion demanded." Above all, "he had a remarkable sense of what was possible, and would always compromise with his ideas if that seemed the only way to obtain it, nor was he ever frightened out of changing his mind by the accusation of opportunism."[84]

Among leaders whose role has been most heatedly debated by Italian historians has been Charles-Albert of the House of Savoy. Was

83. Bolton King. *A History of Italian Unity*, I, pp. vii, 384; J. A. R. Marriott, *The Makers of Modern Italy* (London, 1931), pp. 56–65, 76–7, 80–2.
84. D. Mack Smith, *Italy. A Modern History*, pp. 13–20.

he a dyed-in-the-wool reactionary, who only attuned his policies to meet current liberal demands; or was he a disinterested patriot, who had both Piedmont's and Italy's best interests at heart? N. Rodolico, in a three-volume biography of the 1930s, praises him for his realism and for the spirit of self-sacrifice he displayed even when, as in the crisis after Novara, everything seemed lost. A. Omodeo argues, on the other hand (in a "reply" published in 1940), that the liberal *Statuto* that Charles-Albert promulgated in March 1848, far from being his own handiwork, was forced on him after a bitter dispute by his advisers. He argues, moreover, that, on assuming the leadership of the national war against Austria, he abjured all liberal intentions and attempted to use Lombardy as a pawn to further Piedmont's dynastic ambitions. Why, then, after the Royal army's defeat at Custozza (in July 1848), did the King promise to lend support to the Milanese who were being menaced by Radetzky? According to Rodolico, this was another instance of Charles-Albert's chivalry and abnegation. However, C. Spellanzon, a Lombard historian, in editing Cattaneo's contemporary account of the Milanese insurrection, puts a very different construction on this event. Charles-Albert, he insists, far from being a disinterested knight-errant, was planning to surrender the city to Radetzky. He was prompted, he explains, by his fear of the republican movement in Milan, which threatened to prevent its annexation by the House of Savoy; so the King hoped that he might be able to preserve through diplomacy what he had failed to achieve by force of arms. A more moderate view is that put forward by C. Pischedda (in 1949), who, while conceding that Piedmont had expansionist aims and that these undoubtedly governed Charles-Albert's activities, denied that a deliberate betrayal of the Milanese formed any part of his intentions.[85]

But the leaders—whether Cavour, Mazzini or the King of Piedmont—no longer command so large a proportion of the historians' attention. As Miss Ramm observed in her London Historical Association pamphlet of 1962, there has been a distinct trend away from the "makers" "towards interest in the whole Italian community." This

85. Droz, *L'époque contemporaine*, I, pp. 221–2.

trend she ascribes in part to the experience of Fascism, "which had disclosed weaknesses in Cavour's work and a latent native strength in Italy"; and, in consequence, "interest shifted from Cavour's diplomacy to the deeper movement of the *Risorgimento.* "[86] One aspect of this "deeper movement" that required to be explored was how the Italian people found their way to a sense of nationhood and how far this process had gone by 1848. The older historians had taken all this for granted, and when they took time off from writing about the leaders to write of the Italians as a whole, they tended to see them as an abstraction and to assume (as Settembrini obviously did) that they became conscious of being Italians, in addition to being Lombards, Sicilians or Venetians, almost overnight. This tendency persisted and, even as late as the turn of the century, Bolton King, in writing of the period immediately after Napoleon, supposed that "vague and disorganised though it was, the sense of a common nationality was making quick strides among the people."[87] And thirty years later, Ramm notes, Sir John Marriott, in his *The Makers of Modern Italy,* "leaves the chief political question unanswered: 'why did Italians come to think it was better to live in one large rather than in several small states?' "[88]

So the problem remained for others to probe further. Recent research has tended to confirm the doubts, already expressed by a small number of writers over a century ago, that the Italians' sense of nationhood had gone very far by 1848. "In 1848," writes Ramm, "there were insurrections in all the Italian states, but no one would now contend that the object of the rebels was a united Italy." And, as an extreme example of this opinion, she cites Mr. A. J. P. Taylor's view that the tobacco riots in Milan in January and the rising that followed in March were due "simply to the running-down of the Austrian bureaucratic machine" and were the result of "administrative failure, not oppression." Ramm believes this to be an exaggeration, as she does Mr. Mack Smith's assertion that there was "a

86. A. Ramm, *The Risorgimento,* p. 3.
87. B. King, *op. cit.,* I. p. 12.
88. Ramm, *loc. cit.*

complete absence of national consciousness in Italy" at the time of the post-Napoleonic Restoration. Nevertheless, she goes a long way to meet them. Having considered each region of the peninsula in turn— moving from Lombardy to Venice, from Venice to Tuscany, from Tuscany to Naples and Sicily, and so up to Rome and the Papal States —in each one of which she observes similar parochialisms and similar local antipathies at work, she concludes her survey with the conclusion:

There was, then, no singleness of purpose, no clearness or largeness of aim, to justify our considering the uprisings of 1848–49 truly nationalist. Nor was the war of March to August 1848 and March 1849 in any sense, on either side, a national struggle.[89]

Ramm picks out for special mention the rivalries between Sicily and Naples that, far from contributing to a larger Italian unity, appeared to threaten to tear the Kingdom of the Two Sicilies apart. The main proponent of the "separatist" view had been Croce, whose opinion was that the Sicilian revolt of January 1848, like its forerunner of 1820, had the express purpose of achieving Sicily's independence from Naples. The matter was debated by Italian historians and others during the centenary year. A Frenchman, Ferdinand Boyer, showed that foreign observers at Palermo in 1848 were struck by the local parochialism of the Sicilians, many of whom, they believed, would have gladly accepted a ruler at the hands of the British. This was, of course, a point in favor of Croce. But some Italian liberal historians of Naples and Sicily have taken quite a contrary view. G. Frivella-Valla, for example, argued, in a paper presented to a conference on the events of 1848 held at Palermo, that there were two opposing tendencies at work: on the one hand, the Neapolitan government's economic policies, by discriminating against Sicilian produce, aroused hostility to Naples; but, on the other, among liberals and democrats there was an overriding concern to establish an autonomous state, linking Sicilians and Neapolitans, within the framework of a federal

89. Ramm, *op. cit.*, pp. 7, 11–14.

Italy. Another historian, R. Romeo, has supported this conclusion by pointing to the degree of nationalism already reached in the Two Sicilies by 1848 and to the community of interest firmly established between the liberals of Naples and Palermo.[90] In the wider context of the Italian national movement as a whole, Valsecchi adds a point that has some relevance for the debate, whether centered on the Sicilies or on any other part of the country. "In the present stage of our researches," he writes, "one can only insist that the slow growth of an 'industrial revolution', even in the most economically developed regions, prevented Italy from attaining that same maturity of national consciousness that was evident in the more advanced of the European countries."[91]

But, meanwhile, Italian historians have, like the German, the French, the Czech and Hungarian, begun to turn the searchlight of social and economic enquiry onto their national and revolutionary past; with them, too, this has been a mainly postwar development and closely associated with the commemorations of the centenary year. Before then, as in so many other areas of scholarship, Croce's liberal idealism had largely held the field. But now historians, like N. Rodolico and D. Damarco, opened up new horizons by exploring the social conflicts and clash of economic interests that could be shown to underlie the national movements and the struggles of parties and leaders. Thus Rodolico, in a study of Italian social attitudes in the half-century leading up to 1848, has contrasted the opposing attitudes of town and country and laid bare the hostility of country-dwellers towards the urban *bourgeoisie* and the skill with which the Austrian authorities were able to exploit it. Others have explored the spread of socialist ideas in the national movement (particularly strong in Tuscany), the part played by the common people in revolutionary events, and the degree to which the fear of communism (as it so evidently did in France and Germany) paralyzed the liberals and stimulated the turn to counterrevolution among the Italian middle class.

90. Droz, *op. cit.,* p. 222.
91. Valsecchi, "L'évolution politique," p. 276.

These new methods have been used, perhaps most fruitfully of all, by D. Demarco in his studies of the years of revolution in the Papal States. His most important works are *Una rivoluzione sociale: La Republica romana del 1849* (Naples, 1944) and *Pio IX e la rivoluzione romana de 1848: Saggio di storia economica-sociale* (Modena, 1947). The titles in themselves, even in the original Italian, convey clearly enough the radical change that has taken place in the treatment of such a theme since the days of Berkeley, Woodward, or Trevelyan. The author, in fact, is not so much interested in the vices or virtues of Pius, in the heroism of Garibaldi or the motives of Louis Napoleon, as in the economic background or in the social consequences that flowed from the event. In his book on Pius IX, he argues that the situation of the masses was not substantially affected by the reforms carried out after 1846; despite the liberal professions, the abuses of the Old Regime persisted and were, indeed, aggravated by an economic crisis. In his "Social Revolution," he shows that the fall of the Papal government was not due, as claimed by previous scholars, so much to the intrusion of external influences as to the desire of the masses to improve their conditions of life. The Republic, he maintains, made serious efforts to relieve poverty and destitution; and the Mazzinian liberal program, with its distribution of Church lands for the benefit of the poorer peasants, had begun to yield results. So the Republic fell, he continues, not because of the superiority of French arms; but because of the hostility that its reforms had aroused in parts of the Roman population: both among the upper classes and among the numerous retainers and pensioners of the old ruling families within the lower clergy, and among the small tradespeople and city poor.[92]

Thus the old Crocean type of history has, in a sense, been stood on its head; and, once more to quote Ramm, the new historians "have had more opportunity . . . to discuss the interplay of individual men and group movements, to show how individuals both shaped and were dependent upon social forces."[93]

92. Droz, *op. cit.*, pp. 220–1.
93. Ramm, *op. cit.*, p. 3.

31. Balance Sheet of Revolution

The revolutions of 1848, unlike those of 1640, 1789, and 1917, have generally been written off as failures, either wholly or in part. Opinions have varied widely as to the degree of that failure, and some generations and some historians have been more convinced of it than others. It was natural that the former revolutionaries themselves, the survivors of 1848, as they looked back from the "reaction" that had universally set in by the early 1850s, should have taken a somewhat jaundiced view and believed that all they had fought for had been in vain; men, for example, like the eleven members of the Provisional Government in France who, already by "the last day" of 1848, had (in the reprobatory words of the Marquis of Normanby) "been restored to the political insignificance which was their portion at its opening." Some of them, including Lamartine and Louis Blanc, left memoirs in which, in reviewing the recent past, they deplored its failures and the opportunities missed. Proudhon, who was an anarchist rather than a socialist, believed that the Paris workmen had been duped and betrayed by their "natural" leaders, the *bourgeoisie;* and, in calling for the next stage in the Revolution, he addressed them as follows from his cell in the Consciergerie prison in 1851:

Business men of France, the initiative in the progress of humanity is yours. The untutored workingman accepts you as his masters and models. Is it possible that, after having accomplished so many revolutions, you have yourselves become counter-revolutionaries, against reason, against your own interest, against honor?

In Italy, the Mazzinian liberal, Giuseppe Montanelli, who had played a leading role in the Tuscan events, was equally pessimistic and uncertain for the future. Seeing the Pope reinstalled in Rome and Victor-Emanuel firmly enthroned in Piedmont, he believed that the only hope for Italy lay in the education of the people and in social and economic reform. "The Italian revolution," he wrote in 1851, "is not only a national revolution. Without the Pope in Italy we could have limited our aims to a war of territorial independence . . . The European revolution means the reform of the economic-social conditions of Europe, and hence Italy cannot hope for redemption except by putting into practice the principle underlying this reform." Cavour himself, arriving on the scene a few years later, underlined in his own way this radical-liberal sense of failure, which to him, however, was a happy release. In a speech made in 1855, he condemned the old "revolutionary faction" as something worse than useless for Italy's future; for "the experience of recent years and centuries have shown . . . how little Italy has been assisted by conspiracies, plots, revolutions and disordered movements." And, in Germany, we have seen how Engels, writing after the event, attributed failure to the "betrayal" of the *bourgeoisie* and, more particularly, to that of the "old women" of the Frankfurt Parliament through whose surrender to the forces of conservatism the revolution had suffered a total defeat. Yet he was not given to universal jeremiads, and he believed that the Austrians had fared much better. In Austria, admittedly, as in Germany, Italy and France, the liberal revolution had been defeated and reaction had taken over; but the peasants, at least, had won their freedom and had "succeeded, better than in any other part of Germany." Moreover, he prophesied that "whatever else the Government of Prince Schwarzenberg may be enabled to restore, it will never have the power of re-establishing the feudal servitude of the peasantry." And, in this case, he proved to be entirely right.[94]

Historians, looking back on these events from a safer distance in time, have had the usual advantages of hindsight and of the experience of intervening years. But, of course, a great deal has depended on the point from which they looked back. In the latter part of the nineteenth century, for example, it was in general as natural to take an optimistic view of the outcome of 1848 as it had been to be pessimistic in 1851. For Italy and Germany had won their national unity; France, after the despotic interlude of Napoleon III, had resumed her liberal, Republican course; and even the Austrian Empire had made some sort of concession to Hungarian nationalism, at least, in the Dual

94. Marquis of Normanby, *A Year of Revolution*, II, pp. 382–3; B.-J. Proudhon, *General Ideas of the Revolution of the Nineteenth Century* (New York, 1970); Woolf, *The Risorgimento*, pp. 57–60; Engels, *Revolution and Counter-Revolution*, pp. 42–3.

Monarchy of 1867. So, even if liberalism had taken an obvious knock, the success of nationalism was now evident for all to see; and historians were inclined to see the outcome of 1848 as a purely temporary defeat and as a stepping-stone to the greater triumphs of the 1870s rather than as a graveyard of liberal and socialist ideals. There were, of course, dissenting voices, such as those raised by German nationalist critics of the Frankfurt Parliament or, in Italy, by Neapolitans or neo-Mazzinians; or, in England, by Lord Acton with his gloomy forebodings of the danger of nationalism to liberty at large. Yet these were, at this stage, the exception and went generally unheeded.

But the mood changed, if only briefly, with the confrontation of the Great Powers in the First World War; and Ramsay Muir (whose book on national self-government we considered in an earlier chapter) was only one of many liberal Englishmen to whom it seemed that nationalism, as in Germany, might take a wrong turn. But Imperial Germany gave way to the Weimar Republic; and Weimar, as we have seen, raised fresh hopes for the legacy of 1848 both in Germany and elsewhere. It was the time of Veit Valentin's *Deutsche Revolution,* with its tribute to Germany's liberal past, and the time that John Hawgood, an American, wrote his article in *History,* extolling the virtues and practical good sense of the Frankfurt Parliament which had previously been so much maligned. A few years earlier, Lord Elton had, in his *The Revolutionary Idea in France,* given a new slant and a new significance to the "year of revolutions" by writing that "what is dynamic and distinctive in the Revolution of 1848 belongs to the new, economic Revolution." It was the time, too, that, in spite of the new Fascist regime in Italy, Croce wrote in his old, familiar style:

Nor ought the antinational and antiliberal reactions that closed the process of these revolutions lead us to consider them as a failure . . . [For] an actual failure, in the particular sense of the word, takes place only when a principle is abandoned because it has proved fallacious or because it is worn out; whereas the national-liberal revolutions of 1848 confirmed their own principles, supplied them with new and better-suited forms, and thus bore them magnificently forward on the path of activities.

One old-style liberal, however, did not share his view; for it was also at this time that Trevelyan (perhaps more sharply responsive to current events in Italy?) wrote that "1848 was the turning point at which modern history failed to turn."[95]

But Trevelyan's pessimism was more than outmatched by some historians of the 1940s. With the advent of Hitler to power in Germany, with Germany's military occupation of Europe and the experience of the Second World War, the mood once more changed sharply and new retrospective judgments, attuned to the more recent events, were made of the nature and outcome of 1848. Namier considered that "the year 1848 proved in Germany that union could not be achieved through discussion and by argument, that it could be achieved only by force"; and he even termed the luckless German Liberals the "forerunners" of Hitler. Taylor, too, was obsessed by the German example; but, unlike Namier, he extended his pessimistic picture of Germany to the revolution as a whole. "Never," he wrote, "has there been a revolution so inspired by a limitless faith in the power of ideas; never has a revolution so discredited conservative ideas, the failure of the revolution discredited liberal ideas. After it, nothing remained but the idea of Force, and this idea stood at the helm of Germany history from then on."[96] Others, though equally pessimistic and equally responsive to the pressure of current events, appeared to be less obsessed by the defeated Germans than by the victorious Russians. Thus G. P. Gooch, another Englishman, in a commemorative address of 1948, rejected Namier's and Taylor's theme of the German "bogey" and put another in its place. "The outstanding political achievement," he declared, "of the German people in the nineteenth century was the creation of a nation-state, and the Year of Revolution was a milestone on the road." And the defeat of liberalism, he added, had not, in the long term, left its most indelible mark on Germany, for "today the chief foes of constitutional and national liberty are no longer Habsburgs and Hohenzollerns, but men

95. Hawgood, "The Frankfurt Parliament of 1848," p. 147; Lord Elton, *The Revolutionary Idea in France 1789–1871* (London, 1923), p. 117; Croce *History of Europe*, p. 169; Melvin Kranzberg, (ed.) *1848. A Turning Point?* (Boston, 1959), p. ix.
96. Namier, *Vanished Supremacies*, p. 29.

of non-German blood."[97] Henri Brunschweig, a Frenchman, in an article of the same year, adopted a similarly apocalyptic view of the revolution of 1848:

The two blocs which trouble liberals today—whose formation they wish to prevent, whose boundaries they see passing from the Vistula to the Oder or from the Oder to the Elbe—these blocs were formed in 1850, when the moral unity of the continent was shattered by the international revolution of 1848, and their boundary lies along the Rhine.[98]

And, four years later, Mrs. Priscilla Robertson, an American, published her book *Revolutions of 1848* at the height of the Cold War. "Out of 1848 and its struggles," she wrote, "no important new freedom was wrested"; and "when the 48ers failed they were beaten physically by the terrified conservatives, and also beaten intellectually by the theories of Marx." It is true, she added, that the Austrian serfs won their freedom, "but did this make up for the extra repression on all other Austrian subjects?" So, in Germany and elsewhere, through a succession of failures and the eclipse of old values by new, men lost faith in freedom, turned from idealism to cynicism, and thus prepared the way for "totalitarianism," whose appeal "comes partly from its indifference to these problems which had seemed so unyielding to solution." And "today," she concludes, "millions of classless, stateless people crowd the continent in hatred and despair—and in a way they are the end product of the futility and ruthlessness of the 1848 revolutions."[99]

But, as the dust settled from these traumas and turmoils of the immediate post-war years, historians have been inclined to make a more sober appraisal of the failures and achievements of 1848. The failures have been generally accepted as being evident enough: the failure of liberalism (most strikingly in Germany); the shattering of immediate hopes; the eclipse for many years to come of that "democ-

97. Kranzberg, *1848*, pp. 80–86.
98. Henri Brunschweig, "The Revolution of 1848," in *Revolution in Modern European History*, H. Lubasz (ed.) (New York, 1966), pp. 86–92.
99. Priscilla Robertson, *Revolutions of 1848. A Social History* (Princeton, 1952), pp. 416–19.

ratic and social Republic" of the Parisian artisans; and (with a variety of qualifications) the weakness, cowardice or "betrayal" of the *bourgeoisie*. Yet, against these, there have been chalked up a number of credits on the other side of the slate. Even Namier, for all his antipathy towards Germans and his mild contempt for "intellectuals", concluded the later of his two essays on "1848": "None the less, 1848 remains a seed-plot of history. It crystallized ideas and projected the pattern of things to come; it determined the course of the century which followed." Professor Talmon—like Namier no great friend of revolution—also refutes the charge of "utter futility" that has been levelled against the ideas of 1848 (he calls them "the Messianic spectre" or "political Messianism"); for "looked upon from the vantage point of the twentieth century, the high tide of political Messianism ceases to be a phantom and delusion, and again begins to appear as a vital reality, a significant act in a vast and immensely real drama." Valsecchi, too, argues in his own way that 1848 was a "seed-plot" or a "milestone" rather than a dead-end or a point of no return: "Historians have spoken," he writes, "of a 'second Restoration.' But such an expression has no more than a purely formal significance. One would search in vain, in the reaction following 1848, for any design to re-construct Europe, for any attempt to re-form any systematic balance of power. The protagonists of a second Restoration were by no means animated by a common set of objectives and intentions. In spite of an apparent return to the past, the disintegration of the system of 1815 continued unabated." And Hans Rothfels, a German-born American (and he was writing already in 1948), wrote simply: "The year 1850 no more restored the status of 1847 than 1815 had returned to 1788."[100]

M. Pouthas, in a more detailed survey of debits and credits, almost repeats the phrase: he, too, considers that "the turmoil, brief though it had been, left the Europe of 1851 very different from the Europe of 1847." Yet, on the purely *political* issues (constitutional, liberal and democratic gains), the results were on the whole rather slim. Pouthas, in fact, argues that the countries that benefited most were in the main

---

100. Namier, *Vanished Supremacies*, p. 30; Talmon, *Political Messianism. The Romantic Phase* (London, 1960), p. 31; Valsecchi, *op. cit.*, p. 283; Kranzberg, *1848*, p. 71.

among those which the revolution had not touched. Thus both Belgium and Holland achieved parliamentary regimes, and Belgium administrative and electoral reforms in addition. Denmark and Sweden received constitutional government, the first in 1849, the second in 1851. Switzerland became a federal state and, in the author's words, "a kind of laboratory for political experiments." Yet there were gains, too, in the countries of revolution: most notably in France, but also in Germany and Italy. Thus France retained her "universal" suffrage, Piedmont the provisions of Charles-Albert's *Statuto,* and, in theory at least, the constitutions of all the German states had been liberalized and the vote given to adult males (though, in practice, its operation was generally circumscribed). Meanwhile, in Austria, the whole state system was strengthened by Schwarzenberg and she became "a modern state such as Joseph II had dreamed of." As for nationalism in France and Italy, its eventual gains were beyond dispute. In Italy, even the "reaction" played a positive role by forging the bonds of unity in a common front against the hated "Tedeschi," and the national movement, once Cavour took over, never looked back. In Germany, likewise, there was a national revival after the Crimean War, and this continued, uninterrupted, until the new Prussia-dominated Germany was created by Bismarck. In both countries, it was a case of the part taking over the whole: Cavour's Piedmont in the one case and Bismarck's Prussia in the other. (And here M. Duroselle adds in his *L'Europe de 1815 à nos jours,* "with consequences that were soon to be seen.")

There remain the *social* results of the revolution, and these M. Pouthas considers to have been the most considerable and the most significant of all. The urban and industrial workers, admittedly, did not do too well: in fact, in France, they lost nearly all they had gained under the Second Republic and "a policy of public assistance . . . replaced a social policy"; and, as the most notable and far-reaching consequence of all, he has to point to the cold comfort of "the proletarianization of the masses" which, in his view, the revolution "either set in motion or hastened." But the position of the land-workers and peasants was radically transformed, and this he believes to have been the revolution's most remarkable achievement. In words reminiscent of those used by Engels a century before, he notes that "the different assemblies had abolished the feudal system, and the forces of reaction dared not return to it"; and this affected half of Europe (the most notable exception, until the 1860s, being Russia). In Prussia, feudal dues were finally abolished by a law providing for the cession and transfer of Silesian tenures; but in the Austrian Empire the reform was more thorough, as there it began from scratch. Other land problems, such as the division of large estates into small peasant holdings, were more intractable and remained to be settled later—as in Austria, southern and central Italy, Brandenburg and Prussia. "But at least the individual had been set free. 1848 did for Europe what 1789 had done for France." So, even though the author sees 1848 more as "an end" than "a beginning," the credits prove, in the aggregate, to be fairly impressive.[101]

Yet this is only a broad statement of accounts; and, useful as it is as a corrective to the gloomy, and often ill-supported, judgments of the 1940s, it leaves plenty of the problems still bothering historians unanswered. So, as in so much else that has been touched on in this volume, there remains ample scope for further research, assessment and debate. Some of the outstanding problems are those Professor Gooch had in mind when he wrote that "it is too soon to conclude that the world has heard the last of the ideas and ideals of 1848."[102] But there are other problems besides, such as those more *material* problems that the new direction of research, stimulated though not created by the discussions of the centenary year, have opened up in France, Hungary, Italy and elsewhere.

101. Pouthas, "The Revolutions of 1848," pp. 411–15; J.-B. Duroselle, *L'Europe de 1815 a nos jours,* p. 101.
102. *Cit.* Kranzberg, 1848 p. 86.

Index

Index

72 73 74   12 11 10 9 8 7 6 5 4 3 2 1